Contemporary Perspectives in Literacy in Early Childhood Education

Edited by

Olivia N. Saracho

and

Bernard Spodek

INFORMATION AGE
PUBLISHING

80 Mason Street • Greenwich, Connecticut 06830 • www.infoagepub.com

Library of Congress Cataloging-in-Publication Data

Contemporary perspectives in literacy in early childhood education /
edited by Olivia N. Saracho and Bernard Spodek.
    p. cm. – (Contemporary perspectives in early childhood
education ; v. 2)
Includes bibliographical references.
  ISBN 1-930608-28-4 (pbk.) – ISBN 1-930608-29-2 (hard)
  1. Language arts (Early childhood) I. Saracho, Olivia N. II. Spodek,
Bernard. III. Series.
  LB1139.5.L35 C66 2002
  372.6–dc21
                          2002007464

ISBN: 1-930608-28-4 (paper); 1-930608-29-2 (cloth)

Printed in the United States of America

Contemporary Perspectives in Early Childhood Education
Advisory Committee

Consulting Editors—Volume 2

Dr. Patricia A. Alexander
University of Maryland

Dr. Marylin Chambliss
University of Maryland

Dr. Alice Galper
University of Maryland

Dr. Frances Hancock
Oviedo, Florida

Dr. Violet Harris
University of Illinois

Dr. William Holliday
University of Maryland

Dr. James Hoot
State University of New York–Buffalo

Dr. Mary Jensen
State University of New York–Geneseo

Dr. Michaelene M. Ostrosky
University of Illinois

Dr. Rebecca Oxford
University of Maryland

Dr. Wayne Slater
University of Maryland

Dr. Debra Suarez
University of Maryland

CONTENTS

INTRODUCTION:

CONTEMPORARY THEORIES OF LITERACY

Olivia N. Saracho AND Bernard Spodek

In 1997, Congress charged the Director of the National Institute of Child Health and Human Development (NICHD) to confer with the Secretary of Education and assemble a national panel to determine the status of research-based knowledge, embodying the efficiency of different procedures for reading instruction for young children. The National Reading Panel (NRP) was established and charged with reviewing the research pertaining to critical skills, environments, and early developmental interactions that contribute to young children's acquisition of reading skills. In determining the efficiency of reading instructional procedures, the Panel conducted a review of the research literature. It found around 100,000 reading studies that were published since 1966 and 15,000 before 1966. It was unlikely the panel could critically analyze all of the studies.

The panel identified important topics by publicly announcing, planning, and holding regional hearings in Chicago, Portland, Oregon, Houston, Texas, New York, and Jackson, Mississippi for teachers, parents, students, and policymakers during 1998. They communicated various crucial themes at the regional hearings:

1. The importance of the role of parents and other concerned individuals, especially in providing children with early language and literacy experiences that foster reading development;

2. The importance of early identification and intervention for all children at risk for reading failure;
3. The importance of phonemic awareness, phonics, and good literature in reading instruction and the need to develop a clear understanding of how best to integrate different reading approaches to enhance the effectiveness of instruction for all students;
4. The need for clear, objective, and scientifically based information on the effectiveness of different types of reading instruction and the need to have such research inform policy and practice;
5. The importance of applying the highest standards of scientific evidence to the research review process so that conclusions and determinations could be based on findings obtained from experimental studies characterized by methodological rigor with demonstrated reliability, validity, replicability, and applicability;
6. The importance of the role of teachers, their professional development, and their interactions and collaborations with researchers, which should be recognized and encouraged; and
7. The importance of widely disseminating the information that is developed by the Panel (National Reading Panel, 2000, pp. 1–2).

This volume identifies and critically analyzes research studies related to the critical skills, environments, and adult interactions that contribute to young children's literacy development. The volume reflects the reformation that has emerged in the language and literacy education of young children. Prior to the 1960s, few studies were available on pre-first-grade literacy. Then studies began to emerge in the 1960s focusing on the reading readiness paradigm and on the conventional assumption that literacy development was only introduced when children experienced formal reading instruction in school (Sulzby & Teale, 1986). Fortunately, Durkin (1966) found that there were children reading before first grade and determined that the reading readiness paradigm was theoretically and pragmatically incongruous. Others followed Durkin's footsteps. Sulzby and Teale (1986) identify the following concepts about young children's acquisition of literacy learning:

1. Literacy development originates well before children are introduced to formal instruction.
2. The notion that reading precedes writing or that writing precedes reading is a fallacy.
3. Literacy blooms in "real-life" settings and by performing real-life activities that are used to "get things done."

4. The purposes of literacy for young children are as important in learning about writing and reading as are the dimensions of literacy.
5. Children's cognitive development is important to their acquisition of literacy during the years from birth to six.
6. Children learn written language when they actively engage in their world.

Competent teachers throughout the United States suggest that prior to attending school, children have acquired a distinctive culture, a collection of experiences, and a group of abilities related to literacy (Vacca & Vacca, 2000). Many prekindergarten children have been in a group setting for three and four years such as a child care setting where teachers and caregivers teach them reading and writing.

In 1998 the International Reading Association (IRA) and the National Association of the Education of Young Children (NAEYC) (1998) approved a position statement on young children's literacy development that advocated a continuum for children's literacy development regardless of age. Teachers need to provide young children with instruction that matches their developmental level and that establishes new proficiency in both oral and written language.

These views have resulted from transformations in developmental theories related to literacy, language, and cognition, in the understanding of the diverse populations that are presently in the regular classrooms, and in the nature of reading instruction. For example, lately, L.S. Vygotsky's (1962, 1978) theory has been recognized by western educators, particularly in the area of language and literacy. Vygotsky distinguishes between "natural" and "cultural" development. Cultural development permits individuals to acquire constructs of cultural behavior, incorporating reasoning patterns. Language and literacy development is a construct of cultural development, which occurs within a sociohistoric context. Children's learning is affected by the bodies of knowledge conceived within the culture. These forms of knowledge are conveyed from the more sophisticated to the less sophisticated in a culture, from adults and older children to younger children.

A fundamental notion in Vygotsky's theory is the idea of the "zone of proximal development (ZPD)," which characterizes the domain of the children's ability to achieve with some support. This type of support has been characterized as "scaffolding" or providing assistance to children as they advance in their learning. Consequently, within Vygotsky's theory, education reinforces and advances development as they incorporate what they learn into their developmental framework. This view of development incorporating learning has had a strong impact on contemporary perceptions of language and literacy education, as can be noted in the chapters in this volume.

Literacy materializes in children's lives at a very young age. By the time children are two and three, they have advanced from babbling to comprehensible speech, attending to print in books and constructing inscriptions in their aims to write. Most older two's and younger three's make writing-like and drawing-like doodles and discernible letters or letter-like figures (National Research Council, 1998). Most three's can apply symbols in one instance or domain, but they might be incapable of applying their proficiency in all circumstances and domains without extraordinary practice. The prekindergarten and kindergarten teachers' informal reading instruction has a substantial impact on the children's emerging reading. In providing an effective literacy program, teachers need to integrate reading, writing, speaking, and listening.

INNOVATIVE STRATEGIES IN READING INSTRUCTION

The concern for improving the success of school children in learning to read has led increasingly in the last decade to suggestions that formal reading instruction should begin earlier, moving that instruction from the primary grades down into the kindergarten. This movement of the primary curriculum downward led to the need for position papers such at those related to "developmentally appropriate practices" by the National Association for the Education of young Children (Bredekamp & Copple, 1997) and the position statement on young children's literacy development by the International Reading Association and the National Association of the Education of Young Children (1998).

The emergence of contemporary theories of learning on language development and the acquisition of literacy guides the current reform of reading instruction. Emergent literacy has been substituted for the concept of reading readiness. The realization that all language skills need to be balanced has guided the integration of children's literature within reading instruction. The early childhood years, the phase before teachers initiate formal reading instruction is important in nurturing competent, literate students. This phase has led to the family literacy movement. Parents as well as early childhood education teachers need to be perceptive in their approach to language development and literacy instruction. They need to know how to select developmentally appropriate literacy strategies and activities that include writing, story reading, creative dramatics, art, or any content area. Teachers need to be aware of the cultural and linguistic knowledge that children have, child rearing styles in teaching family literacy, and the importance of physical and social arrangements in the classroom. They need to develop a professional knowledge base that differs from the one that teachers of young children used several years ago.

In the first chapter Olivia N. Saracho describes the different roles teachers assume to promote literacy in the context of play in the classroom. The studies she reviews indicate that the teachers' roles include those of discussion leader, storyteller, examiner, instructional guide, informer, learning center monitor, decision-maker, storyteller, guiding play, promoting literacy-related play, monitoring children's play, facilitating children's play, interacting in children's play, inquiring during children's play, initiating children's play, extending children's play, engaging children in discussion, and making decisions during play.

The second chapter, "Hypermediating Literacy Activity: How Learning Contexts Get Recognized," by Kris D. Gutierrez and Lynda Stone, presents the theoretical construct of hypermediation to illustrate how literacy learning strategies can constrain and even prevent deep or substantive learning, especially among culturally and linguistically diverse children. They describe hypermediation as the discursive practice in which excessive and non-strategic assistance is provided in a learning activity. They allege to the importance of attending to the social organization of the learning context and the ways in which the practice of hypermediation can inadvertently reorganize both context and the learning activity. They particularly describe how hypermediation often leads to a transformation of the participation structures of the literacy activity in ways that render even robust and productive assistance strategies become needless or inappropriate to the learning goals. Instead the literacy programs are characterized by reductive literacy practices, teaching skills in isolation of literate practices, and prohibiting or severely limiting the use of the child's primary language in meaning making activities. Through participation in such activities, English language learners and other working class children are socialized to unproductive understandings and uses of literacy. In particular, reductive literacy practices do not recognize differences and diversity as resources for learning. Such practices identify English as the target of learning and fail to recognize that language is the most powerful mediator in the learning activity. The authors make the reader aware of the needs of culturally and linguistically diverse children in the schools.

In the third chapter, "Creating Opportunities for Discourse: Language and Literacy Development for At-risk Children," Barbara Wasik, Mary Alice Bond, and Annemarie Hindman describe how opportunities for discourse contribute to the development of language and literacy skills in at-risk children. They discuss (1) research related to at risk children's language development, (2) the ways in which book reading can promote discourse, and (3) suggestions for intervention to improve language and literacy skills of at risk children through discourse.

In the next chapter Jon Shapiro, Jim Anderson, and Ann Anderson discuss storybook reading as a form of literacy that serves as social practice. The authors recognize that what counts as literacy can differ markedly from one context to another. They believe that literacy practices differ across contexts and make universal assumptions about the importance of any particular literacy practice or event is unwise and can disadvantage some children. They also assume that literacy practices are socially constructed, particularly literacy events or activities or practices are quite heterogeneous.

The next three chapters focus on family literacy. In his chapter, Trevor H. Cairney explains that today early childhood educators need to know how to cater to the needs of all students and acknowledge and build on the rich cultural diversity present within any early childhood setting. He acknowledges that children live in a world of diverse opportunities for learning, in which literacy is of crucial importance. Cairney reviews the family literacy initiatives, focusing on building effective relationships between home, school, and community. He reviews and classifies family literacy studies in three broad categories: (1) home/school programs (initiatives that attempt to strengthen the relationship between home and school); (2) intergenerational programs (that attempt to bring about change in families by strengthening the literacy of adults and children); and (3) partnership initiatives (attempts to develop more effective partnerships between home and school).

In "Engaging Children in the Appropriation of Literacy: The Importance of Parental Beliefs and Practices" Susan Sonnenschein considers two related aspects of home-based influences on children's literacy development, parental beliefs about literacy and learning, and the activities available at home to the children. Her review of the literature identifies systematic differences due to sociocultural groups in parents' beliefs about the importance of education, how children learn and their own involvement in the schooling process. Her review suggests the type of literacy activities and interactions that are important in helping children become better readers.

In "Promising Perspectives and Practices in Family Literacy," Olivia N. Saracho reviews the (1) importance of parent-child interactions in developing literacy, (2) language and literacy theories that have emerged on home literacy strategies, and (3) value of extensive interventions in effective family literacy programs. Family members can reinforce the children's literacy learning when they are presented with literacy experiences in a myriad of settings and contexts.

The final chapter of the language and literacy volume provides a glance to the future of the language and literacy area of early childhood education. Over the years the fields of language and literacy for young children have encountered continued curriculum change, which are described in this volume. Early childhood scholars, researchers, and educators need to be cognizant of any innovations due to results in language and literacy studies. They need to create the knowledge and skills needed to adhere to an early childhood education literacy that is sensitive to the needs of young children in contemporary society.

REFERENCES

Bloome, D., Katz, L., Solsken, J., Willett, J., & Wilson-Keenan, J. (2000). Interpellations of family/community and classroom literacy practices. *The Journal of Educational Research, 93*(3), 155–162.

Bredekamp, S., & Copple, C. (Eds.). (1997). *Developmentally appropriate practice in early childhood programs* (rev. ed.). Washington, DC: National Association for the Education of Young Children.

Durkin, D. (1966). *Children who read early: Two longitudinal studies.* New York: Teachers College Press.

International Reading Association & the National Association of the Education of Young Children. (1998). Learning to read and write: Developmentally appropriate practices for young children. *The Reading Teacher, 52,* 193–216.

National Research Council. (1998). *Preventing reading difficulties in young children.* Washington, DC: National Academy of Sciences.

National Reading Panel. (2000). *Teaching children to read: An evidence-based assessment of the scientific research literature on reading and its implications for reading instructions.* Bethesda, MD: The National Reading Panel.

Saracho, O.N. (1986). Teaching second language literacy with computers. In D. Hainline (Ed.), *New developments in language CAI* (pp. 53–68). Kent: Croom Helm.

Sulzby, E., & Teale, W.H. (Eds.). (1986). *Emergent literacy: Writing and reading.* Norwood, NJ: Ablex.

Vacca, R.T., & Vacca, J.L. (2000). *Reading and learning to read.* New York: Longman.

Vygotsky, L.S. (1962). *Thought and language.* Cambridge, MA: MIT Press.

Vygotsky, L.S. (1978). *Mind in society: The development of higher psychological processes.* Cambridge, MA: Harvard University Press.

CHAPTER 1

TEACHERS' ROLES IN PROMOTING LITERACY-RELATED PLAY

Olivia N. Saracho

What teachers know and understand about content and students shapes how judiciously they select from texts and other materials and how effectively they present material in class. Their skill in assessing their students' progress also depends upon how deeply they understand learning, and how well they can interpret students' discussions and written work. No other intervention can make the difference that a knowledgeable, skillful teacher can make in the learning process. (National Commission on Teaching and America's Future, 1997, p. 8)

For the past few decades the interest for improving the quality of performance in early childhood teachers has increased. Research show that early childhood teachers have a significant impact on young children's learning. Many studies identify the attributes of good teachers, such as personal characteristics that affect good teacher performance. For example, Ruddell (1997) examines the personal characteristics of teachers who have an extraordinary positive effect on their students' development. He shows that these teachers are (1) warm, caring, and flexible; (2) sensitive to individual needs and motivations; (3) demanding with high expectations; (4) enthusiastic about teaching; (5) supportive of intellectual excitement; (6) considerate of alternative points of view; (7) concerned for students as persons; (8) attentive to students' academic and personal problems; (9) con-

1

scious of making instruction personally relevant; and (10) emphasizing logical and strategy-oriented instruction, clear writing, and critical thinking. In a longitudinal study (a 35-year period) of effective urban teachers, Haberman (1995) presents a set of characteristics that differentiate the more effective teachers from the less effective.

1. *Persistence.* Effective teachers assume that they have the responsibility to "find ways of engaging all their students in learning activities. They persist in trying to meet the individual needs of the problem student, the talented, the handicapped, the frequently neglected student ... persistence is reflected in an endless search for what works best with each student ... teaching can never be 'good enough' since everyone should have learned more in any activity. The basic stance of these teachers is never to give up trying to find a better way of doing things" (p. 779).

2. *Protecting learners and learning.* Effective teachers frequently share a hobby or other lifelong learning activity (e.g., opera, philately, Save the Wolves, computers) with their students as a form of motivating their learning. Such sharing directs these teachers to bring up into the curriculum eventualities which "frequently brings them into noncompliance with the extremely thick bureaucracies of urban schools" (p. 779). If the principal confronts them about such non-traditional activities, teachers arbitrate their activities because "they see protecting and enhancing students' involvement in learning activities as their highest priority" (p. 779). They also attempt to see how to immerse students rather than to emphasize "covering the curriculum."

3. *Application of generalizations.* Effective teachers have a complete view of their teaching—the relationship between long-term goals and their daily teaching practice.

4. *Approach to "at-risk" students* is considered the most important component in differentiating the more effective teachers from the less effective teachers. Effective teachers list poverty, violence, drugs, and other variables as elements in low-achievement; identify inappropriate curricula, poor teaching, and bureaucratic schools as motives; and "...believe that, regardless of life conditions their students face, they as teachers bear a primary responsibility for sparking their students' desire to learn" (p. 780).

5. *Professional versus personal orientation to students.* Effective teachers will have students in their classrooms whom they are not able to love and students who fail to love the teachers. However, they should be able to teach these students. "They use terms such as caring, respect, and concern, and they enjoy the love and affection of stu-

dents when it occurs naturally. But they do not regard it as a prerequisite for learning ... "Genuine respect is the best way to describe the feeling Star teachers have for their students" (p. 780).

6. *Burnout: Its causes and cures.*   Effective teachers know how to defend themselves from brainless, disrupting bureaucracies and learn how to perform in the system and how "to gain the widest discretion for themselves and their students without incurring the wrath of the system ... they set up networks of like-minded teachers, or they teach in teams, or they simply find kindred spirits. They use these support systems as sources of emotional sustenance" (p. 780).

7. *Fallibility.*   Effective teachers view their mistakes and their students' errors as an integral component to learning.

8. *Teaching style.*   Effective teachers' preconception is to "coach" instead of involving themselves in "directive teaching."

9. *Explanations of success.*   Effective teachers focus on the students' attempts rather than their aptitude.

10. *Organizational ability.*   Effective teachers are concerned in planning and gathering materials for their teaching.

11. *Emotional stamina.*   Effective teachers have the capacity to endure in spite of violence, death, and other crises.

12. *Basis of rapport.*   Effective teachers make students an integral part of the classroom so that it is "my" classroom or "our" classroom rather than "their" classroom.

13. *Readiness.*   Effective teachers focus on the students' individual differences instead of assuming that all students are functioning at the same level.

14. *Physical stamina.*   Effective teachers work hard.

An earlier and large-scale study of professional effectiveness compliments Haberman's (1995) findings. This study used the Behavioral Events Interview (BEI) to create a "grounded theory" of job competencies by working backwards from the criterion of superior performance "to identify the characteristics of people who perform at these levels" (Spencer & Spencer, 1993, p. 135). These competencies are presented below in descending sequence of importance.

1. *Impact and influence.*   Individuals adjust their demonstration and language to the audience, build credibility, and use individual effect strategies such as humor, body language, and voice.

2. *Developing others.*   Individuals accept the students' ability and apply innovative teaching approaches to be flexibly responsive to individual needs, especially "allowing students to use individualized ways to learn or to meet requirements" (p. 189).

3. *Interpersonal understanding.* Individuals listen and are cognizant of the students' dispositions and feelings, background, interests, and needs.

4. *Self-confidence.* Individuals feel confident of their own capacities and assessments to solve problems and failings as well as to raise questions and provide suggestions to superiors.

5. *Self-control.* Individuals are stress-resistant, have stamina, and protect their own emotions from disrupting their work.

6. *Other personal effectiveness competencies.* Individuals make correct self-assessment, learn from their mistakes, sincerely like people, are positive of others, and exhibit "intrinsic enjoyment of their work and a strong commitment to the process of learning and to the mission of their school" (p. 191).

7. *Professional expertise.* Individuals broaden and apply their professional knowledge.

8. *Customer service orientation.* Individuals search "to discover the student's underlying needs and match available or customized services to that need" (p. 193).

9. *Teamwork and cooperation.* Excellent individuals collect input from their students, award credit to and collaborate with others, and possess a "concern to help children and their desire to develop their own skills led teachers into mutually beneficial dialogue with other professionals" (p. 194).

10. *Analytical thinking.* Individuals form inferences, conceive causal relationships, systematically assess complicated problems, and especially think "about the connections in the subject matter and how to get them across to students" (p. 195).

11. *Conceptual thinking.* Individuals have the capacity to detect patterns, analyze situations, and "make connections between course work and their students' lives and to make complex material clear and vivid" (p. 195).

12. *Flexibility.* Individuals adjust their style and strategies base on the situations, in which "flexibility was critical for teachers..." (p. 196).

13. *Directiveness/Assertiveness.* Individuals determine barriers, challenge problem behavior, and vocalize no when it is indispensable. Thus, "the best teachers have established boundaries so well that they don't focus on directiveness" (p. 196).

The studies report the different characteristics, beliefs, attitudes, and interpersonal skills of effective regular teachers. Several studies show a relationship between aspects of formal teacher preparation and quality of teaching or student outcomes (National Reading Panel, 2000). For example, the analyses of the National Assessment of Educational Progress (NAEP) show that, based on the NAEP tests, teachers with more professional training tend to implement teaching practices that are related with higher reading achievement (Darling-Hammond, 2000). Teachers of young children need to have special knowledge and skills that complicate the identification of effective early childhood teachers.

Several researchers (e.g., Cho & Saracho, 1997; Saracho, 1984, 1988a,b) have examined teachers and their instruction for approximately two decades. Results of these studies suggest that teaching is more than observable behaviors (Saracho, 1988a-d). The teacher's thought processes regarding teaching and the conceptions that drive these processes are also important characteristics to consider in identifying effective teachers. Ruddell's (1997) teachers' rank building trust with students through personal contact as extremely important. These teachers plan their instruction based on their observation of students, student portfolios, regular individual conferences, and parent involvement programs. These teachers' curriculum is student-oriented. The concentration of these teachers in knowing everything about each student is supported by others (e.g., Goldstein, 1999; Noddings, 1984; Tappan, 1998) as critical in both developing a caring relationship and nurturing a productive relationship. Lampert (1985) explores how ideal teachers manage to teach in a way that, as a manager, teachers can determine how to do something and how practice and creation are blended together in the management system. The critical issue then becomes the determination of "something" in relation to these teachers' practice in literacy teaching and learning guides.

Teachers approach diverse compositions of their practice differently and children's voices, epistemologies and relationships that indicate their socialized experience (Allington, 1991; Allington & Johnston, 2000; Allington & Woodside-Jiron, 1999; Johnston, 1999). Stipek and her colleagues (Stipek, de la Sota, & Weishaupt, 1999) specify that: "Even if basic skills acquisition is educators' exclusive goal ... powerful developments in preadolescents can interfere with learning, [and] ... cannot be ignored" (p. 433). They claim that neglecting to acknowledge issues of a broader intellectual and social development until adolescence may be too late. They recommend intertwining classroom practices that impact on children's social development, which may be considered "nonacademic." However, others stress that these competencies and ascribed relationships and dispositions must be integrated into the children's literacy development. Actually, the discursive classroom surroundings have compelling consequences on literacy relationships, identities, and epistemologies (Johnston, 1999; Johnston, Layden, & Powers, 1999). Ruddell (1997) indicates that teachers assume that the most important characteristic of their teaching is to develop trust by means of personal contacts with students, although the instructional programs of these teachers fail to identify this characteristic as influential in teaching. Duffy and Hoffman (1999) advocate that researchers focus on obtaining more knowledge of the complexity of classroom life, teacher effectiveness, teacher decision making, teacher development across the career span, and in particular how more effective teachers plan and modify instruction to meet the students' individual needs. Saracho (2001, in press) suggests that the roles of the teacher in a literacy-related play environment can be explored. Both are important components in the children's literacy development.

LITERACY AND A PLAY ENVIRONMENT

American schools have established an important goal: All children will achieve *thoughtful literacy* capabilities. However, most schools are aiming on the development of *basic literacy* rather than *thoughtful literacy*. *Basic literacy* is when children are required to read and recall, write neatly, and spell accurately. In contrast *thoughtful literacy,* is when children read, write, and think in complex and critical means. Reading requires individuals to recognize words, infer their meanings, and comprehend the context of the words' grammatical structure, speech phrasing and intonation, literary forms and devices, and print practices (National Reading Panel, 2000). In an attempt to assure that all children acquire *thoughtful literacy,* schools are requiring that students reach a designated level of reading proficiency on some new state-sponsored assessment to be promoted to the next grade. To raise the stakes, several states compensate teachers whose students perform well on the selected assessments. The instruments differ from state to state. Linn (2000) states, "I am led to conclude that in most cases the instruments and technology have not been up to the demands that have been placed on them by high-stakes accountability" (p. 14). With today's high-risk measures centered on young children, there is a boastful promise for a more *thoughtful literacy,* which increases the importance in young children's literacy experiences.

The world is flooded with print. Young children daily are absorbed with print that is elusive but motivates young children to learn to read for personal and social purposes. Presently preschoolers are much more attuned to and conscious of print and its potentials. In 1958 James Hymes stated that reading "sells itself" to young children because print messages are "in the limelight" constantly. Common living "beats the drums" for literacy as the children's world is clogged with print that is no where equivalent to any formal instructional program (Vacca & Vacca, 2000). However, this current concentrated goal raises an obstacle in young children's literacy development, because there has been relatively little research on the nature of literacy instruction in early childhood classrooms.

Researchers (e.g., Goodman, 1986; Roskos & Neuman, 1998; Saracho, 1993, 2001; Saracho & Spodek, 1996) suggest that initial reading instruction should be provided in a natural context, where the functional purpose of language and literacy is emphasized rather than skill acquisition (Saracho, 1993, 2001). The approach of the natural context can be facilitated through children's play. Thus, initial reading instruction can be smoothly introduced in play environments. Several studies (e.g., Jacob, 1984; Pellegrini, 1985; Roskos & Neuman, 1998; Saracho & Spodek, 1996) demonstrate a relationship between children's literacy and their play. For example, Saracho's (2001) study concentrates on play activities that promote reading and writing in a kindergarten classroom. These play activities encourage children to invent symbols and messages in their writing. The teachers create a literate environment with literacy play experiences that promote the children's literacy development. They set up play centers (e.g., language, library, writing) that concentrate on language and literacy development including pretend reading, learning the letters of the alphabet, and writing stories. During play young children can apply social conventions and skills that are essential for reading and writing (Isenberg & Jacob, 1983; Neuman & Roskos, 1990). Researchers (e.g., Anderson & Stokes, 1984; Isenberg & Jacob, 1983; Jacob, 1984; Pellegrini, 1985; Roskos, 1988) assert that reading and writing activities can be integrated with the children's play activities.

When young children play, they inquire into the meaning of the written language (Roskos & Neuman, 1998). They usually play with language and thinking or test the literacy functions and its applications (Saracho, 2001). Jacob (1984) shows that kindergarten children figure out how to use written language in their play. In Woodward's (1984) study children write and use shopping lists, buy goods with food stamps, and get prescriptions from a doctor. The classroom's environment or physical structure is an essential factor in sociodramatic play. Props (such as notepads, pencils, aprons, or thermometers) compliment the classroom environment and motivate young children to assume their desired roles in play. Appropriate writing materials, such as paper, markers, pencils, stamp pads can motivate young children to write frequently (Morrow & Rand, 1991; Neuman & Roskos, 1992; Roskos & Neuman, 1998; Schrader, 1985; Vukelich, 1990).

A play environment can also motivate young children to write and promote their literacy development. A play environment that includes literacy experiences that help children to acquire knowledge about the uses and qualities of print can promote children's literacy development. Vukelich (1994) shows how children who play in a print-rich environment are able to identify words, even in a list that does not include graphics or/and context of the play environment. Children who play in a literacy-enriched environment interact and employ a new language as they plan, negotiate, draft, and carry out a "script" of their play (Levy, Wolfgang, & Koorland, 1992). They also create constructive hypotheses concerning written language as a "sense-making" activity (Saracho, 2001) and become "meaning makers" (Wells, 1986).

Strickland and Morrow (1989) also suggest that literacy experiences in a play environment can cultivate the children's literacy development. Play environments need to focus on the children's interests to promote their literacy development (Saracho, 2001). For example, in sociodramatic play children are able to read and write to affirm their pretend play, to communicate, and to account for details within play experiences. Neuman and Roskos (1989) conclude that children capitalize on literacy to (1) investigate their environment, (2) intermingle with others, (3) communicate, (4) verify events, and (5) deal with text (Roskos, 1988). Saracho and Spodek (1996) show that teachers in kindergarten classrooms are able to provide a play environment with play centers that include a language or literacy element which helps children to identify inconsistencies between print and nonprint and to prompt them to create symbols and messages. The National Research Council (1998) hypothesize that teachers can help develop the children's language and literacy using play-based literacy instruction when teachers:

- allow enough time and space for play in the classroom,
- provide the needed material resources,
- develop children's background knowledge for the play setting,
- scaffold the rehearsals of dramatic retellings, and
- become involved in play settings as to guide the children's attention and learning through modeling and interaction (p. 184).

Teachers can design a satisfactory literacy program for young children using their interests and experiences to motivate them to listen, write, read, and speak. Teachers need to provide children with literacy experiences where they are required to receive and express ideas in children's literature, poetry, storytelling, puppetry, and creative dramatics. These oral language experiences can focus on written communication skills where children learn to connect the spoken and written word. Children can also learn to receive and express ideas, impressions, and feelings in speaking and writing (Saracho, 1987a, 1993; Saracho & Spodek, 1996, 1998). A literacy program can provide teachers with directions on means of cultivating the children's learning and teaching situations that focus on their literacy capabilities. In this literacy program, teachers assume important and fundamental roles in the children's literacy development.

THE ROLES OF THE TEACHERS IN THE CLASSROOM

Teachers of young children perform a variety of roles in the classroom. Several researchers (e.g., Bae, 1991; Cho, & Saracho, 1997; Saracho, 1984, 1987b, 1988a-d) have identified the roles teachers assume in the classroom. For example, Saracho (1984) identifies the following roles of the teacher.

1. *Diagnostician* is when teachers identify the children's strengths and needs in planning the children's learning experiences.
2. *Curriculum designer* is when teachers use theories and practices of early childhood education to design the curricula for young children.
3. *Organizer of instruction* is when teachers use long-range and short-range planning to organize the classroom activities and appropriate accessible resources in meeting their educational goals.
4. *Manager of learning* is when teachers design a learning environment that provides relevant and interesting learning experiences.
5. *Counselor/Advisor* is when teachers continuously interact with children to give them caretaking emotional support, instructional guidance, and socialization skills.
6. *Decision maker* is when teachers carry out a variety of decisions about children, materials, activities, and goals.

Saracho's studies (1987b, 1988a-d) verify these roles among several early childhood teachers in different settings. Her studies have identified the roles of the teacher as curriculum designer, organizer of instruction, and counselor/advisor. Although the role of decision-maker is supported in her studies, it is often combined with the other roles. These studies contribute to an awareness of the roles teachers assume in the classroom, provide a synthesis of theory and practice, and describe characteristics of competent teachers of young children. Bae (1991) and Saracho (1984, 1988a,b) conclude that competent teaching goes beyond recognizable behaviors. Cho and Saracho (1997) explore the teachers' thought processes that affect their teaching and their beliefs that cause these processes. Defining the roles of the teachers can generate a theoretical framework for identifying competent teachers. Saracho (1988a,b) suggests that the descriptions of the different roles might offer important information that contributes to the theory, knowledge, and practice for effective teaching.

The roles of the teacher help us conceptualize and determine the way literacy emerges in young children. Each role embodies a component of both performance and decision-making that influences the children's literacy development (Saracho, in press).

ROLES OF THE TEACHERS IN THE
CHILDREN'S LITERACY DEVELOPMENT

Teachers encounter a complicated process at all grade levels when they teach reading comprehension strategies to students. They need to understand the content of a text, how to select the most effective strategies for individual students, the kinds of content that can be used with particular students, and an effective way to teach and model the use of different literacy strategies.

Over the last 20 years, studies on comprehension strategies have concentrated on teaching one strategy at a time; recent studies have explored the effectiveness of several combined comprehension strategies. When students read, teachers need to know a variety of ways to teach and provide students with flexible instructive feedback. The National Reading Panel (2000) suggests that teachers use the *direct explanation approach* and the *transactional strategy instruction*. The *direct explanation approach* refers to the teachers' capacity to clarify explicitly the logic and cognitive means connected with effective reading comprehension. They help students (1) to consider reading to be a problem solving function that requires the application of strategic thinking and (2) to learn to think strategically to solve comprehension problems. *Transactional strategy instruction* also refers to the teachers' capacity to provide specific instructions of thinking processes. Additionally, it enhances the teachers' capability to promote the students' discussions where they interpret text in a group and develop a fuller understanding of the cognitive processes that develop reading comprehension. General guidelines for teachers that emerge from research evidence on comprehension instruction suggest that teachers assist students "by explaining what it is they are teaching; what to do, why, how, and when; by modeling their own thinking processes; by encouraging students to ask questions and discuss possible answers among themselves; and by keeping students engaged in their reading via providing asks that demand active involvement" (National Reading Panel, 2000, p. 4–125).

The interaction between teachers and students has an impact in learning. According to Wilkinson and Silliman (2000), "the language used by teachers and students determines what is learned and how learning takes place ... [and] exerts a profound effect on students' development of language and literacy skills" (p. 337). Talk between teacher and student can be personalized. Teachers in Ruddell's (1997) study use conversation— real conversation—to learn about each student. They also motivate students to use each other's ideas. Authority is more balanced with consolidated talk. Such talk also prompts authentic inquiry processes on a general topic of conversation such as "How could we find that out?" The inquiry is focused on making meaning and the means for doing so. Generalizing conversations about the process of making meaning and accomplishing meaningful ends require both teachers and students to endlessly model and articulate strategies. In addition, when students specify the process they apply to resolve problems, they place themselves in a free position in relation to learning.

Several teachers inspire students to create identities around this freedom and make comments such as "As writers, how can you solve this problem?" (Ivey, Johnston, & Cronin, 1998). Cantrell (1999) describes how more meaning-centered third grade teachers cultivate students to be more successful on a variety of reading and writing measures. Teachers immerse children in discussion, ask inferential questions (that often lead to discussion), and combine subject areas with one another's and with children's experiences, which make instruction personally and socially meaningful. These practices contribute to the teachers' foundation of trust and respect in the classroom. Apparently this process goes both ways. When teachers listen to students' discussions and experiences, teachers provide some degree of respect. They manage instruction by mainly being conversational. However, other teachers use different means to teach reading and writing.

Research on reading and writing suggest that teachers analyze their selection of appropriate activities and materials to promote the children's literacy development within a classroom. Pressley, Wharton-McDonald, Mistretta-Hampston, and Echevarria (1998) examine the teachers' selections of materials and methods for teaching reading and writing. Several teachers choose a basal reading series, others choose trade books in theme oriented curriculum units, while others choose a reading/writing workshop model. Homework assignments vary in importance from experimenting on immersion in content to exercises on emerging aspects of written text. Writing activities vary remarkably both in depth of genres and size of pieces written. Amount of book reading and scope of reading differ with each teacher. However, these teachers' instructional programs fail to account for their effectiveness.

Several researchers (for example, Ruddell, 1997; Thomas & Barksdale-Ladd, 1995) who asked students to nominate effective/outstanding literacy teachers report that some of these teachers' characteristics seem to be distinct beliefs and theories concerning teaching and learning which include that (1) reading and writing help children learn to read and write; (2) all children are able to learn to read and write; (3) modeling is an ideal approach in teaching literacy; (4) reading and writing are intertwined instructionally; (5) children learn from their peers in cooperative environments; (6) print-rich environments are essential in literacy learning; (7) children need to experience daily various types of reading such as shared reading, independent reading, and guided reading; (8) observations of students provide information for individual teaching; and (9) children need to be provided with choices for ownership which often leads to learning. Ruddell (1997) asked students to nominate former teachers who had an extraordinary positive effect on their literacy development. The teachers in Ruddell's (1997) study plan their instruction according to their (1) observations of students, (2) collected materials in the student portfolios, (3) regular scheduled conferences with students, and (4) parent involvement program which integrates reading and writing with content area instruction. In summarizing his work on "influential" teachers, he shows that teachers (1) apply explicitly conceived instructional strategies that present opportunities to monitor and give feedback to students; (2) possess in-depth knowledge of reading and writing practices and ways to teach them; (3) recurrently employ internal motivation; and (4) sparsely apply external motivation. The teachers in this study are more student-oriented than curriculum oriented.

Although intuitively parallel with other descriptors, such constructs fail to assist novice teachers or their colleagues. It is essential to keep in mind that competent teachers concentrate on meaning and its composition by integrating reading and writing into the subject areas.

Hess and Holloway (1984) classify five broad areas that may motivate the children's literacy development:

1. *Valued placed on literacy* refers to when someone reads and stimulates children to read.
2. *Press for achievement* refers to when adults convey to children their expectations for their achievement, provide reading instruction, and respond to the children's reading enthusiasms and interest.
3. *Availability and instrumental use of reading materials* refer to when the children's literacy experiences include children's reading and writing materials.
4. *Reading with children* refers to when adults read to, listen to, and help children with their school's oral reading.
5. *Opportunities for verbal interaction* refer to when adults interact with children in divergent ways.

The children's intrinsic interests, their real-life experiences, and the integration of literacy experiences into all content areas can promote their literacy development through children's literature and environmental print that concentrate on oral language experiences that introduce the development of written communication skills. During the reading and listening of a story, children will acquire ideas and impressions that will help them to understand the relationship between the spoken and written word. Teachers need to provide children with a variety of learning alternatives in literature, poetry, storytelling, puppetry, and creative dramatics where children receive and express ideas (Saracho, 1987a). Recurrent story reading and storytelling using felt boards, puppets, and props can stimulate young children's interest in books.

In helping young children to acquire literacy skills, teachers perform a variety of roles such as lecturers, storytellers, group discussion leaders, traffic directors, mediators of conflicts, psychological diagnosticians, custodians, assigners of academic work, and file clerks (Saracho, 2001, in press). They rely on the children's interests in offering literacy experiences in teaching children to listen, write, read, and speak. In this process teachers assume the role of storyteller in guiding play and in literacy-related play.

Role of Storyteller

The adult's approach (e.g., techniques, feedback strategies) in storybook reading enhance the children's interactions and understanding of stories (Morrow, 1988; Ninio & Bruner, 1978; Pellegrini, Brody, & Sigel, 1985; Schieffelin & Cochran-Smith, 1984; Snow & Goldfied, 1983; Teale, 1984; Wells, 1986). An adult or a more competent peer encourages the child by "scaffolding" literacy learning such as serving as an ideal model for reading aloud. Adults assist the children's level of reading development (Morrow & Rand, 1993). They minimize the extent of assistance when children become independent readers.

Role of Guiding Play

The latest research on emergent literacy has focused on instructional strategies that are developmentally appropriate practices of child development. Piaget (1926) encourages educators to focus on the interaction between the child's thoughts and actions and its social and physical environment. Vygotsky (1978) indicates that children learn when they internalize the world's social interactions, although the roles of the teachers that motivate literacy development during the children's play need to be studied (Christie, 1991). Knowledge of these roles can provide important knowledge on the effectiveness of the children's literacy development within the play context. During children's play, teachers can facilitate learning by becoming supportive rather than directive with their teaching (Spodek & Saracho, 1998).

Most "play training" investigations examine the adults' roles in children's play, primarily for the purposes of enhancing the effects on play (e.g., see Christie & Johnsen, 1983, for a complete review). Studies on play intervention, or play training, provide evidence that teacher intervention continues the intricacy of children's play (Rosen, 1974; Smilansky, 1968; Smith & Syddall, 1978; Tizard, Philips, & Plewis, 1976; Williamson & Silvern, 1990). Most studies do not include the roles of the adults as they influence the children's play development (Smith & Syddall, 1978). Most play intervention studies contribute to knowledge about play but exclude the teacher's impact in the context of literacy-related play. For example, Spidell (1985) identifies the preschool teachers play interventions as conversation, participation, demonstration, environmental modification, praise, redirection, maintenance, and instruction. Her study does not report the outcomes of play interventions or the relationship between the children's play and the interventions used.

Play training studies show an increase in the affective, cognitive, social, and creative domains as well as intelligence scores when such studies promote the children's imagination and sociodramatic play (Dansky, 1980; Saltz, Dixon, & Johnson, 1977; Williamson & Silvern, 1990). Play training techniques can also be used to enrich peer interaction and group problem solving skills. They can also improve the children's language skills, verbal fluency, comprehension, and recall of play training (Dansky, 1980; Freyberg, 1973; Lovinger, 1974; Williamson & Silvern, 1990) interventions. It seems that play interventions should be an essential component of the early childhood curriculum.

Roles in Literacy-Related Play

A few studies explore interventions in children's spontaneous literacy-related play (Christie & Enz, 1991; Morrow, 1991; Vukelich, 1989). Since these studies use adults rather than the children's classroom teachers, the studies are conducted outside the natural context of the classroom. The duration of the play interventions are only for a short period of time (i.e., three weeks) and exclude the teachers' roles or strategies that contribute to the children's emerging literacy. These studies are similar to those in "play training" and fail to directly relate to the role of the teacher in promoting literacy development during the children's play. The researchers eliminate the teacher's role in promoting literacy during play, because of its perceived reality. Although some researchers indicate that adults who intervene in the children's play enhance their social and cognitive development (Bruner, 1983; Smilansky, 1968; Vygotsky, 1967), others assume that active teacher intervention in children's play tend to stifle it, thus cheating children of their right and need to play on their own terms (Fein, 1985).

Practitioners can remove themselves from children's play, assuming a "noninterfering" role (Johnson, Christie, & Yawkey, 1999), although Morrow (1991) believes that such anxieties can motivate early childhood caregivers to be hesitant to intervene in children's spontaneous interactions with print. Holdaway's (1979) developmental view of literacy learning suggests that the teachers' intervention in children's play can deliberately provide a model for children to imitate literacy behaviors, support their literacy attempts, and finally exit to allow the children to practice these behaviors in their own play.

Effective profiles of the roles teachers assume to foster literacy in children's spontaneous play are uncommon. A few researchers (e.g., Roskos & Neuman, 1993; Saracho, 2001, in press; Saracho & Spodek, 1998; Schrader, 1990) have analyzed the adult's behaviors in literacy-related play.

In considering this instructional context, Saracho (in press) examines how teachers influence young children's literacy engagement, including the types of teacher interactive patterns that seem to facilitate the children's learning environmental and functional print. Her study focuses on the roles teachers undertake to promote literacy. She identifies the roles that teachers assume and, within those roles, the strategies they use to promote literacy in the context of play. In her first study, the teachers assume the roles of discussion leader, storyteller, examiner, instructional guide, informer, learning center monitor, and decision maker:

1. *Discussion Leader.*   The teacher and the children engage in a discussion which is lead by the teacher. The children provide input into the discussion. In this discussion, the teacher introduces new concepts or/and reviews familiar ones to help children understand the new material.

2. *Storyteller.*   The teacher reads or tells the story while the students listen and respond when they listen to the story. She motivates the children to predict the events of the story and participate in the telling of the story, asks questions about the story, allows sufficient time for children to respond, monitors their listening comprehension, and rereads the story to help them verify their responses and predictions. The children can respond by predicting, putting the story in sequential order, providing the main ideas, identifying the characters, and describing the setting. Most of the storytelling experience occurs in the library area. In the library area the teacher engages in reading to the children, while they sit on the carpet and listen to the story.

3. *Examiner.*   The teacher asks questions about a new concept that she is teaching or reviewing. She monitors the children's responses, clarifies concepts, or expands their knowledge of the concepts that

she is teaching or reviewing. In examining the children, the teacher uses concrete experiences to help the children relate to the concept in a meaningful way.

4. *Instructional guide.* The teachers guide the children's learning such as helping them to associate the letter sound or objects in the proper setting or to associate picturers with words. They plan appropriate experiences, set up the learning environment, and display materials that will motivate them to learn.

5. *Informer.* The teacher provides new or reviews old information with the children. The teacher will introduce new concepts to the children or review old information to help the children make a transition from the familiar concepts to the new concepts. Often times teachers use riddles or raise questions to provide children with clues.

6. *Learning center monitor.* The teachers monitors the activities, materials, instructions, and interactions in the learning centers in order that effective learning occurs. As they monitor the children's learning in the centers, the teachers join a conversation to elaborate on what they are discussing, interact with the children to keep them interested, add materials to challenge the activities, change activities when children lose interest, and keep quiet when they are not needed. The teachers monitor the learning centers using flexible judgement in order that optimum learning occurs.

7. *Decision maker.* The teacher makes spontaneous or reflective decisions in relation to children, materials, activities, and goals. Teachers perform the role of *thinker and actor* (Spodek & Saracho, 1994). Their act ions are based on their thoughts.

Saracho (in press) supports these results in a different study. In examining the roles of the teachers during literacy-related play, she identifies and describes the roles teachers assume to support literacy learning in children's play. These roles include those of constituent, promoter, monitor, storyteller, group discussion leader, and instructional guide in children's learning. In a later study Saracho (no date) shows that teachers assume the roles of monitoring, facilitating, interacting, inquiring about, initiating, and extending children's play as well as engaging children in discussion and making decisions during play.

1. *Monitoring Children's Play.* Teachers systematically observe and assess the children's play in relation to literacy-play materials and language. They also support the children's literacy-play and provide appropriate assistance related to literacy.

2. *Interacting in Children's Play.* Teachers determine the purpose of children's play, interact accordingly, and attempt to include the children's environment such as the community.

3. *Inquiring During Children's Play.* Teachers focus the children's attention on some element in their play and redirect the children's learning using questions, and/or direct their attention to an important domain.

4. *Extending Children's Play.* Teachers extend children's play by joining their play and providing (1) specific physical features (print and objects) and goal-directed behaviors; (2) highly informative collaborative interactions; and (3) descriptions through verbal cues, play context, and theme to present the lesson.

5. *Initiating Children's Play.* Teachers establish a play environment, provide reasonable play opportunities, and display some type of novelty.

6. *Engaging Children in Discussion During Play.* Teachers discuss an important and appropriate topic or concept that develops during the children's play.

7. *Facilitating Children's Play.* Teachers select, organize, and present objects, materials, and props according to the assigned concepts or themes.

8. *Decision maker.* Teachers make spontaneous or reflective decisions in relation to children, materials, activities, and goals.

There are only a few studies that have examined the teachers' roles in the children's literacy development through spontaneous play. Most of the studies use adults (such as mothers or caregivers) rather than the children's classroom teachers. Such studies generally transpire outside the natural context of the classroom environment, which make the results harder to generalize to the classroom.

SUMMARY

Teachers assume many roles in a learning situation. These roles demand that teachers learn and assimilate professional knowledge and skills to employ the principles and practices of literacy development in early childhood education. The studies reported in this review suggest that a literacy-related play environment can foster children's literacy in their play rather than imposing formal instructional techniques. However, when teachers promote children's literacy during their spontaneous play, teachers have to be discreet when they intervene in literacy-related play to assure that children's play continues to be spontaneous. Teachers in the studies seem to assume simultaneously a combination of roles in their perceptions of children's spontaneous play and children's emerging literacy interests, skills, needs, and especially their language.

Emergent literacy in a literacy-rich environment calls for teachers to offer abundant opportunities for children to practice reading, writing, speaking, and listening—from symbolic play activities to communication in an endless variety of forms and media. Teachers who establish a literacy related play environment to promote the children's learning incorporate writing centers, writing activities, and print labels continually. Most of these possibilities are offered in the children's dramatic play (Saracho, n.d.).

Early childhood teachers must have an absolute grasp of the roles that they assume in the children's literacy learning. The National Assessment of Educational Programs, *Who Reads Best*, advocates that the students' performance must achieve a higher level of thinking skills (Applebee, Langer, & Mullis, 1988). Evidence suggests that literacy knowledge on cognitive strategies give the teachers the required knowledge to help their students to acquire an advance understanding of the reading process (Saracho, 1983, 1993, 2001).

REFERENCES

Allington, R.L. (1991). The legacy of "slow it down and make it more concrete." In J. Zutell & S. McCormick (Eds.), *Learner factors/teacher factors: Issues in literacy research and instruction; 40th Yearbook of the National Reading Conference* (pp. 19–30). Chicago: National Reading Conference.

Allington, R.L., & Johnston, P.H. (2000). *What do we know about effective fourth-grade teachers and their classrooms?* National Research Center on English Learning and Achievement. Report award #R305A60005. U.S. Department of Education, OERI, or the Institute on Student Achievement.

Allington, R.L., & Woodside-Jiron, H. (1999). The politics of literacy teaching: How "research" shaped educational policy. *Educational Researcher, 28*(8), 4–13.

Anderson, A., & Stokes, S. (1984). Social and institutional influences on the development and practice of literacy. In H. Goelman, A. Oberg, & F. Smith (Eds.) *Awakening to literacy* (pp. 24–37). Portsmouth, NH: Heinemann.

Applebee, A.N., Langer, J.A., & Mullis, I.V. (1988). *Who reads best: Factors related to reading achievement in grades 3, 7, and 11.* Princeton, NJ: Educational Testing Service.

Bae, S. (1991). *Student teachers' thought processes: The evolution of two student teachers' professional beliefs during their student teaching period.* Unpublished Doctoral Dissertation, University of Illinois.

Bruner, J. (1983). Play, thought and language. *Peabody Journal of Education, 81*, 115–118.

Cantrell, S.C. (1999). Effective teaching and literacy learning: A look inside primary classrooms. *The Reading Teacher, 52*, 370–378.

Christie, J. (1991). Play and literacy development: Summary and discussion. In J. Christie (Ed.), *Play and early literacy development*. Albany: SUNY Press.

Christie, J., & Enz, B. (1991, April). *The effects of literacy play interventions and pre-schoolers' play patterns and literacy development.* Paper presented at the annual meeting of the American Educational Research Association, Chicago.

Christie, J., & Johnsen, E. (1983). The role of play in social-intellectual development. *Review of Educational Research, 53,* 93–115.

Cho, B., & Saracho, O. N. (1997). The development of the early childhood teacher's role rating scale in Korea. *International Journal of Early Childhood Education, 2,* 19–36.

Dansky, J.L. (1980). Cognitive consequences of sociodramatic play and exploration training for economically disadvantaged preschoolers. *Journal of Child Psychology and Psychiatry and Allied Disciplines, 21*(1), 47–58.

Darling-Hammond, L. (2000). Teacher quality and student achievement: A review of state policy evidence. *Education Policy Analysis Archives* [On-line], *8*(1). Available: http://epaa.asu.edu/epaa/v8n1/

Duffy, G.G., & Hoffman, J.V. (1999). In pursuit of an illusion: The search for a perfect method. *Reading Teacher, 53*(1), 10–16.

Fein, G. (1985). Learning in play: Surfaces of thinking and feeling. In J. Frost & S. Sunderlin (Eds.), *When children play: Proceedings of the International Conference on Play and Play Environments.* Wheaton, MD. Association for Childhood Education International.

Freyberg, J.T. (1973). Increasing the imaginative play of urban disadvantaged kindergarten children through systematic training. In J.L. Singer (Ed.), *The child's world of make-believe: Experimental studies of imaginative play* (pp. 129–154). New York: Academic Press.

Goldstein, L.S. (1999). The relational zone: The role of caring relationships in the co-construction of mind. *American Educational Research Journal, 36*(3), 647–673.

Goodman, Y. (1986). Children coming to know literacy. In W. Teale & E. Sulzby (Eds.), *Emergent literacy* (pp. 1–14). Norwood, NJ: Ablex.

Haberman, M. (1995). Selecting 'Star' teachers for children and youth in urban poverty. *Phi Delta Kappan, 76*(10), 777–781.

Hess, R.D., & Holloway, S. (1984). Family and school as educational institutions. In R.D. Parke (Ed.), *Review of child development research: The family* (Vol. 7, pp. 179–22). Chicago: University of Chicago Press.

Holdaway, D. (1979). *The foundations of literacy.* Portsmouth, NH: Heinemann.

Isenberg, J., & Jacob, E. (1983). Literacy and symbolic play: A review of the literature. *Childhood Education, 59*(4), 272–276

Ivey, G., Johnston, P.H., & Cronin, J. (1998, April). *Process talk and children's sense of literate competence and agency.* Paper presented at the annual meeting of the American Educational Research Association, Montreal, Canada.

Jacob, E. (1984). Learning literacy through play: Puerto Rican kindergarten children. In H. Goelman, A. Oberg, & F. Smith (Eds.), *Awakening to literacy.* Exeter, NH: Heinemann.

Johnson, J.E., Christie, J.F., & Yawkey, T.D. (1999). *Play and early childhood development.* Boston: Allyn & Bacon.

Johnston, P.H. (1999). Unpacking literate "achievement". In J. Gaffney & B. Askew (Eds.), *Stirring the waters: A tribute to Marie Clay.* Portsmouth, NH: Heinemann.

Johnston, P.H., Layden, S., & Powers, S. (1999, April). *Children's literate talk and relationships.* Paper presented at the annual meeting of the American Educational Research Association, Montreal, Canada.

Lampert, K.W. (1985). Using dialogues to teach the interpretive process. *Journal of Teaching Writing, 4*(1),19–30.

Levy, A.K., Wolfgang, C.H., & Koorland, M.A. (1992). Sociodramatic play as a method for enhancing the language performance of kindergarten-age students. *Early Childhood Research Quarterly (Special Issue: Research on Kindergarten), 7,* 245–262.

Linn, R.L. (2000). Assessments and accountability. *Educational Researcher, 29*(2), 4–16.

Lovinger, S.L. (1974). Sociodramatic play and language development in preschool disadvantaged children. *Psychology in the Schools, 11,* 313–320.

Mathes, P.G., & Torgesen, J.K. (2000). A call for equity in reading and instruction for all students: A response to Allington and Woodside-Jiron. *Educational Researcher, 29,* 4–21.

Morrow, L. (1988). Young children's responses to one-to-one story readings in school settings. *Reading Research Quarterly, 23,* 89–107.

Morrow, L. (1991). Relationships between adult modeling, classroom design characteristics and children's literacy behaviors. In J. Zutell & S. McCormick (Eds.), *Learner factors/teacher factors: Issues in literacy research and instruction.* Chicago: National Reading Conference.

Morrow, L.M., & Rand, M.K. (1991). Promoting literacy during play by designing early childhood classroom environments. *Reading Teacher, 44*(6), 396–402.

Morrow, L.M., & Rand, M.K. (1993). Preparing teachers to support the literacy development of young children. In B. Spodek & O.N. Saracho (Eds.), *Yearbook in early childhood education: Language and literacy in early childhood education* (Vol. 4, pp. 178–195). New York: Teachers College Press.

National Commission on Teaching and America's Future (1997). *Doing what matters most: Investing in quality teaching.* New York: National Commission on Teaching and America's future.

National Reading Panel. (2000). *Teaching children to read: An evidence-based assessment of the scientific research literature on reading and its implications for reading instructions.* Bethesda, MD: The National Reading Panel.

National Research Council. (1998). *Preventing reading difficulties in young children.* Washington, DC: National Academy of Sciences

Neuman, S.B., & Roskos, K. (1989). Preschoolers' conceptions of literacy as reflected in their spontaneous play. In S. McCormick & J. Zutell (Eds.), *Cognitive and social perspectives for literacy research and instruction* (pp. 87–94). Chicago: National Reading Conference.

Neuman, S.B., & Roskos, K. (1990). Play, print, and purpose: Enriching play environments for literacy development. *The Reading Teacher, 44,* 214–221.

Neuman, S.B., & Roskos, K. (1992). Literacy objects as cultural tools: Effects on children's literacy behaviors in play. *Reading Research Quarterly, 27,* 203–225.

Ninio, A., & Bruner, J. (1978). The achievement and antecedents of labeling. *Journal of Child Language, 5,* 1–14.

Noddings, N. (1984). *Caring: A feminine approach to ethics and moral education.* Berkeley, CA: University of California Press.

Pellegrini, A.D. (1985). Relations between preschool children's symbolic play and literate behavior. In L. Galda & A. Pellegrini (Eds.), *Play, language and stories* (pp. 79–97). Norwood, NJ: Ablex.

Pellegrini, A., Brody, G., & Sigel, I. (1985). Parents' book reading habits with their children. *Journal of Psycholinguistic Research, 14*, 509–521.

Piaget, J. (1926). *The language and thought of the child.* New York: Harcourt, Brace, & World. (Original work published 1923).

Pressley, M., Wharton-McDonald, R., Mistretta-Hampston, J., & Echevarria, M. (1998). Literacy instruction in 10 grade fourth- and fifth-grade classrooms in upstate New York. *Scientific Study of Reading, 2*, 159–194.

Rosen, C.E. (1974). The effects of sociodramatic play on problem-solving behavior among culturally disadvantaged preschool children. *Child Development, 45*, 920–927.

Roskos, K. (1988). Literacy at work in play. *The Reading Teacher, 55*, 107–121.

Roskos, K., & Neuman, S.B. (1993). Descriptive observations of adults' facilitation of literacy in young children's play. *Early Childhood Research Quarterly, 8*(1), 77–97.

Roskos, K., & Neuman, S.B. (1998). Play as an opportunity for literacy. In O.N. Saracho & B. Spodek (Eds.), *Multiple perspectives on play in early childhood education* (pp. 100–115). Albany, NY: State University of New York Press.

Ruddell, R. (1997). Researching the influential literacy teacher: Characteristics, beliefs, strategies, and new research directions. In C. Kinzer, K. Hinchman, & D. Leu (Eds.), *Inquiries in literacy theory and practice; 46th yearbook of the National Reading Conference* (pp. 37–53). Chicago: National Reading Conference.

Saltz, E., Dixon, D., & Johnson, J. (1977). Training disadvantaged preschoolers on various fantasy activities: Effects of cognitive functioning and impulse control. *Child Development, 48*, 367–380.

Saracho, O.N. (no date). *Teachers' roles in promoting literacy in the context of play in a kindergarten classroom with Spanish-speaking children.* College Park: University of Maryland.

Saracho, O.N. (1983). Cognitive style and Mexican American children's perceptions of reading. In T. Escobedo (Ed.), *Early childhood education: A bilingual perspective* (pp. 201–221). New York: Teachers College Press.

Saracho, O.N. (1984). Perception of the teaching process in early childhood education through role analysis. *Journal of the Association for the Study of Perception, International, 19*(1), 26–39.

Saracho, O.N. (1987a). Evaluating reading attitudes. *Day Care and Early Education, 14*, 2325.

Saracho, O.N. (1987b). An instructional evaluation study in early childhood education. *Studies in Educational Evaluation, 13*, 163–174.

Saracho, O.N. (1988a). An evaluation of an early childhood teacher education curriculum for preservice teachers. *Early Child Development and Care, 38*, 81–101.

Saracho, O. N. (1988b). A study of the roles of early childhood teachers. *Early Child Development and Care, 38*, 43–56.

Saracho, O. N. (1988c). Using observation to study the roles of the teacher. *College Student Journal, 22*(4), 396–400.

Saracho, O. N. (1988d). Assessing instructional materials in an early childhood teacher education curriculum: The search for impact. *Reading Improvement, 25*(1), 10–27.

Saracho, O.N. (1993). Literacy development: The whole language approach. In B. Spodek & O.N. Saracho (Eds.), *Yearbook of early childhood education: Early childhood language and literacy* (Vol. IV). New York: Teachers College Press.

Saracho, O.N. (2001). Exploring young children literacy development through play. *Early Child Development and Care, 167.*

Saracho, O.N. (In press). Roles of the teachers during literacy-related play. *International Journal of Early Childhood Education.*

Saracho, O.N., & Spodek, B. (1996). Literacy activities in a play environment. *International Journal of Early Childhood Education, 1,* 7–19.

Saracho, O.N., & Spodek, B. (1998). A play foundation for family literacy. *International Journal of Educational Research, 29,* 41–50.

Schieffelin, B., & Cochran-Smith, M. (1984). Learning to read culturally: Literacy before schooling. In H. Goelman, A. Oberg, & F. Smith (Eds.), *Awakening literacy.* Portsmouth, NH: Heinemann.

Schrader, C.T. (1985). *Written language use within the context of young children's symbolic play.* ERIC Document (264 595).

Schrader, C. (1990). Symbolic play as a curricular tool for early literacy development. *Early Childhood Research Quarterly, 5,* 79–103.

Smilansky, S. (1968). *The effects of sociodramatic play on disadvantaged school children.* New York: Wiley.

Smith, P.K., & Syddall, S. (1978). Play and non-play tutoring in preschool children: Is it play or tutoring which matters? *British Journal of Educational Psychology, 48,* 315–325.

Snow, C., & Goldfield, B. (1983). Turn the page please: Situation specific learning. *Journal of Child Language, 10,* 551–570.

Spencer, L.M., & Spencer, S.M. (1993). *Competence at work: Models for superior performance.* New York: Wiley.

Spidell, R.A. (1985). *Preschool teachers' interventions in children's play.* Unpublished doctoral dissertation, University of Illinois.

Spodek, B., & Saracho, O.N. (1994). *Right from the start: Teaching children ages three to eight.* Boston: Allyn & Bacon.

Spodek, B., & Saracho, O.N. (1998). The challenge of educational play. In D. Bergen (Ed.), *Play as a medium for learning and development* (pp. 11–28). Olney, MD: Association for Childhood Education International.

Stipek, D., Sota, A.D.L., & Weishaupt, L. (1999). Life lessons: An embedded classroom approach to preventing high-risk behaviors among preadolescents. *The Elementary School Journal, 99,* 433–451.

Strickland, D., & Morrow, L. (1989). Environments rich in print promote literacy behavior during play. *The Reading Teacher, 43,* 178–179.

Tappan, M. B. (1998). Sociocultural psychology and caring pedagogy: Exploring Vygotsky's "hidden curriculum." *Educational Psychologist, 33*(1), 23–33.

Teale, W. (1984). Reading to young children: Its significance for literacy development. In H. Goelman, A. Oberg, & F. Smith (Eds.), *Awakening to literacy.* Portsmouth, NH: Heinemann.

Thomas, K.F., & Barksdale-Ladd, M.A. (1995). Effective literacy classrooms: Teachers and students exploring literacy together. In K.A. Hinchman, D.J. Leu, & C. Kinzer (Eds.), *Perspectives on literacy research and practice* (pp. 169–179). Chicago: National Reading Conference.

Tizard, B., Philips, J., & Plewis, I. (1976). Staff behaviour in pre-school centres. *Journal of Child Psychology and Psychiatry, 17*(1), 21–33.

Vacca, R.T., & Vacca, J.L. (2000). *Reading and learning to read.* New York: Longman.

Vukelich, C. (1989, December). *A description of young children's writing in two play settings with and without adult support.* Paper presented at the 39th National Reading Conference, Austin, TX.

Vukelich, C. (1990). Where's the paper? Literacy during dramatic lay. *Childhood Education, 66*(4), 205–209.

Vukelich, C. (1994). Effects of play interventions on young children's reading of environmental print. *Early Childhood Research Quarterly, 9,* 153–170.

Vygotsky, L.S. (1967). Play and its role in the mental development of the child. *Soviet Psychology, 5*(3), 6–18.

Vygotsky, L.S. (1978). *Mind in society.* Cambridge, MA: Harvard University Press.

Wells, G. (1986). *The meaning makers.* Portsmouth, NH: Heinemann.

Wilkinson, L.C., & Silliman, E.R. (2000). Classroom language and literacy learning. In M.L. Kamil, P.B. Mosenthal, P.D. Pearson, & R. Barr (Eds.), *Handbook of reading research* (Vol. 3, pp. 337–360). Mahway.

Williamson, P., & Silvern, S. (1990). The effects of play training on the story comprehension of upper primary children. *Journal of Research in Childhood Education, 4,* 130–134.

Woodward, C.Y. (1984). Guidelines for facilitating sociodramatic play. *Childhood Education, 60,* 172–177.

CHAPTER 2

HYPERMEDIATING LITERACY ACTIVITY:

How Learning Contexts Get Reorganized

Kris D. Gutierrez and Lynda Stone

INTRODUCTION

An important new emphasis in educational reform centers on helping teachers create classroom learning communities in which students develop academic literacy both in and across content areas by participating in rigorous learning activities. Within this focus, the "language of" and the "language in" the classroom play a central role both in creating and sustaining robust learning contexts, as well as in promoting and supporting individual student learning. In this chapter, we discuss this relationship between knowledge construction, classroom talk, and social activity in instructional settings. In particular, we hope to illustrate the distinction between appropriately mediated instruction and forms of assistance that constrain authentic or accountable talk that advances learning (Michaels, 2001).

We present the theoretical construct of hypermediation to illustrate how particular assistance strategies can potentially impede deep or substantive student learning.[1] Here hypermediation is the discursive practice in which excessive and/or non-strategic assistance is provided in learning activity. Drawing on our ethnographic work in urban classrooms, we document how hypermediation often leads to a transformation of the participation structures of literacy activity in ways that render otherwise robust and productive assistance strategies unnecessary or inappropriate to learning goals. In doing so, the importance of attending to the social organization of the learning context and the ways in which the practice of hypermediation can inadvertently reorganize both context and the learning activity is highlighted.

We believe the practice of hypermediation should be of particular significance to educators today as we observe hypermediation occurring at all levels of educational practice. We have documented how voter initiatives have overlegislated educational change (Gutierrez, Asato, Santos, & Gotanda, in press) and have reported the particular negative consequences of legislative and state-mandated reforms on large numbers of linguistically and culturally diverse children (Gutierrez, Baquedano-Lopez, & Asato, 2001). We have also noted that the excessive intrusion on instructional decision making also serves to deskill teachers and to devalue the experience and expertise so many of them bring to the classroom (Gutierrez, 2000; Stone, 1999).

Most notably, these recent studies reveal that many young children, particularly linguistically and culturally diverse children, do not participate in robust classroom literacy activity. Instead, new literacy programs in many underperforming schools teach skills in isolation of literate practices and prohibit or severely limit the use of the child's primary language in mean-making activities. Such narrow conceptions of literacy and learning lead to practices that are disconnected from socially constructed systems of learning (Gutierrez, Baquedano-Lopez, & Turner, 1997). Of significance, these practices socialize English language learners and other working class children to unproductive understandings and uses of literacy[2] (Gutierrez, Baquedano-Lopez, & Asato, 2001; Moll, 2000). This relationship between classroom social practices and literacy learning, however, is not always evident to both teacher and classroom participants. This point is central to understanding why and how the teacher, as in the case study that will follow, unintentionally helps reconstruct literacy activities that undermine her own instructional goals.[3]

In the following section we present a case study of the literacy practices of one second-third grade urban classroom populated primarily by immigrant Latino students who had recently transitioned from Spanish to English language instruction, and several African-American and Pacific Islander children. The children in this classroom were representative of the larger school population in this port-of-entry school district that housed many immigrant Latino families who came to the area in search of service jobs provided by the nearby airport and the surrounding hotels. Although English was the language of instruction in this classroom, the teacher, Ms. Cole, had some understanding of Spanish and attempted to use it when the need arose. She had extensive teaching experience in urban schools and believed strongly in implementimg a wide range of literacy activities that valued meaningful talk and participation across and within tasks.

There were so many wonderful things to note about the classrom, its participants, and the school, including the high level of parent participation in school activities (Gutierrez, 1992, 1993). Perhaps, this is what makes this case study so compelling. If hypermediation can occur in classrooms that try to construct robust literacy activities, what might occur in the many current classrooms that employ more narrow and restricted notions of literacy learning?

We draw on a corpus of oral and written classroom narratives, both formal and informal, to illustrate how hypermediation occurs. We have documented that hypermediation can take several different forms and can range from assistance that is undifferentiated across contexts of use and tasks to scaffolding strategies that interfere or complicate learning, for example. In all, hypermediation reconstitutes the learning activity and limits the opportunity for students to develop linguistic practices and habits of mind that advance deep learning.

Like other narratives, classroom narratives are created and reshaped with each participant turn in the telling. In this way, these narratives are locally organized and their outcome is influenced by turn-taking patterns of students and teacher, the nature and amount of overlapped speech, and by the moment to moment interaction among participants (Ochs & Capps, 2001). Thus, classroom narratives can be highly sensitive to the nature of scaffolding during the telling of the narrative. The classroom narrative, then, can be a rich site for studying hypermediation.

Classroom narratives are also a rich source for understanding many important developmental phenomena (Mischler, 1995). These narratives can serve as one means of documenting the effectiveness of literacy activities, as well as the ways classroom culture and practices are both constituted and revealed in the narratives that participants construct. Further, narratives have the potential for revealing the relationship between the construction of literacy knowledge and the various social positions taken up by participants (Ochs, personal communication, 1995, 2000). Since narratives are used to communicate meaning, they are also a rich locus for knowledge construction, i.e., sociocultural, content, and linguistic knowledge. Thus, as they unfold, narratives can become the windows through which to observe the role of talk in the social construction of knowledge through moment-to-moment interaction in the classroom.

It is important to note that there are many different kinds of narratives and various methods of analyzing their dimensions (Jefferson, 1978;

Labov, 1972; Mishler, 1995; Ochs & Capps, 2001; Preece, 1987). Moreover, narrative forms also vary across cultures (Goodwin, 1990; Ochs, Taylor, Rudolph, & Smith, 1992; Rogoff, 1990). While it is well documented that all normal children narrate their personal experiences, they are socialized to various forms and uses of narratives according to the sociocultural norns and expectations of their various communities (Heath, 1982; Ochs, 1988; Ochs & Schieffelin, 1994). This point is essential to understanding that children will demonstrate competence in creating narratives in a variety of ways (Berman, 1995; Goodwin, 1990; Invernizzi & Abouzeid, 1995).

Such differences may be highlighted in classrooms populated by students who bring different linguistic practices to the classroom. This may be particularly true in classrooms that privilege a narrow range of narrative practices that are not congruent with the valued narrative practices of working-class children, especially many culturally and linguistically diverse children (Heath, 1982, 1983, 1985). This tension may be further exacerbated if the normative understanding of narrative structure in the classroom mirrors the normative patterns found in middle class Anglo homes, as is often the case in U.S. classrooms. Here the preferred normative narrative pattern reflects a high degree of linearity in which the telling of past experiences occurs through sequentially ordered clauses that capture the temporal unfolding of events (Labov, 1972; Labov & Waletsky, 1967). As we will illustrate later in the chapter, this incongruence also highlights the power asymmetry that already exists between teacher and children in classrooms and may devalue the knowledge and linguistic practices that many children have been socialized to value. Of significance, the classroom narratives we documented were most often a first draft of an attempt to make sense of an experience, a form of throat-clearing. In this way, these classroom narratives were not polished narratives and thus were vulnerable to hypermediation and its reorganization of the learning activity.

We find Ochs and Capps' (2001) work on personal narratives to be the most relevant to our analysis here as the narratives we recorded over a two-year period in this classroom were most often personal events recounted by the children. According to Ochs and Capps (2001), personal narratives can be characterized as:

> interactional accounts of a temeporal progression of events, whose contents and ordering are subject to dispute, flux, and discovery, whose boundaries reach beyond the past to concerns in the present and possible futures. The plot line of these narrative may or may not encompass a beginning, middle, and end, given that the plot is what interlocutors are attempting to craft and that life events are not necessarily coherent nor immediately resolvable. (p. 57)

Personal narratives then are not a homogeneous genre but vary in their quality as tellable accounts and fall along a continuum of possibilities according to certain narrative dimensions: tellership, tellability, embed-dedness, linearity, and moral stance (Ochs & Capps, 2001). In addition, children's narrative skills can be evaluated in terms of genre, topic, inter-locutors' participation, and activity setting.

THE SOCIAL CONSTRUCTION OF
CLASSROOM NARRATIVES

As Ochs and Capps (2001) aruge, "the telling of a personal narrative is a social activity that varies in breadth and type of participation of the inter-locutor" (p. 32). Although one individual often prevails in telling a per-sonal experience, other interlocutors often contribute vocally and nonvocally to the shaping of the narrative (Goodwin, 1984). Thus, narra-tives are not the product of one individual, but rather are co-shaped by participants, teller and recipients, as they attempt to make sense out of ongoing talk. The co-constructed nature of narratives suggests that partici-pants take up various social roles in order to create narratives or co-nar-rate. Thus, in the moment-to-moment co-narration of children's classroom stories, for example, roles or "footings" are assumed by the participants in relation to the structure of the narrative activity (Goffman, 1981). These footings include an "Introducer" (the initiator of the story), a "primary recipient" (the person/s for which the story is oriented), and the "prob-lematizer" (one who comments on or evaluates narrators' actions). Ochs and Taylor (1992) argue that these are the most empowering roles avail-able in narrative activity. These roles are illustrated in Figure 1.

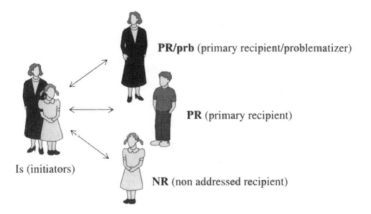

Figure 1.   The participation structure of narratives.[1] (Note: We want to clarify that this is the preferred narrative structure in the classroom, not the normative struc-ture of all narratives.)

The above diagram displays how classroom participants often organize themselves in relation to the telling of a student's narrative. This narrative organization entails participation roles that structure talk in relation to who can say what, when and to whom (Goffman, 1974). The participation roles, e.g., initiator of a story, bring certain rights and obligations organized by many cultural expectations of the particular activity setting (Cazden, 1986; Ochs, 1988). For example, a narrative event often grants the teller a long turn at talk. In classrooms, however, the teacher may determine the time student narrators are allocated to share stories.

In classroom settings where children tell stories, it is not uncommon for the primary problematizer to be the teacher. However, there are occasions in which both peers and teacher take up the role of problematizer. In classroom settings, teacher and students are expected to participate by displaying attention and comprehension through body alignment, verbal behavior, and gestures (Goodwin, 1984). An important point here is that while there are specific roles taken up in narrative activity, the social organization of narrative is not predetermined, but rather the social organization is influenced by and influences the development of these roles.

Thus, by examining classroom narrative activity, we can understand how the social architecture or the social organization of the classroom mediates learning, power and identity (Michaels, 1985). For example, the selection and display of events and responses during narrative events reveal aspects of identity of the teller and the recipients (Goffman, 1974). Children as well as adults select a sequence of past events to highlight and make clear the "plot" or main story line of a narrative. During this selection, aspects of self and individual agency are revealed and jointly constructed (Bruner, 1991).[4]

To clarify the relationship between the participation structures of classroom narrative events, the forms of mediation utilized, and knowledge and identity construction, we provide an exemplar of a prototypical narrative found in the focal classroom of this study. The following example is taken from a class time activity in which students are taking turns sharing their experiences. Some students share riddles while others share personal experiences. In this classroom, student narratives are often stories of events through which students construct accounts about past experiences or classroom themes. While stories may also refer to present or future events related to the narrated past, they generally center around a problematic event that motivates the author to tell the story.

In this particular excerpt, one African-American student, Marcie, stands and begins to tell a story about a recent family experience. Marcie is a new student to the school this year. She is an energetic and competent student who confidently displays her knowledge and actively engages in classroom discussion and events. However, the teacher and her peers did not always meet her narratives with enthusiasm. As we observed Marcie across the year, we documented numerous instances of Marcie's bid to participate— that is, to answer the teacher's question or to share stories of her experiences. However, both her teacher and peers often met Marcie's participation with sighs of exasperation, as Marcie rarely provided the one or two-word response or phrase expected in the student response slot. Instead, Marcie often provided detailed responses or embedded her answers or tagged them onto elaborate narratives of her life.

Although the ways various communities construct narratives are not the central focus of this chapter, we believe it is essential to point out that cultural expectations and social practices influence the rhetorical shape of individual's personal narratives. Thus, we should expect that all children's narratives span what Ochs and Capps (2001) call "the tellability continuum." Like many children in the class, Marcie's forms of participation and narrative style did not conform to conventional classroom participation norms (Champion, Seymour, & Camarata, 1995; Heath, 1982). However, our analysis shows that Marcie's linguistic practices, classroom behavior, and class work regularly displayed high levels of competence.

Reported Event:[5]

1	Marcie:	[Teacher (.) I can't wait 'til tomorrow
2		['cause my uncle is coming( )
3		[((standing and looking at the teacher at front of the room))
4	Teacher:	O:h that's wonderful
5	Marcie:	[We didn't hardly get to see 'im when he got off the plane
6		[((looking at the teacher))
7	Teacher:	Sorry (.) say that again
8	Marcie:	My auntie
9		she was sorta kinda like snotty
10		she just [took him off
11		[((glances at student in front of her, then back to the teacher))
12		she went to go put 'im at-
13		pick him up at the; (0.0) airport
14		and she said that she was gonna come get my mo:m
15		(.)
16		to go with her but she didn't
17		[she went on
18		[((looks down at student at her table))
19		and she went to her house
20		and then the next day?
21		he went to sleep

```
22              (.) hhh
23              and my mom she kept on calling him
24              and he-
25              her son kep on u:h
26              (.)
27              kep on [u:h saying that he wasn't there
28              [((glances down at her hands, then back to teacher))
29              but he really was.
30    Teacher: Huh
31     Marcie: And he ke-
32              he said (.) that he wasn't there
33              (0.0)
34              but he really was
35              [and than that da?y
36              [((looks quickly around the class at her classmates))
37              (0.0)
38              the next da?y after he came?
39              [they went to( )
40              [((rocks slightly))
41              (0.0)
42              they went ( )
43              uncle (.) 'cause then tomorrow he might come back
44    Teacher: >Well maybe she was upset< that he had to leave
45     Marcie: [(0.0)
46              No ((quietly))
47              [(0. 0)
48              [((looks straight forward))
49              [NO it was my auntie
50              [((looks at teacher then leans onto chair back))
51                          she was the one that [took him way out there
52              [((passes right hand over her head))
53              and my mom she was ma:d
54              she didn't-(.hhh)
55              she didn't even let him call my auntie: or [nobody
56              [((shakes head no))
57          S: I don't know why it's strange
58     Marcie: She was sno-
59              she was snotty
60              ((laughs, looks down and slides back down into seat))
61    Teacher: Sorry
62              (0.0)
63              [well I'm glad he's coming back though
64              [((timer goes off))
```

65	Marcie:	[She might ( ) I hope so
66		[((sitting in seat, looking at the teacher))
67	Teacher:	Okay
68		Marcie is anyone else sharing from your table?
69	Marcie:	[Maribel
70		[((looking down at something in her hand))
71		[The class moves on to next person who will be sharing.]

The above story displays common characteristics found in the social organization of classroom narratives. Once the narrative begins, Marcie or the initiator's turn at talk is much longer than most conversation or classroom talk. This long turn is characteristic of narratives as the teller constructs an account of a past experience. However, the primary recipient and problematizer in this setting is the teacher. Thus, students' focused attention on the teacher is not unexpected since there are powerful socialization processes found in normative classroom practices that encourage students to orient their talk toward the teacher rather than toward other students. The responses of the teacher as primary recipient assist Marcie in telling her story by providing appropriate displays of attention and understanding during a turn-constructional unit. For example note below how the teacher responds to Marcie's opening:

> Marcie: Teacher (.) I can't wait 'till tomorrow
> 'cause my uncle is coming to town
> (((Standing and looking at the teacher at the front of the room))]
> Teacher: O:h that's wonderful
> Marcie: We didn't hardly get to see 'im when he got off the plane.

In this excerpt, the teacher uses the particle "oh" to display the receipt of information and then evaluates this information with a favorable assessment, "that's wonderful". Utilizing these conversational strategies, the teacher co-participates in Marcie's narrative account by demonstrating that she is monitoring the ongoing talk and accepting Marcie's story as newsworthy. In this way, Marcie and the teacher work together as initiator and primary recipient to produce a narrative through multiple turns at talk.

In this process of co-narration, the various participation roles are accomplished during the interactional sequences of talk. For example, the teacher assumes the role of problematizer by proposing an alternative explanation of why Marcie's mother was troubled, "Well maybe she was upset that he had to leave." Of particular interest is Marcie's response to the teacher's attempt to provide an alternative theory to her story, "No.

NO, it was my auntie." Through repetition, intonation and emphasis, Marcie disagrees with the teacher and attempts to clarify the teacher's interpretation. By stating again emphatically that the issue was not that the Uncle had to leave but rather that the Auntie did not give her mother an opportunity to visit with her own brother, Marcie assumes an agential role.

It is this clarification response that serves as an agential act and challenges the teacher's proffered theory. Marcie does not acquiesce to the teacher's interpretation but rather inserts her understanding of a past event and continues the narration with an elaborate explanation. This exchange had the consequence of providing an opportunity space for Marcie to draw on prior knowledge and to be actively engaged in elaborate discourse. Here, as in so many instances we observed throughout the year, Marcie displays the importance of telling her story; yet, it was this same agential stance that contrasted her with other students who did not challenge different interpretations of their particular narratives.

Thus while we can argue that participation in the construction of these narratives has academic benefits, a microanalysis of the above narrative also instructs us about the various consequences of such seemingly benign narrative activities. In other words, these narrative activities are not only literacy learning activities; they are also the means through which children make sense of who they are, about whose knowledge counts, and how their knowledge can be used in develop (Apple, 1993; Baker & Luke, 1991; Gutierrez, Baquedano-Lopez, Alvarez, & Chiu, 1999).

THE REORGANIZATION OF NARRATIVE

The longitudinal data of this classroom demonstrate that the normative role of problematizer in the narrative, while productive in one instance, can become the means through which the students' narratives are reorganized and, ultimately, reauthored over time.[6] As we observed over the course of the study, the repeated attempts to revise Marcie's narrative and her subsequent resistance, also contributes over time to the social construction of Marcie's as an annoying and problematic student. Ultimately, we noted that this discursive construction of Marcie into a distanced author had cognitive and social consequences (Gutierrez, Larson, & Kreuter, 1995; Morrison, 1992). Marginalizing Marcie limited the nature and frequency of opportunities to co-narrate and theorize about her own past experiences and to work collaboratively with her peers.

In the following section, we discuss how the social reorganization of the student narrative is accomplished in this case by the teacher assuming and redefining the various roles. To make this process of narrative transformation evident, we focus on another routine classroom literacy activity, Author's Chair.

As conceptualized, Author's Chair is a classroom literacy activity designed to help students better understand the literacy process by allowing them to assume the various roles of reader, writer, listener, and critic/editor (Graves, 1984). Author's Chair, often a productive instructional activity that grows out of writing process pedagogy, is designed as an interactive instructional context in which students' written stories are presented by student authors who use this public occasion as a means of co-narrating, co-cognizing and co-revising their narratives. In this way, students and teacher as audience serve as coauthors in the community construction of text (Duranti, 1985). This interactive activity, then, is characterized by group membership in which shared knowledge and high levels of participation help define what counts as writer, reader, and member in this particular literacy practice.

In our ethnographic studies of literacy in urban schools, we have observed that there are as many variations of Author's Chair as there are classroom communities who participate in this literacy activity; nevertheless, there are some commonly implemented practices. Typically, students write texts both individually or in small groups. Once students have completed drafts of narrative texts, the social and spatial organization of the classroom shifts so that students, although still seated at their group tables, orient their attention to the center of the room. One student, seated in a special chair at the front of the room, assumes the role of author, reads aloud his or her text, and then directs the question and comment portion of the activity. The audience, comprising of student peers, is then provided opportunities to co-construct the author's text by raising questions, adding details, or commenting on the general effectiveness of the read text. The teacher serves as a member of the critical audience. Of particular import is that there are abundant occasions for mediating both the author and the students' learning.

In this chapter, we use Author's Chair to illustrate how narratives, especially in this context, become the discursive structures through which roles and normative practices of the classroom are established and reestablished. We present the complete text of Marcie's formal narrative as read to the class to provide the context for subsequent discussion and ultimate revision of her narrative. Next, we show how the reauthoring of her text occurs through the discursive practice of hypermediation in this classroom, i.e., the transformation of the participation structures of narrative activity, the monitoring and assessment of her narratives, and the intended imposition of the teacher's text. Specifically, we use the following data samples to illustrate how the reorganization of the narrative structures of this classroom activity became the means through which the teacher controls the social construction of knowledge.

This particular narrative activity required students to read aloud their own versions of Rudyard Kipling's *Just So Stories.* The assignment specifically directed students to create a fanciful tale in which a problematic event in an animal's life leads to a transformation in the animal's physical characteristics. As designed, this activity provides occasions for students to draw on their own imagination and interpretation of Kipling's stories. Through reading their texts to the class, students may incorporate their peers' comments and address their critical questions. In this way, children can use their knowledge to construct elaborated texts in a particular genre, to construct critical questions that lead to productive revision and the development of a repertoire of sense-making strategies and behaviors.

AUTHOR'S CHAIR: SOCIALIZING MARCIE

We draw the following samples of Marcie's formal narratives and the discussion around the presentation of her narrative from a routine Author's Chair activity. As the activity begins, Marcie, seated at the front of the room in a chair facing the other students, reads her "Just So Story." Throughout this portion of the activity, the teacher stands at the front of the classroom to Marcie's left. In the text below, Marcie is reading her narrative as the teacher and children listen.

Example 1: How the Baby Seal Got Her Fur

72	*(Marcie is seated at the front of the* class, *waiting for the teacher to tell her to start))*
73	Marcie: Okay one um
74	*((clears throat))*
75	wait
76	(the title is (.) how the baby seal got its- her fur.
77	*[((looks down as she reads from her journal))*
78	(1.6)
79	once upon a time,
80	(1.3)
81	[once upon a time
82	*(((points to words on the page as she reads))*
83	the >baby seal< ha:d (.) skin like dolphins:.
84	(1.5)
85	one day a ma:n- a man came to the jungle.

86	he: had a lot of magic.
87	he went a big cave (.)
88	he put a lot of materials (.) in- in the- in the cave for the **animals.**
89	all the animals (1.0) <went to ge:t they fur>
90	the other (.) materials
91	(1.2)
92	[material (.)
93	*[((reaches behind her head with her right hand))*
94	and the- (1.0) they-
95	(.)
96	[animals went to get (.) <they fur and other materials>.
97	*[((follows words with her finger as she continues reading))*
98	the mother seal got (.) h-her baby some fur
99	because she wanted her baby to feel warm.
100	(.)
101	she zip it up a:nd then-
102	(0.2)
103	and that- and that's how (1.0) that's how the seal °"got it's fur"°.
104	*((looks up and smiles slightly when she finishes))*
105	*((students clap))*

Marcie's narrative conforms to the teacher's directions for this particular writing activity, that is, it is a fictional account of how a baby seal got its fur. Marcie's narrative employs conventions commonly found in fantasy story lines, such as "once upon a time" to create a nonfiction, fairytale-like setting. In addition to creating an imaginary situation, the problematic event of her story, a mother's concern to keep her baby warm, motivates the mother to use the materials of the "man with a lot of magic" to resolve the dilemma of keeping her child warm. Thus, Marcie links congeries of events into a meaningful whole around the plot (Polkinghorne, 1988). Consequently, Marcie has created a complete and complex narrative (cf. Champion, Seymour, & Camarata, 1995; Goodwin, 1990; Labov & Walesky, 1967; Stein & Glenn, 1979).

   As the following excerpts will illustrate, however, the teacher reconstructs Marcie's fictional account as unsatisfactory. Through a series of questions, explanations and elaborations the teacher, now in the role of problematizer, very subtlety shifts the roles and responsibilities of the student participants. These discursive practices hypermediate the production of meaning and transform the practice into one in which the teacher assumes primary responsibility for the construction of the children's text. This potential to establish a hierarchy exists since narrative is a social practice that is constituted both by social organization and by the text of that social organization. Moreover, this reciprocal relationship explains why the teacher's appropriation of the student text results in the simultaneous control of the social organization of narrative. It is the complex and interdependent development of narrative structure that is captured in the excerpt below.

Example 2: Distancing Marcie

106	Teacher:	Oka↑y (.) very nice ladies (.) °good idea°
107		questions or comments for Marcie,
108		can you sit down please
109		questions or coMMents about her story.
110		(0.8)
111	Marcie:	[((covers her face with her journal)
112	Teacher:	Ernie?
113	Ernie:	[Uh- what did the:: (.) um the Magic Man?
114		[((looking at Marcie at the front of the room))
115		[the one that went to the jungle?
116		[((waves and points with finger))
117		(1.0)
118		what did he travel in.
119	Marcie:	What
120	Student?:	Yeh
121	Ernie:	[What did he travel, like in what.
122		[((has hand raised, then waves it above his head as he looks at Marcie))
123	Student?:	You know( )
124	Teacher:	HOW did he travel?
125	Ernie:	[Yeah in what (.) a boat
126		[((looking at teacher))
127	Marcie:	[You know like in the Greedy Zebra book,
128		[((looking at the teacher))
129	Teacher:	Uh huh↑
130	Marcie:	[It's like one of those (kind of things).
131		[((waves hand in a circle))
132	Student?:	0::h
133	Marcie:	It's like one of those magical things
134	Teacher:	Do You want to put that down at the bottom of your
135		paper to add?
136	Marcie:	[Okay
137		[((turns to look behind her for something to write with))

138   Teacher: [Let me get you a pencil=
139   *[((standing to one side of the classroom))*
140   Marcie: *[((begins to write on her paper))*

The rules for Author's Chair established in this classroom call for the student author to direct and to respond to peer responses and contributions. Contrary to the intent of Author's Chair, both the textual and spatial organization of the discussion around Marcie's text are reoriented over time so that students' questions initially directed to Marcie are ultimately redirected to the teacher. Note that from the onset of the activity, the teacher occupies both the physical and cognitive space reserved primarily for the author. Thus, while the teacher invites students to co-participate in the critique of Marcie's story (Lines 106–109), the social organization of this requesting activity places the teacher in a position of authority in relation to topic selection. The teacher's request for student responses to Marcie's story is intended to assist Marcie; however, the teacher discursively creates different understandings about who directs the activity, who elicits participation, and who ratifies students' contributions. Specifically, the teacher's subsequent selection of one student, Ernie, serves to construct the teacher rather than Marcie as the initiator and primary recipient and author.

This role shift is engendered by the use of a commonly found pattern of discourse in this classroom. Through the use of reformulation of children's talk, the teacher scaffolded unnecessarily students' understanding of ongoing talk. For example, rather than simply revoicing Ernie's question (lines 113–118), the teacher reformulates a question that already had been clarified by Marcie, Ernie and a peer (line 124). Consequently, the group of children reorient their talk and alignment toward the teacher. Of significance is that Marcie never regains her role as principal author and, thus, director of the activity, despite later attempts to assert her authority "You know like in the Greedy Zebra book," (line 127).

Inasmuch as a single attempt to mediate learning is rarely a form of hypermediation, this teacher's repeated attempts to regulate how and when the author uses peer comments function as excessive scaffolding or mediation. In this setting, teacher elicitations such as "Do you want to put that down at the bottom of your paper to add?" (Lines 134–135), followed by "Let me get you a pencil" (Line 138) allowed little opportunity for the author to evaluate the merit and relevancy of the students' comments. Although this instructional language appears tentative, it is, in fact, a non-negotiable request, i.e., a command that does not encourage children to develop multiple interpretations of texts. Moreover, our data reveal that over time children were socialized to accept these suggestions as routine directives.

In doing so, the teacher radically reshapes the content and meaning of the narrative, as well as limits the potential for the author and peers to co-construct knowledge during narrative activity. Furthermore, the tightly circumscribed roles of the reorganized narrative do not allow for productive co-participation and, thus, limit the social enactment of narrative activity— one means by which the management of information about self, i.e., identity, is accomplished with the assistance of others (Collins, 1988). As a result, the co-narration of past events provides one site where identity is developed, as children and adults create a storied canvas in which children's current and past identities are shaped and reshaped. The redesignated roles of student and teacher are displayed in Figure 2.

The reorganization of roles displayed above shows pictorially how hypermediation results in the teacher assuming all of the roles of the narrative over time and the students assuming secondary positions in the telling of their stories. Consequently, hypermediation in the literacy activity reorganizes both the narrative and the literacy activity and, thus has significant consequences on the nature of knowledge construction as students participate in literacy events. It is through participation in storytelling activities that the cultivation of complex understandings of literacy such as theory-building, i.e., the interpretation of everyday events, occurs. However, as the above illustration shows, opportunities to co-participate fully in theory-building activity in the construction of narratives are limited by the more hierarchical participation structures of the reorganized narrative. Thus, the potential for participation in routine yet rich classroom literacy events in which young children can engage in literate acts such as perspective-taking, metacognition, analytical thinking and theory reconstruction is

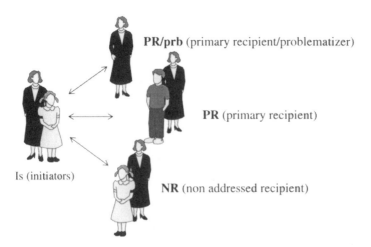

Figure 2.   Reorganized narrative participation roles.

not realized (see Stone & Gutierrez, in press; Ochs et al., 1992 for a fuller discussion). Indeed, our research shows that young children can engage productively in such literate acts (Gutiérrez, Baquedano-López, & Alvarez, 2001; Gutierrez, Baquedano-Lopez, & Tejeda, 2000).

There are also social consequences from hypermediation. Through the reorganized participation structures, the narrative can also function as the means through which power is redistributed and the authoritative roles are reappropriated by the teacher. As we will illustrate in the data sections that follow, the teacher transforms the participation structure of narratives and gradually assumes the roles of initiator, author, primary recipient and problematizer. This final segment of this classroom narrative elucidates the gradual socialization of the children into roles that limit their potential for choice, i.e., agency, their potential for productive participation in complex thinking. As the teacher's role as problematizer grows, she has multiple opportunities to hypermediate, that is, to mediate consistently and unproductively. Here hypermediation and instructional directives change the normative narrative role of problematizer and eventually shift the nature of all the roles. Consider the following data segment.

Example 3: Teacher as Preemptory Problematizer

141	Teacher: Amanda?
142	Amanda: Where did it take place at↑
143	Marcie: [In the jungle
144	((looking at Amanda, smiling))
145	I already said it
146	((Looks down at her paper))
147	Teacher: She might have missed that
148	that's fine (.)
149	Juan?
150	Juan: U:: m
151	(0.0)
152	[forgot
153	((looks from Marcie to the teacher, then lowers his head))
154	Marcie: We'll call back on you later.
155	Teacher: Elisa did you have a comment?
156	(0.0)
157	um Elisa?
158	Elisa: Um like (.) what-how-u:h
159	how was he in the jungle the seal
160	[((looking at Marcie, rocking in her chair))
161	Teacher: How -why was who in the jungle honey

162   Elisa: [The seal]
163   ((*looks at the teacher*))
164   Teacher: **Why would a SEAL BE in the jungle.**
165   That's a good question.
166   Marcie: [() it's not-you know like the rain forest is?
167   ((*looking at the teacher*))
168   Teacher: Yes.
169   Marcie: [You know like when you have like the:-
170   [((*looks around the room, taps pencil on notebook*))
171   (.)
172   [you know like when (.) the land have like,
173   [((*looks back to the teacher*))
174   like a lot of trees and a lot of [grass and stuff
175   [((*waves hand*))
176   [and then they have like a little (.) water thing?
177   [((*looking at the teacher, shifting slightly in her chair*))
178   Teacher: Okay,
179   (.)
180   so maybe near the rain forest [there] could be some um
181   (.) salt water
182   Marcie: [Yeah.]
183   [((*nods head, looking at teacher*))
184   Teacher: [=don't they live in salt water seals?
185   [((*appears to be asking the researcher*))
186   Marcie: [((*Looks at researcher, then down at her paper and draws in
                 the margin*))
187   Researcher: [I think so
188   [((*from off camera*))
189   Teacher: I think so
190   so we need to have
191   some- some near some [ocean probably
192   Marcie: [((*looks up from her paper to the teacher*))
193   Teacher: =because I think seals (.) I THINK they like salt water.
194   (0.0)
195   Marcie: ((*squints left side of face and looks down at her paper*))
196   Teacher: You know what I'm saying (.) like ocean water?
197   Marcie: [Yeah.
198   [((*looks down at the paper, then quickly back to teacher*))
199   Teacher: I don't think they live-
200   Student?: ( ) ocean
201   Marcie: [But 'kept ( )]
202   [((*looking at the teacher*))
203   Teacher: [I don't think they live in lakes and things] (.) sorry?

204   Marcie: [(.)
205   *[((looking toward classmates))*
206   Teacher: So we need to be somewhere near an ocean.
207   Marcie: *((Stops smiling and slightly wrinkles her face))*
208   Student?: (It's) a big ocean.
209   Teacher: So you might want to say (.) that the jungle,
210   (0.0)
211   had an ocean or a bay (.) or
212   Student?: ( )
213   Teacher: =something like that.
214   (0.0)
215   Marcie: [It had like a big pond, or something like that
216   *[((looking at the teacher))*
217   Teacher: Um (.) but ponds usually aren't salt water.
218   [1 think that's the- the problem.
219   Marcie: *[((looking down, drawing circles on her paper))*
220   Student?: ( )
221   Teacher: - She said-near the beach
222   (0.0)
223   Marcie: *((looks at student off camera and smiles))*
224   Teacher: =so there could be a jungle that borders on the beach?
225   Marcie: Yeah: (.) it's like the baby, [(.) you know when they
                 have the
226   *[((sits up straighter, looking at the teacher))*
227   (0.0)
228   [I was thinking that
229   *[((squinting, slouches and looks down when she finishes))*
230   Teacher: And sometimes near the jungle there are islands,
231   so he could be (.) swimming out to the islands or some-
                 thing.
232   (0.0)
233   okay good.

In the above segment the teacher continues to utilize questions, explanations and elaborations; we argue that as she expands her role of problematizer she assumes control of all the narrative roles. However, it is the
teacher's concern for the use of factual knowledge, despite the fact that
this was a fanciful story, which leads to hypermediation in which the
teacher privileged content over agency-despite the fanciful genre. Thus,
the agential potential of these student roles is minimized by the teacher's
reinterpretation of students' texts. We argue that this intrusive form of
assistance expands the common role of problematizer to include the multiple roles of narrative. Ochs (personal communication, 1995) contends

that this hypermediation is akin to the excessive interpretation that adults often employ when they underestimate the skills of young children. This pervasive underestimation, in this setting, once again mitigates children's agency in this activity. Here, the teacher reappropriates both student text and over time the entire activity.

However, as the class discussion above also illustrates, Marcie's fanciful account is not ultimately ratified. Interestingly, the narrative, which by all standards fulfills the performative, structural and textual requirements of this narrative assignment, becomes the context for reestablishing the official script of the classroom, that is, reestablishing and securing the teacher's authority over knowledge construction (Gutierrez, Rymes, & Larson, 1995). Through intertextual processes that occur within and across the various social spaces, the teacher's narrative over time emerges as the student's text, even though this was not the teacher's instructional goal.

This encroachment into Marcie's narrative, ostensibly to assist her, is unwarranted insofar as Marcie demonstrates competence through her literate acts (Green & Dixon, 1993); here, literate actions include the sociocultural knowledge of what it means to participate successfully in this academic community. For example, when Marcie responds to Juan ("We'll call back on you later," (line 154) after he has attempted to contribute comment to her narrative (lines 150–152), she ventriloquates (Bakhtin, 1981) a common feature of the teacher's discourse practice. Clearly Marcie's understands how to scaffold peer participation and provide a space for student reflection. Simultaneously, in asserting her claim to the author's chair, however, she competes with the teacher's directive role. From this situated perspective, Marcie's struggle to retain authority over her own narrative can be seen as her struggle to retain agency over her own learning, her own sociocultural history. Nonetheless, the teacher's immediate use of an elicitation reinstates her own directive role (lines 155–157). Consequently, when the teacher controls who gets a turn to talk, the children have few occasions to orient to the student author and, instead, reorient to the teacher. For example, note that in the following excerpt, there is no interactional space for student selection, uptake, or elaboration:

> Teacher: Juan?
> Juan: U::m
> (0-0)
> [forgot
> [(((looks from Marcie to the teacher, then lowers his head))
> Marcie: We'll call back on you later.
> Teacher: Elisa did you have a comment?
> (0.0)
> u::m Elisa?

As this activity unfolds, the continual instantiation of her directive role leads to an expansion of the role of problematizer. As authority over knowledge shifts to the adults in the course of the negotiation of meaning (Lines 184–191), Marcie is gradually distanced from her own narrative and, therefore, her own role as author. This distancing makes it more difficult for Marcie to retain authority over her own text. The delegitimation of Marcie's contributions, that is, the interpretation of her own text, occurs through her treatment of Marcie's challenges to the reauthoring of her narrative. It is the teacher's nonresponse to student contributions or attempted contributions and her expansion of Marcie's explanation that reorganize the activity and the narrative. For example, when Marcie offers a plausible answer to a student question (Lines 166; 169–177), the teacher provides an elaborate solution to the question and sustains control over the discourse. The teacher accomplishes this control through her preemptory actions in which she both overlaps Marcie's bid to provide a rival hypothesis (marked conversationally by "[But 'cept ( )]" and ignores her bid to participate (line 203). In this way, it is the teacher's ratification that legitimates bids to participate and Marcie's bids to challenge the teacher's revision of her narrative.

As the teacher takes over the role of primary problematizer, she also assumes the role of initiator and primary recipient. In this way, the normative role of problematizer works to re-author rather than coauthor Marcie's narrative. Consequently, Marcie and the other children are not encouraged to draw from their linguistic and cognitive resources to build literacy knowledge, as the responsibility for coauthoring the narrative falls heavily on the side of the teacher. Hence, while children do co-participate in this activity, the student's prior experience, a resource for complex literate thinking, is neither available nor legitimate to use in this context. The potential for rich and productive literacy learning in which children develop comprehensive literacy skills and strategies, including critical literacy is unfulfilled. Ultimately, the opportunity to participate in a form of transformative praxis is not realized (Freire & Macedo, 1987; Lankshear & McLaren, 1993).

RETHINKING THE SOCIAL ORGANIZATION OF LEARNING

In presenting these reauthored narratives we illustrate most dramatically how hypermediation undermines productive literacy learning. The instructional strategies designed to assist children's literacy learning through participation in classroom literacy activities usually attributed to reform-oriented practice, i.e., high levels of student talk participation and co-participation, the student's prior knowledge and experience, in fact, were mitigated by the teacher's nonstrategic and undifferentiated attempts to scaffold the children's narratives. In this way, the strategies she designed to mediate learning instead resulted in a form of hypermediation that limited the children's literacy learning and the potential for using children's narratives as sources for building complex understandings, i.e., theory-building, perspective-taking, and coherent and sustained discourse production.

The tension between mediating productively and hypermediating, evident in the data, arise from competing explanations of learning and literacy learning in particular, as well as conflicting views of curriculum as social practice (Apple, 1993; Baker & Luke, 1991; Gutierrez, 1993). The contradictions inherent in the teacher's views of learning and instruction are made visible in the ways the learning activities are organized and mediated. In particular, the pull between the teacher's desire to instruct and the children's desire to co-participate in the construction of narratives results in classroom social practices that emphasize teaching over learning and, thus, become indistinguishable from traditional literacy practices. Controlling the social organization of participation, in effect, limits the learning opportunities provided through participation in these classroom narrative activities.

Rather than problematizing Marcie or vilifying the teacher, we hope that by making these tensions and contradictions visible teachers will more readily understand and critique the sociocultural and historical specificity of their own classroom practices. In particular, it is in the unfolding of the social practices of the classroom that teachers can observe the complex relation of knowledge construction, social activity, and discursive practices. As educators, we also need to understand the social and cognitive consequences of these fundamentally related processes, particularly in urban school contexts where the potential for the marginalization of students and their discourses exists. As Heath (1985) has argued "Researchers and schools are a long way from understanding that it is first necessary to understand what people do in language, before we try to decide what institutions want to make them do" (p. 18).

The high social cost attributed to such unproductive contexts for learning becomes evident in light of the rapidly changing nature of our society, its technologies, its workplaces, and its diverse citizenry. Without understanding how curricular, instructional and learning theories are enacted in the social practices of the classroom, it becomes more difficult for schools to respond effectively to the increasing linguistic and cultural diversity in the student population. We must rethink the social practices of the urban classroom if we are to develop more productive forms of literacy learning, especially for linguistically and culturally diverse student populations. Otherwise, hypermediation may become a normative practice in classrooms where children's sociocultural and linguistic practices are neither valued nor understood.

NOTES

1.   The construct of hypermediation was conceptulized as we conducted microanalysis of the discourse practices of a cohort of elementary school classrooms over a two-year period in Los Angeles (Gutierrez, 1994) and subsequently in work with Lynda Stone and Joanne Larson. We wish to acknowledge Joanne Larson's contribution to the transcription and early analysis of these data.

2.   In particular, reductive literacy practices do not recognize difference and diversity as resources for learning. Moreover, such practices identify English as the target of learning and fail to recognize that language is the most powerful mediator in learning activity. See Gutierrez, Baquedano-Lopez, and Asato ((20001) and Gutierrez, Asato, Santos, and Gotanda (in press) for a fuller discussion of reductive literacy practices.

3.   We thank Ms. Cole for allowing us to share her story. She believes it would be instructive to other teachers. It is important to note that she was a very experienced, knowledgeable, and caring teacher who is a strong advocate for the ways research can inform classroom practice. We also recognize that teachers are part of institutions and institutional practices that are often imposed on them. In this way, we do not view teachers as problems or as the focal point of educational criticism.

4.   The construct of identity used here assumes that identity arises from social interaction and not from internal individual processes.

5.   The following transcription conventions, adapted from Atkinson and Heritage (1984) are used in the examples given:

Colons denote sound stretch ("U::m"); Underlining denotes emphatic stress ("Don't shout out"); Brackets indicate overlapping speech, for example:

> S: [It's clean now
> T: [Na::w, it's a good guess

Equal signs indicate closely latched speech, or ideas, for example,

> T: Someone=
> S: =Michael Jackson

Intervals of silence are timed in tenths of seconds and inserted within parentheses; short, untimed silences are marked by a dash when sound is quickly cut off ("We've got a- current events quiz") or with a period within parentheses (.). Rising intonation within an utterance is marked with an arrow ("to ↑ start with"); Utterance final rising intonation is marked with a question mark, continued intonation with a comma, and failing intonation with a period; Degree signs indicate lowered volume (°you shut up°); Items written entirely in capitals are of a higher volume ("HAH HAH"); Descriptions of the speech are italicized within double parentheses *(((imitating)))No:::.)*. Single parentheses surround items of doubtful transcription; and boldface indicates items of analytic focus.

6. We make the distinction between co-authoring and re-authoring. We acknowledge that narratives are socially constructed and, thus, co-authored (Goodwin, 1984; Jefferson, 1978). Re-authoring, however, refers to the displacement of the initiator of the story in the course of the construction of the narrative.

REFERENCES

Apple, M. (1993). *Official knowledge: Democratic education in a conservative age.* New York: Routledge.

Atkinson, J.M., & Heritage, J. (1984). *Structures of social action.* Cambridge: Cambridge University Press.

Baker, C., & Luke, A. (1991). *Towards a critical sociology of reading pedagogy.* Philadelphia: John Benjamins.

Bakhtin, M. (1981). *The dialogic imagination.* Trans. Caryl Emerson & Michael Holquist. Austin: University of Texas Press.

Berman, R. (1995). Narrative competence and storytelling performance: How children tell stories in different contexts. *Journal of Narrative and Life History, 5*(4), 285–314.

Bruner, J., (1991). The narrative construction of reality. *Critical Inquiry, 18,* 1–21.

Cazden, C. (1986). Classroom discourse. In M. Wittrock (Ed.), *Handbook on research on teaching.* New York: American Educational Research Association.

Champion, T., Seymour, H., & Camarata, S. (1995). Narrative discourse of African American children. *Journal of Narrative and Life History, 5*(4), 333–352.

Collins, R. (1988). Theoretical continuities in Goffman's work. In P. Drew & A. Wootton (Eds.), *Erving Goffman: Exploring the interaction order* (pp. 41–63). Oxford: Polity Press.

Duranti, A. (1985). Sociocultural dimensions of discourse. In T.A.V. Dijk (Ed.), *Handbook of discourse analysis, Vol. 1: Discipline of discourse* (pp. 193–230). New York: Academic Press.

Freire, P., & Macedo, D. (1987). *Literacy: Reading the word and the world.* South Hadley, MA: Bergin and Garvey.

Giroux, H. (1983). *Theory and resistance in education: A pedagogy for the opposition.* New York: Bergin and Garvey.

Goffman, E. (1974). *An essay on the organization of experience: Frame analysis.* Boston: Northeastern University Press.

Goffman, E. (1981). *Forms of talk.* Philadelphia: University of Pennsylvania Press.

Goodwin, C. (1984). Note on story structure and the organization of participation In J.M. Atkinson & J. Heritage (Eds.), *Structures of social action: Studies in conversation analysis* (pp. 225–46). Cambridge: Cambridge University Press.

Goodwin, M. (1990). He said she said: Talk as social organization among Black children. Bloomington: Indiana University Press.

Graves, D. (1984). *A researcher learns to write: Selected articles and monographs.* Exeter, New Hampshire: Heinemann.

Green, J., & Dixon, C. (1993). Talking knowledge into Being: Discursive and social practices in classrooms. *Linguistics and Education, 5*(3&4), 231–240.

Gutierrez, K. (2000). Teaching and learning in the 21st Century. *English Education, 32*(4), 290–298.

Gutierrez, K. (1994). *Scripts, counterscripts, and the construction of context in literacy activities for elementary school-aged Latino children. Perspectives on literacy, schooling and power.* Sociolinguistics Session, XII World Congress of Sociology, Bielefeld, Germany.

Gutierrez, K. (1993). How talk, context, & script shape contexts for learning: A cross case comparison of journal sharing. *Linguistics and Education, 5*, 335–365.

Gutierrez, K. (1992). A comparison of instructional contexts in writing process classrooms with Latino children. *Education and Urban Society, 24*(2), 224–262.

Gutiérrez, K., Asato, J., Santos, M., & Gotanda, N. (in press). Backlash pedagogy: Language and culture and the politics of reform . *The Review of Education, Pedagogy, and Cultural Studies.*

Gutiérrez, K., Baquedano-López, P., & Alvarez, H. (2001). Literacy as hybridity: Moving beyond bilingualism in urban classrooms. In M. Reyes & J. Halcon (Eds.), *The best for the children: Critical perspectives on literacy for Latino students* (pp. 122–141). New York: Teachers College Press.

Gutiérrez, K., Baquedano-López, P., & Alvarez, H. (2000). The crisis in Latino education: Challenging the current debate. In C. Tejeda, C. Martinez, & Z. Leonardo (Eds.), *Demarcating the borders of Chicana(o)/Latina(o) education* (pp. 213–233) Cresskill, NJ: Hampton Press Inc.

Gutierrez, K., Baquedano-Lopez, P., & Asato, J. (2001). "English for the children": The new literacy of the old world order, language policy and educational reform. *Bilingual Research Journal, 24*(1 & 2), 87–112.

Gutiérrez, K., Baquedano-López, P., Alvarez, H., & Chiu, M. (1999). A cultural-historical approach to collaboration: Building a culture of collaboration through hybrid language practices. *Theory into Practice, 38*(2), 87–93.

Gutiérrez, K., Baquedano-López, P., & Tejeda, C. (2000). Rethinking diversity: Hybridity and hybrid language practices in the third space. *Mind, Culture, and Activity, 6*(4), 286–303.

Gutiérrez, K., Baquedano-López, P., & Turner, M.G. (1997). Putting language back into language arts: When the radical middle meets the third space. *Language Arts, 74*(5), 368–378.

Gutierrez, K., Larson, J., & Kreuter, B. (1995). Cultural tensions in the scripted classroom: The value of the subjugated perspective. *Urban Education, 29*(4), 410–442.

Gutierrez, K., Rymes, B., & Larson, J (1995). Script, counterscript and underlife in the classroom: James Brown versus Brown v. Board of Education. *Harvard Educational Review, 65*(3) 445–471.

Heath, S.B. (1985). The cross-cultural study of language acquisition. *Papers and Reports on Child Language Development, 24*, 1–21.

Heath, S.B. (1983). *Ways with words: Language, life, and work in communities and classrooms.* Cambridge: Cambridge University Press.

Heath, S.B. (1982). What no bedtime story means: Narrative skills at home and school. *Language and Society, 11*, 49–76.

Invernizzi, M.A., & Abouzeid, M.P. (1995). One story map does not fit all: A cross-cultural analysis of children's written story retellings. *Journal of Narrative and Life History, 5*(1), 1–19.

Jefferson, G. (1978). Sequential aspects of storytelling in conversation. In J. Schenkein (Ed.), *Studies in the organization of conversational interaction* (pp. 219–248). New York: Academic Press.

Labov, W. (1972). The transformation of experience in narrative syntax. In W. Labov (Ed.), *Language in the inner city* (pp. 352–396). Philadelphia: University of Pennsylvania.

Labov, W., & Waletsky, J. (1967). Narrative analysis: Oral versions of personal experience. In J. Helm (Ed.), *Essays on the verbal and visual AIU* (pp. 12–44). Seattle, WA: American Ethnological Society.

Lankshear, C., & McLaren, P. (1993). *Critical literacy: Politics, praxis. and the postmodern.* Albany: State University of New York Press.

McNeil, L. (1986). *Contradictions of control: School structure and school knowledge.* New York: Routledge.

Michaels, S. (2001). Personal communication. Athens, Greece.

Michaels, S. (1991). The dismantling of narrative. In A. McCabe & C. Peterson (Eds.), *Developing narrative structure* (pp. 303–351). Hillsdale, NJ: Erlbaum Publishers.

Michaels, S. (1985). Hearing the connections in children's oral and written discourse. *Journal of Education, 167*(1), 36–56.

Michaels, S. (1981). Sharing time: Children's narrative style and differential access to literacy. *Language in Society, 10*, 423–442.

Mishler, E.G. (1995). Models of arrative analysis: A typology. *Journal of Narrative and Life History, 5*(2), 87–123.

Moll, L. (2000). Inspired by Vygotsky: Ethnographic experiments in education. In C. Lee & P. Smagorinsky (Eds.), *Vygotskian perspectives on literacy research: Constructing meaning through collaborative inquiry* (pp. 256–268). New York: Cambridge University Press.

Morrison, T. (1992). *Playing in the dark: Whiteness and the literacy imagination.* New York: Vintage Books.

Ochs, E. (2000). Personal Communication, University of California, Los Angeles.

Ochs, E. (1995). Personal Communication. University of California, Los Angeles.

Ochs, E. (1988). *Culture and language development: Language acquisition and language socialization in a Samoan village.* Cambridge: Cambridge University Press.

Ochs, E., & Capps, L. (2001). *Living narrative: Creating lives in everyday storytelling.* Cambridge, MA: Harvard University Press.

Ochs, E., & Schieffelin, B. (1994). Language acquisition and socialization: Three developmental stories and their implications. In B.G. Blount (Ed.), *Language, culture, and society* (pp. 470–512). Prospect Heights, IL: Waveland Press, Inc.

Ochs, E., & Taylor, C. (1992). Family narrative as political activity. *Discourse and Society, 3*(3), 301–340.

Ochs, E., Taylor, C., Rudolph, D., & Smith, R. (1992). Storytelling as a theory building activity. *Discourse Processes, 15*, 37–72.

Preece, A. (1987). The range of narrative forms conversationally produced by young children. *Child Language, 14*, 353–373.

Polkinghorne, D.E. (1988). *Narrative knowing and human sciences.* Albany: State University of New York Press.

Rogoff, B. (1990). *Apprenticeship in thinking.* New York: Cambridge University Press.

Stein, N.L., & Glenn, C.G. (1979). An analysis of story comprehension in elementary school children. In R. Freedle (Ed.), *New directions in discourse processing* (pp. 53–120). Norwood, NJ: Ablex.

Stone, L.D. (1999). Sharing, discovering, and creating: Practice into theory and theory into practice. *Kindergarten Education: Theory, Research, and Practice, 4*(1), 21–40.

CHAPTER 3

CREATING OPPORTUNITIES FOR DISCOURSE:

Language and Literacy Development in Economically Disadvantaged Children

Barbara A. Wasik, Mary Alice Bond, and Annemarie Hindman

INTRODUCTION

Literacy development is a complex process that begins long before children engage in formal reading instruction (Snow, Burns, & Griffin, 1998; Teale & Sulzby, 1986; Whitehurst & Lonigan, 1998). Pre-literacy skills such as phonological and linguistic awareness, letter recognition, and familiarity with the function of print in literature and in the environment, establish a solid foundation for literacy learning. However, the most important variable that contributes to success in literacy is the development of language skills (Snow et al., 1998; Wells, 1986). As they approach the task of reading, children with well-developed vocabularies and strong oral language skills are equipped to understand the meaning of individual words and, by extension, entire texts (Metsala & Ehri, 1998).

The preschool years are a critical time for language development, as children's vocabularies are rapidly expanding and their understanding of the structure of language is becoming increasingly sophisticated. It is important during this time that children have opportunities to interact with linguistically competent adults and peers in order to facilitate their language development (Bus, van Ijzendoorn, & Pellegrini, 1995; Hart & Risley, 1999; Jordan, Snow, & Porche, 2000; Scarborough & Dobrich, 1994). Through discourse with adults and peers, children learn new words, receive feedback on their language, and use language as an effective communication tool. Children from language-rich environments enter school with the solid foundation of language skills needed to communicate with others and comprehend many of the words they will encounter as beginning readers.

Children raised in poverty, however, often enter school without the language skills necessary for literacy development and are consequently less prepared for learning than are their more advantaged peers. Limited exposure to books and print-related experiences is considered one explanation for the lack of language and literacy skills among children in poverty. However, as recent research has shown (Lonigan & Whitehurst, 1998; Wasik & Bond, 2001), it is not simply book reading that contributes to the development of language and literacy skills. It is the discourse that occurs around book reading and other similar interactions that creates the broad, rich context in which children learn and use language. Discourse, defined as reciprocal verbal interactions, encourages children to engage in conversations that result in developing language skills.

The purpose of this chapter is to discuss how opportunities for discourse contribute to the development of language and literacy skills in children in poverty. In order to accomplish this, a discussion of research related to language development in children in poverty is first presented. Second, the ways in which book reading can promote discourse are discussed. Third, other opportunities and activities that facilitate discourse are presented. Finally, suggestions for intervention to improve the language and literacy skills of children of poverty through discourse are provided.

LANGUAGE DEVELOPMENT AND CHILDREN IN POVERTY

Compared to their more advantaged peers, children reared in poverty have less access to opportunities to develop language and literacy skills (Snow et al., 1998; Wells, 1986). In a longitudinal study, Hart and Risley (1995) reported that, by the age of 3, children in poverty had more limited vocabularies and oral language skills compared to children from high- and middle-income homes. Snow et al. (1998) also reported that children in poverty lacked necessary pre-literacy skills as they entered kindergarten. These findings are consistent with the Carnegie Foundation report *Ready to Learn: A Mandate for the Nation* (Boyer, 1991), which found that 35% of the children entering school did not have the educational skills necessary to succeed. Of these children, a disproportionate number were from low-income homes. Other research indicates that socioeconomic status is one of the strongest predictors of performance differences in children at the beginning of the first grade (Alexander & Entwisle, 1988), and that this gap persists as children progress from elementary to high school (Puma, Karweit, Price, Ricciuti, Thompson, & Vaden-Kiernan, 1997).

For children in poverty, limitations in language development are, in large part, the result of three important factors: (a) inadequate or infrequent discourse with adults, (b) limited exposure to literacy experiences, and (c) conflicting perceptions and practices regarding language and literacy at home and at school. Consequently, the language and literacy experiences of children in poverty are often inconsistent with the expectations of the school culture.

As part of a longitudinal study, Hart and Risley (1995) examined both the quality and quantity of parent-child discourse in welfare, working-class, and professional families. Their data showed that children in welfare families received less than half as many language experiences in each hour of their lives as did their working-class peers, primarily a result of less talking in welfare families. However, the quality of the language also varied by social class. In their interactions, professional families used a high frequency of multiclause sentences, more questions, more varied verb tenses, and a greater variety of verb tenses compared to low-income families, thereby providing a more enriching language experience for their children. This suggests that both the amount and the quality of talk do affect the development of young children's language skills.

One criticism regarding Hart and Risley's (1995) findings concerns how the quality of language was assessed. Critics argue that the quality of language was judged based on what is expected for white, middle-class children (Coll et al. 1996). Therefore, the linguistic and cultural differences that exist between different social classes and races were not acknowledged. As children in poverty learn language, however, the structure of their language and their vocabulary is often not the same compared to children in middle-class homes. In addition, there is an incongruity between the language that children in poverty learn at home and what is expected in school. Children in poverty arrive in school with language that does not sufficiently facilitate their understanding of books and experiences that reflect the middle-class, white culture.

Another factor influencing disadvantaged children's language development is that families living in poverty often have limited access to the kinds of literacy experiences that help young children develop strong language skills (Bowman, Donovan, & Burns, 2001; Snow et al., 1998; Wells, 1986). As a result, children in poverty often enter school insufficiently prepared to learn about language and literacy and, ultimately, at risk for failing to learn to read. Based on a longitudinal study, Wells (1986) suggested that the lack of literacy experiences in disadvantaged children's homes contributed to a deficit in the knowledge of cultural literacy necessary for school success.

Wells (1986) documented the language and literacy development of 32 high-, middle-, and low-income children from Bristol, England, from age 1 until their last year of elementary school. The results from this study suggest that, before children entered school, there were no clear differences between the middle- and lower-class groups in their rate of language development, in the range of meaning expressed, or in the range of functions for which language was used. However, once the children began school, differences not previously apparent became very salient. Children from low-income families did not perform as well on many school-related literacy activities, including reading and writing tasks. There appeared to be an incongruity between the expectations of the home and those of the school with regard to language development. Wells (1986) argued that the linguistic disadvantages of some low-income children were not the result of poor command of or experience with oral language. Rather, these deficits were a consequence of the low value that their parents placed on literacy, as evidenced by the parents' limited use of these literacy skills and by the absence of books in the home. In contrast, children who were more successful in school were likely to have access to books and to have parents who read on their own and to their children. Wells asserted that this lack of exposure to literacy experiences contributed to limitations in language skills and knowledge about print and reading.

In support of Wells' observations, more recent research by Neuman and Celano (2001) demonstrated that high-poverty areas are characterized by a paucity of literacy materials and activities. Neuman and Celano (2001) conducted an ethnographic survey of literacy opportunities available in a low-income community in Philadelphia, Pennsylvania, and found a profound lack of literacy opportunities available to children and families. Like Wells, Neuman and Celano suggested that this inadequate access to books and other literacy opportunities contributes to children in poverty not acquiring the language and literacy skills needed to succeed in the culture of school.

Cultural differences between the home and the school, particularly regarding styles of communication, can further complicate the language and literacy learning that these children so desperately need. Heath's (1983) work suggests that language development is strongly influenced by the home and community in which a child is reared. The language that children learn at home is intimately tied to the culture of their community, and this language may not always overlap with the language of the school. What is valued in one domain or cultural context may not necessarily be valued in another. Problems arise when people, especially children, need to interact in both the culture of home and the culture of school where similar values are not shared.

There is often discontinuity between the expectations of a child's community and the expectations of a child's school (Delpit, 1990). Michaels (1986) found one particularly salient divergence in the ways in which African-American and white children told oral stories. During a "sharing time," children of both races were asked to share stories with the class. African-American and white children differed in the style of topical development of their stories, and their teachers differentially evaluated their stories. White children produced more literate, topic-centered narratives, which focused on a single object or event. African-American students tended to produce more oral, episodic narratives, which centered simultaneously on multiple objects and events. Results showed that stories by African-Americans were more likely to be negatively evaluated by their Caucasian teachers. In a related study that examined the race of the teachers as well as the children, Cazden (1988) found that white teachers, without knowing the race of the children they were evaluating, uniformly rated African-American children's narratives as inferior to those of white children. In contrast, African American teachers rated the children equally.

Taken together, these data suggest that children in poverty enter school ill-equipped to communicate in the language of the classroom. Children's linguistic limitations can be attributed partly to the lack of adequate scaffolding experiences in conversations between adults and children, which, if properly executed, would allow young speakers to expand their vocabularies by hearing new words and using them in meaningful ways. Second, families and children in poor communities often lack literacy experiences and materials in their general environment and in their homes. Children who are not frequently exposed to printed words lose many opportunities to develop the skills that support literacy learning in the classroom. Finally, the discontinuity between language expectations of the classroom and those of the home may impair the language and literacy learning of young, impoverished children. From an early age, children in poverty lack well-developed language and literacy skills, which inhibits their progress in school.

BOOK READING AND LANGUAGE DEVELOPMENT

Book reading is one of the most important activities in providing a context for language development in young children (Dickinson & Snow, 1987; Dickinson & Tabors, 1991; Sénéchal, LeFevre, Thomas, & Daley, 1998; Snow, 1983). Although there has been some controversy concerning the precise causal nature of early book reading and later literacy and academic skills (Scarborough & Dobrich, 1994), most scholars agree that shared book reading contributes in important ways to early literacy and language development (Bus et al., 1995; Lonigan, 1994; Payne, Whitehurst, & Angell, 1994; Snow et al., 1998). Book reading provides the context for rich conversations between a child and an adult. During book reading, interactions frequently extend beyond the text of the story and invite dialogue between the adult and the child. Adults and children ask questions, discuss vocabulary words, and predict what may happen next. Wells (1986) found that approximately 5% of the daily speech of 24-month-old children occurred in the context of story time. Similarly, the most frequent context for mothers' labeling objects with their 2-year-olds was during book reading (Ninio & Bruner, 1978). Moreover, these book-related interactions resulted in increased vocabulary development.

Another important aspect of book reading is that it presents children with decontextualized language (Dickinson & Snow, 1987; Snow, 1983). Decontextualized language communicates information or ideas that lie beyond the personal experiences of the reading audience, and therefore requires that readers think abstractly. Through book reading, children not only learn new information and vocabulary words that they might never encounter in their daily affairs and interactions, but also explore the conventions of printed words and the syntactic structure of language. Children's decontextualized language skills have been shown to be related to conventional components of literacy such as decoding, understanding story narratives, and print production (Dickinson & Snow, 1987).

STRATEGIES THAT ENHANCE
DISCOURSE DURING BOOK READING

In an effective book reading experience, the adult and child talk about the book, ask questions about its content, and together engage in a dialogue concerning either that content or related information. Research suggests that adults can use particular strategies during book reading to promote greater opportunities for discourse, which in turn facilitates the development of children's language and literacy skills. Among these are asking questions, using non-immediate talk, which is talk that goes beyond the text of the book, and rereading a text with children. In the following sections, a discussion of these book-reading strategies will be presented.

Questioning Strategies

Asking children questions during book reading engages them in conversations about the text. The types of questions asked, the timing of the questions, and the feedback given to the questions significantly affect what children learn during book reading, and can be particularly effective tools for developing children's vocabulary. Sénéchal (1997) assessed the effects of three reading conditions on children's vocabulary knowledge. Thirty 3- and 4-year-olds were assigned to one of three conditions: a single book reading, a repeated book reading, and a book reading with questioning. In the book, familiar words were replaced with novel words, such as *angling* for *fishing*. The intention of the study was to determine if rereading or questioning during book reading facilitated the acquisition of new vocabulary words. After the reading, children were assessed on their knowledge of the new vocabulary words. Children in the questioning and repeated-reading conditions learned more vocabulary words than did children in the single-reading condition. Children in these conditions also engaged in conversations beyond the content of the book that contributed to their understanding of novel words, an indication that these strategies encouraged children to delve more deeply into the book and extract more from the reading.

Work by Whitehurst suggests that asking open-ended questions facilitates discourse during book reading. In a series of influential studies, Whitehurst and his colleagues (Arnold, Lonigan, Whitehurst, & Epstein, 1994; Payne, Whitehurst, & Angell, 1994; Valdez-Menchaca & Whitehurst, 1992; Whitehurst, Arnold, Epstein, Angell, Smith, & Fischel, 1994; Whitehurst, Epstein, Angell, Payne, Crone, & Fischel, 1994; Whitehurst, Falco et al., 1988) demonstrated that a program of shared reading, termed *dialogic reading*, can produce substantial changes in low-income preschool children's language skills. Dialogic reading involves a series of procedures in which the adult asks open-ended questions, creates opportunities for the children to participate in storytelling, and actively listens to and encourages a discussion about the story.

The dialogic reading program emphasizes several principles about book reading which are summarized by the acronym CROWD. The C stands for the use of completion prompts, which invite children to answer fill-in-the-blank questions related to the story content. The R stands for the practice of using recall prompts to aid in the recall of the story. The O stands for the use of open-ended questions, and the W represents the practice of asking Wh-questions, including why, where, and what queries. The dialogic reading training program encourages adults to replace questions that call for a simple "yes" or "no" response with more open-ended queries that prompt children to use language to communicate their opinions and ideas. Finally, the D stands for the distancing prompts that connect the story to the child's own experiences. As children become accustomed to these procedures, the adult shifts more of the responsibility for storytelling to the children, and the children initiate the interactions about the stories.

One-to-one interventions using dialogic reading have resulted in significant gains in language skills among children in high-, middle-, and low-income families (Whitehurst et al., 1988). Whitehurst et al. (1988) found that when dialogic reading was implemented with middle-class children, children in the intervention group scored significantly higher on a test of expressive language than did children in the comparison group. When dialogic reading was tested on a group of high-poverty children, the findings were again consistently positive. Valdez-Menchaca and Whitehurst (1992) examined dialogic reading with 20 children attending public daycare centers in Mexico. Children in this daycare were living in poverty with an annual family income of less than $2500. Children in the experimental condition received one-to-one dialogic reading experiences, while children in the comparison group engaged in a perceptual motor task for the same amount of time. After six weeks, the children in the dialogic group demonstrated significantly more growth in oral language skills, as assessed by standard measures of vocabulary and spontaneous measures of verbalizations.

The work of Whitehurst and his colleagues show the positive effects of asking open-ended, provocative questions that invite young children to discuss their ideas and opinions about books. These procedures also provide a model for the way in which young children can ask their own questions. Book reading that supports children engaging in dialogue with the teacher and other children promotes the use of language. Through this scaffolding process, adults help children develop more sophisticated communication skills and incorporate new vocabulary words into their repertoires.

Non-immediate Talk

Although creating opportunities for discourse is important for language development during book reading, the quality of this discourse is more important than the quantity. Talk without direction and meaning will not enhance children's expressive and receptive language skills. High-quality conversations that allow children to take the information in a book and extend it to their own experiences can contribute to the development of language. Essential to these kinds of conversations is non-immediate talk, defined as discourse in which parties make inferences or predictions, connect the text to the world or to other texts, or give explanations and information about print or language. For example, when an adult reads a book about animals with children, the adult might make a connection between the animals in the book and the animals that the children saw during their recent field trip to the zoo. Non-immediate talk supports children's language development because, as children themselves begin to extend ideas beyond their immediate context in a book, they practice using language to link their personal experiences to the words presented in the book.

DeTemple and Snow (1992) observed parents reading to their 3- and 4-year-olds and found that the amount of non-immediate language in the discourse during the book reading predicted children's language and vocabulary skills at 5 years of age. Thirty-nine low-income mothers read books to their children during two home visits, first when the children were $3\frac{1}{2}$ years old, and again when the children were $4\frac{1}{2}$ years old. The book reading sessions were taped, and the content was analyzed to generate information about (a) the amount of maternal talk beyond the written text, (b) the relative roles of the mother and child in requesting and giving information, and (c) the amount of requested or given information that was classified as "non-immediate" talk.

At age 5, all of the children were administered the Peabody Picture Vocabulary Test-Revised (Dunn & Dunn, 1981), a measure of emergent literacy and print knowledge, a story comprehension task, and a sequencing task. The results indicated that there was as a significant positive relationship between mothers' non-immediate talk during book reading and children's performance on all measures.

Haden, Reese, and Fivush (1996) found similar results in a study of 3- and 4-year-olds whose mothers read stories to them. The children's knowledge of print and story understanding was assessed at age 5. Nineteen mothers from middle-class homes were audio-taped, first when their children were 3 years 3 months, and a second time when the children were 4 years 8 months. At 5 years old, the children were administered a literacy assessment which included the PPVT-R, a task exploring concepts of print, and a measure gauging story production, comprehension, and retelling abilities. The utterances during these book-reading sessions were coded as high-, medium-, and low-level, and a cluster analysis was done to categorize the level of utterances. Three types of reading styles were identified: (a) describers who focused on low-level utterances; (b) comprehenders who engaged in more high-level/high-demand, extra-textual talk; and (c) collaborators who confirmed the child's contributions to the dialogue and who elicited the child's commentary about the story.

At 5 years of age, children whose mothers were classified as describers performed lower on measures of receptive language, word recognition, and story comprehension than did children of comprehenders and collaborators. The results indicate that parents who asked questions and made comments that expanded upon the information explicitly stated in the text promoted their children's language and literacy development. These findings imply that children benefit from story time discussion that transcends the simple facts on each page, engaging them instead in examination, predictions, and connections.

Timing of Questioning and Discourse

The timing of discourse during book reading can also have an impact on children's language development. Dickinson and Smith (1994) observed the book reading behavior of teachers in 25 high-poverty preschool classrooms. Videotapes of teachers reading to their classes were coded for types of reading behavior. A cluster analysis revealed three distinct patterns of book reading: (a) a co-constructive approach in which teachers and children engaged in extended, cognitively challenging conversations throughout the book reading; (b) a didactic-interactional approach in which children responded to questions about factual details and produced portions of the text in chorus; and (c) a performance-oriented approach in which the text was read with a selective, limited discussion, followed by extended discussion.

One year after the observations of book readings were conducted, all children were administered the PPVT-R and a story comprehension task. The analysis revealed that children who were in the performance-oriented classrooms performed better on the PPVT-R than children in the other classrooms did. This suggests that having a limited amount of discussion and questioning during the book reading, followed by extensive discussion after the reading, may help children focus on the language and content of the book and then encourage them to reflect on what they have absorbed. In addition, when controlling for the amount of teacher talk during the reading, researchers found that discourse featuring analysis, prediction, and vocabulary-related utterances by both the teacher and the children accounted for half of the variation in the children's PPVT-R scores. Similar results were found when controlling for teacher talk before and after the reading.

The results from this study indicate that constant talk during a book reading experience, even though this talk may be of high quality, might impede young children's abilities to process information. Instead, limited discourse that includes making predictions and inferences during the book reading helps children to focus on the book. Subsequent discussion that goes beyond the information presented in the book further contributes to children's language and literacy growth.

Rereading

Research consistently shows that children learn more from a book when it is read more than once (Morrow, 1988). With each reading, children can attend to another of the many aspects of the book and can further explore unfamiliar words and concepts. During a first reading, children often attend to the pictures in a book, which can be its most salient aspect. On a second reading, children can attend more carefully to the text of the book. On a third reading, children can attend specifically to unfamiliar vocabulary words. As the text becomes increasingly familiar to the children, there are more opportunities to engage in non-immediate talk and make connections to their own experiences (Wasik & Bond, 1999).

Repeated readings of a book can stimulate discourse and contribute to the development of vocabulary. Morrow (1988) found that children who were read a story three times made significantly more comments about the story and asked significantly more questions than children who were read the story only once. Research has also shown that reading a book multiple times can improve vocabulary development in young children (Cornell, Sénéchal, & Broda, 1988; Robbins & Ehri, 1994; Sénéchal & Cornell, 1993; Sénéchal, 1997). In a series of studies, Sénéchal and her colleagues found that rereading stories to young children contributed to the increase in their vocabulary compared to children who had a single reading of a book. Reading a story multiple times increased the amount of discourse children used in discussing the book. Each additional opportunity to think and talk about ideas and words in a book advances a child's language and literacy abilities.

Group Size

Discourse during book reading is also affected by the size of the group involved in the activity. When reading to groups of 10 to 16 young children, typical of a preschool class, teachers must keep the whole audience engaged and on-task. Such large-group settings provide individual children with few opportunities to talk with and listen to others. When dialogic reading was implemented with groups of four children and one adult, researchers found less robust results. Whitehurst, Epstein et al. (1994) examined the effects of dialogic reading on 4-year-olds in Head Start centers. Classrooms were randomly assigned to one of two conditions. One group of classrooms implemented phonemic awareness activities and exposed children, in groups of four, to dialogic reading strategies. In addition, the parents of these children were trained to extend dialogic book reading procedures into the home. The other group of classrooms received the regular Head Start curriculum. As in previous studies (Valdez-Menchaca & Whitehurst, 1992; Whitehurst et al., 1988), the results showed significant effects for writing and concepts of print. Yet unlike the earlier, one-to-one interventions, findings on the language measures merely approached significance. Whitehurst, Epstein et al. (1994) suggested that group interactions may have detracted from the one-to-one contact between the adult and child, thereby limiting valuable opportunities for discourse.

Ideally, one-to-one book reading would allow children to engage in rich discourse with an adult. But although one-to-one book reading may be the best strategy to promote discourse with young children, it has practical limitations in preschool settings. With limited staff, it is difficult to conduct one-to-one book reading during class time. An alternative to one-to-one book reading is to reduce the size of the reading group. Work by Morrow and Smith (1990) compared the comprehension of books by children who were read to (a) one-to-one; (b) in groups of three children; and (c) in groups of 10 children. Children who were read to in small groups of three performed better on comprehension questions related to the stories. Reading books in groups of three allowed children to interact with the adult and each other. Perhaps by increasing the size of the group from three to four children as found in Whitehurst, Epstein et al. (1994), opportunities for discourse become increasingly limited.

Reading at home, one-to-one with an adult, contributes significantly to young children's language development. Whitehurst, Arnold et al. (1994) found that the home intervention, which provided a one-to-one reading experience, was a critical factor in improving language skills. To compare the effects of home and classroom use of dialogic reading, Whitehurst, Arnold et al. (1994) randomly assigned children in low-income daycare to one of three conditions: (a) a classroom and home condition, in which the children were read to by their parents and teachers using dialogic reading; (b) a school-only condition, in which the children were read to only by teachers using dialogic reading; and (c) a control condition, in which the children engaged in play activities other than reading. Parents in the latter two conditions were not trained in the dialogic reading program. In settings where dialogic reading was being implemented with fidelity, children in the home-plus-school dialogic reading condition performed better on measures of expressive language than children in the school-only condition. In an extension of this work, Lonigan and Whitehurst (1998) also found that the combination of dialogic reading in both the home and the school resulted in significant language gains for young children. In general, the one-to-one experiences with dialogic reading contributed significantly to the effectiveness of the intervention and to the literacy development of the children.

STRATEGIES THAT ENHANCE
DISCOURSE BEYOND BOOK READING

Book reading is an essential activity for developing language and literacy skills. However, reading books contributes only a small portion of the discourse that occurs between children and adults (Scarborough & Dobrich, 1994). In order for young children to master new words and language structures, they need to have multiple opportunities to encounter and use language in different contexts. Opportunities for discourse distinct from book readings are especially important for disadvantaged children who, as discussed above, often have less access to literacy materials and experiences. In this section, opportunities beyond book reading that support discourse are presented.

Extending the Discourse of Book Reading

Typically, parents and classroom teachers read a book and, when the book is finished, mention little about its context or vocabulary (Dickinson, 1999). Unless a book is reread or extended into related activities, the book reading becomes an isolated activity. Recent research, however, has shown that when discourse connected to book reading is extended beyond the book through other activities, children's opportunities to use language increase.

In high-poverty preschool classrooms, Wasik and Bond (in press) studied the effects of extending a vocabulary intervention beyond book reading. Teachers in the intervention group were given a set of materials and trained in discourse strategies to increase the amount of conversation between the adult and the children. The materials were organized around specific topics that are commonly used in preschool classrooms such as clothing, the seasons, and starting school. Each box of materials contained two age-appropriate books connected to the topic. The two books contained similar vocabulary words on the selected topic. The box also contained concrete objects that represented the target vocabulary in the books. For example, the garden prop box contained the books, *The Carrot Seed* by Ruth Krauss and *Jack's Garden* by Henry Cole. The box also contained the following objects: seeds, a shovel, a rake, a small version of a garden hose, a watering can, insects, flowers, a stalk of corn, and a carrot. The teacher would introduce the props, have the children label the objects, and then point out these words while reading the stories.

In addition to the books and props, instructions and materials for extension activities were provided. The activities included arts and crafts activities such as making a paper plate garden and painting a garden picture, science activities such as planting carrot or bean seeds, and cooking activities such as making a vegetable platter and eating it during snack time. These activities were to take place after the book reading. The goal was to have the teachers and children continue to talk about the concepts and vocabulary as they were implementing the book-related activities.

In addition to materials, teachers were provided with training in both book reading and discourse strategies. The book reading strategies were similar to those used in Whitehurst's work, in which teachers were trained to ask open-ended questions and to make connections between the book and the children's experiences. In addition, teachers were trained in discourse strategies to be used both during the book readings and the extension activities. For example, teachers were trained to ask questions that prompt children to talk about and use the target vocabulary words, elicit rich language exchanges, and make explicit connections between the book and the extension activities. These strategies were first modeled for the teachers, after which the teachers were observed and provided with feedback on their book reading and discourse behaviors. Teachers in the comparison group were given the books but were not provided with the additional materials or the training.

Findings from Wasik and Bond (2001) indicated that children who had opportunities to extend the concepts and vocabulary beyond the book reading itself increased their performance on expressive and receptive vocabulary measures. Qualitative analysis also revealed that teachers in the intervention group consistently used the new vocabulary both during the book reading and after the book reading activity was complete. This did not occur in the comparison group, where the vocabulary was often used once during book reading and only infrequently after the reading. The results showed that, in comparison to children in the control group, children in the intervention group scored significantly better on receptive and expressive measures targeting vocabulary specific to the intervention books. In addition, children in the intervention group scored better on the PPVT-III, a more general measure of receptive vocabulary.

Extending the discourse about books beyond the reading group itself facilitates the language development of disadvantaged children. Books provide a springboard for discourse, but the activities connected to the book reading allow children to explore language, use book-related vocabulary, and communicate their ideas to a receptive and trained teacher. As Whitehurst's work suggests, isolated book reading events in classrooms may require additional support, either through home interventions or through activities that extend the language beyond the book reading.

Play and Literacy Discourse

Play creates an important context for children's discourse with adults and other children (Roskos & Christie, 2000). During play, children have the opportunity to talk freely about the activities in which they are involved. Research has shown that the physical setting and the available materials of the play environment affect the nature and the content of play (Morrow, 1990; Morrow & Rand, 1991). Structuring the play environment specifically to promote literacy activities increases the likelihood that children will engage in discussion related to literacy events such as reading and writing, discussion that will enhance both their language and literacy knowledge.

In a series of studies, Neuman and Roskos (1990, 1991, 1993, 1994) demonstrated how literacy-rich environments encourage literacy-related discourse during play. Neuman and Roskos (1991) worked with high-poverty preschool classrooms to infuse classroom play with literacy opportunities. To provide ample opportunities for children's interactions, the classroom was reorganized to designate four play areas: the post office, the library, the office, and the kitchen. Relevant literacy props were organized in each play space. For example, the kitchen center included recipe cards, coupons, and cookbooks. Each area was also equipped with printed materials and literacy tools, including pencils, markers, and assorted stationery. Labeling of objects was done extensively throughout these settings as a reference tool for materials, toys, and information.

Children's play behavior was recorded through extensive observations over a two-month period. Verbal interactions were coded for the amount of literacy discourse that occurred during play. Literacy discourse was defined as exchanges in reading- and writing-like activities and behaviors. Three types of discourse about literacy were identified in the play context; children's conversations focused on (a) designating the names of literacy-related objects, (b) negotiating meaning related to a literacy topic, and (c) coaching another child in some literacy task in order to achieve a goal of play. In general, the literacy-rich environment promoted discourse on literacy; children engaged in writing activities, conversations about literacy, and discussions about books and literacy materials. Neuman and Roskos (1991) suggested that the print-rich environment provided special opportunities for preschool interactions centering on the language of reading and writing.

In addition to the physical setting and the materials available during play, the number of children involved in play can affect the quality of the children's discourse. This data was based on the longitudinal Harvard Home-School Study of Language and Literacy Development that followed 84 children from low-income families from age 3 through their early years, dividing them into two cohorts, with the first cohort including 39 children who received home visits (Dickinson & Tabors, 2001). Findings from the Harvard Home-School study have shown that significant discourse can occur in small group activities (Beals, DeTemple, & Dickinson, 1994). As noted previously with regard to book reading, children have greater opportunities to talk, to listen, and to be heard when they work and play in small groups. Analysis of longitudinal data showed that the amount of time teachers reported engaging 3-year-olds in small, teacher-led groups related positively to the children's literacy and receptive vocabulary skills upon reaching kindergarten. The amount of time that 4-year-olds spent in small teacher-led groups related significantly to their story understanding, receptive vocabulary, and emergent literacy skills.

Findings from the Harvard Home-School study also showed that small-group activities, including art and play, provided opportunities for "cognitively challenging talk" (Beals et al., 1994). Children were observed in their classrooms and samples of children's verbal interactions were documented. The children's verbalizations were then coded based on what was cognitively challenging talk. Cognitively challenging talk is defined as (a) talk about abstract or non-immediate topics (such as plans for the future), (b) talk that encourages children to think deeply about issues, and (c) talk about print. The results suggested that the amount of time that 4-year-olds spent in small group activities related significantly to performance on measures of story understanding, receptive language, and emergent literacy. In addition, the longitudinal data suggests that 4-year-olds who engaged in cognitively challenging talk performed better on measures of story telling, emergent literacy, and receptive vocabulary at age 5. Conversations related to knowledge of non-present issues, print concepts, and vocabulary words facilitate children's language and literacy development. In general, the results of this longitudinal study indicate that it was the specific content of the talk, not the overall amount of talk, that contributed to children's successful development of language and literacy skills.

Different approaches to book reading have also been found to influence the use of literacy-related talk during play. Fein, Ardila-Rey, and Groth (2000) compared the use of two book-reading techniques in preschool classrooms. In one group, children acted as authors and "read" stories to their peers. In another group, children actively dramatized the events in the stories. Children in the dramatization group were found to use significantly more print-related language during play than the children in the other group. Researchers observed that children in the dramatization group acted out the stories in books, invented their own stories, and talked about books. For these children, play became an extension of the book reading experience.

Mealtimes and Discourse

Mealtimes present many opportunities for children to engage in discourse with both adults and other children. At home and in schools, mealtime conversations focus on a variety of topics including the day's events, interesting news, and future plans and activities. Research has shown that conversations during mealtime are similar to discourse that occurs during book reading (Beals et al., 1994). Specifically, mealtime conversations often contain the narrative, explanatory, and vocabulary-related talk that is frequently observed during book reading (Beals, 1997).

Mealtime conversations contain both the narrative and explanatory aspects of book reading. Conversations during a meal often consist of someone telling a story about an event. The speaker, like the reader, tells the story, while the listeners ask questions or add comments to help clarify the event. In the Harvard Home-School study, Beals et al. (1994) examined the mealtime dialogue of preschoolers raised in poverty both at school and at home. Conversations were coded for two types of discourse, narrative and explanation. Talk was coded as narrative when the topic involved a past or future event and was coded as explanation when it sought to elucidate some logical connection between objects, events, and ideas.

The observations revealed that a significant amount of mealtime conversation consisted of narrative talk. Of the narrative talk, for 3-year-olds, the mother contributed 40% and the target 3-year-olds contributed 28%. Other family members contributed the remaining 32%. For 4-year-olds, the mother contributed 46% of the narrative talk and the target child contributed 30%. These findings suggest that the mother spoke frequently, while the child questioned or responded to the mother's commentary. This is similar to a book reading scenario in which the mother reads a story and the child either responds to questions that the mother asks or poses questions to clarify the story. The amount of discourse devoted to explanatory talk was also significant. The mother contributed 47% of the explanations in the conversation, and the target child contributed 27%. It appears that, during mealtime discourse, the adult creates the context for the conversation and provides opportunities for the child to respond or question the content of the conversation.

Beals et al. (1994) also found that both the amount of explanatory talk and the number of narratives that 4-year-old children were exposed to during mealtime were positively correlated with their PPVT scores at 5 years of age; children with more exposure to explanatory and narrative talk showed greater receptive language at age 5. Also, the higher the number of narrative utterances and the larger the proportion of narrative to non-narrative talk in mealtime at age 4, the better the children's scores on story comprehension at age 5. These findings suggest that children do not need to offer their own explanations and narratives. Children benefit from hearing explanations and narratives, requesting them, and adding their own comments when appropriate. Similar findings were reported in Beals and Smith (1992).

Mealtime conversations have also been found to facilitate vocabulary development in young children. Beals' (1997) work suggests that (a) during mealtime, children are provided with a broad range of words and supports for learning unfamiliar words, and (b) children of preschool age draw a great deal of information about unfamiliar words from conversations. As most of their word learning is not done through explicit defining of unfamiliar words, children instead extrapolate the meaning of words from the context of the conversation and other cues in the interchange. Mealtime offers many opportunities for this kind of discovery. For example, in one child's mealtime dialogue with her father, the child infers the meaning of the word "license" by drawing upon the content of the conversation and the responses her father made during the conversation. Extended conversations offer children many opportunities both to hear unusual words being used by a more knowledgeable speaker and to connect new words and concepts to what they already know.

Beals' (1997) study also revealed that the frequency of informative use of unfamiliar words at ages three and four was positively correlated with children's PPVT scores at ages 5 and 7. Children who, during their preschool years, were frequently exposed to unfamiliar words being used in informative ways, showed greater vocabularies at ages 5 and 7. Similar to book-reading experiences, rich language interactions that occur during mealtime can facilitate vocabulary development in young children.

SUMMARY

Engaging in discourse facilitates the language and literacy development of young children. Through participating in conversations with adults and peers, receiving feedback on their language, and listening to adult discourse, young children learn new vocabulary words and explore the structural and functional aspects of language. Discourse, therefore, represents an important tool in the promotion of language development in children, particularly those who come to school from disadvantaged backgrounds where literacy experiences are scarce.

The research on language and literacy development suggests that discourse can be encouraged through various contexts. Book reading is considered one of the most important activities related to language and literacy development. Discourse during book reading allows children to expand upon the information presented in the text, clarify the meaning of unfamiliar information, and make connections between the book and their own experiences. Research-based strategies such asking open-ended questions at the appropriate time, talking about information beyond the text, and limiting the number of children included in a single reading group can contribute to language development.

Extending the information and vocabulary from books to other related activities also affects language and literacy development. Making connections from a book to other activities will help reinforce the concepts in a story and provide children with multiple opportunities to interact with the book. Art, music, center activities, and other small-group experiences that allow children to work with the language, vocabulary, and concepts of the books they have read facilitate the development of language. The additional strategy of presenting children with concrete representations of vocabulary words (Wasik & Bond, 2001) and making the connections between the vocabulary in the book and the vocabulary in related activities will promote the development of language.

Playtime and mealtime also provide excellent opportunities for discourse. Print-rich play environments increase the probability that children will integrate literacy materials and events into their play and conversations. Mealtimes foster spontaneous discourse that resembles the valuable talk surrounding book reading. Even though adults contribute much of the talk during these interactions, children gain valuable language skills as they listen to the narratives and explanations of new information or vocabulary words.

Teachers working with children in poverty must structure opportunities for children to engage in discourse with adults and with one another. The following suggestions can increase the opportunities for discourse and language development in young children.

1. Book reading must occur daily. Teachers and families must engage young children in discussions about vocabulary and content both during readings, with well-chosen questions and after, with structured extension of activities. Book reading activities need to engage young children and create opportunities for the children and adults to talk about the content and vocabulary in the book. The experiences that the children learn about from the book need to be connected to other experiences that children have in their classroom and in their daily lives.

2. Teachers need to create both formal and informal opportunities for children to talk and receive feedback on their language. In small group activities, teachers can listen to children, ask questions, and encourage appropriate responses. Specifically, small groups of three children can create the environment that allows young children to

talk and to respond. Informal situations such as transitions between activities, trips to the playground, and meals also provide the opportunities for children and teachers to engage in conversations.

3. Teachers need to model active listening skills for young children. Active listening is learned. Children need to be taught how to listen in order to process the information from other adults and children. Often in a dialogue, young children are concerned with what they want to say, and this interferes with their ability to listen to others talk. Teachers need to model active listening skills that include being quiet as others talk, paying attention to what others say, and asking questions to clarify what is not understood. Turn-taking is also an important part of active listening. Children need explicit guidance in learning to take turns in a dialogue.

4. Teachers need to develop children's vocabulary knowledge through explicit instruction. In classrooms, children in poverty are exposed to many frequently used vocabulary words of which they do not know the meaning. Teachers need to explicitly describe the meaning of words and try to make connections between new and familiar words. Labeling objects in the classroom and describing words that are encountered in books are important ways to teach children unfamiliar words.

5. Finally, teachers must acknowledge cultural and linguistic differences in children and their families. Children of poverty come to school with many skills; however, these skills may not match the expectations of the classroom culture. Teachers need to understand the language and vocabulary of the children they teach and create a bridge between children's home language and the language of school.

Opportunities for discourse guided by these strategies will help children in poverty develop the language and literacy skills needed to succeed in learning to read.

ACKNOWLEDGMENTS

This research was supported under the funding from the Office of Educational Research and Improvement, U.S. Department of Education (Grant No. R-117D-40005). However the opinions expressed are those of the authors and do not necessarily represent the positions or polices of the U.S. Department of Education.

REFERENCES

Alexander, K.L., & Entwisle, D.R. (1988). Achievement in the first two years of school: Patterns and processes. *Monographs of the Society for Research in Child Development, 53* (2, Serial No. 218).

Arnold, D.H., Lonigan, C.J., Whitehurst, G.J., & Epstein, J.N. (1994). Accelerating language development through picture book reading: Replication and extension to videotape training format. *Journal of Educational Psychology, 86,* 235–243.

Beals, D.E. (1997). Sources of support for learning words in conversation: Evidence from mealtimes. *Journal of Child Language, 24,* 673–94.

Beals, D.E., DeTemple, J.M., & Dickinson, D.K. (1994). Talking and listening that support early literacy development of low-income children. In D.K. Dickinson (Ed.), *Bridges to literacy: Children, families, and schools* (pp. 19–40). Cambridge, MA: Blackwell.

Beals, D.E., & Smith, M.W. (1992, April). *Eating, reading, and pretending: Predictors of kindergarten literacy skills.* Paper presented at the Annual Meeting of the American Educational Research Association, San Francisco, CA.

Bowman, B.T., Donovan, M.S., & Burns, M.S. (2001). *Eager to learn: Educating our preschoolers.* Washington, DC: National Academy Press.

Boyer, E.L. (1991). *Ready to learn: A mandate for the nation* (Carnegie Foundation Special Report). Lawrenceville, NJ: Carnegie Foundation for the Advancement of Teaching/ Princeton University Press.

Bus, A.G., van Ijzendoorn, M.H., & Pelligrini, A.D. (1995). Joint book reading makes for success in learning to read: A meta-analysis on intergenerational transmission of literacy. *Review of Educational Research, 65,* 1–21.

Cazden, C.B. (1988). *Classroom discourse.* Portsmouth, NH: Heinemann.

Coll, C.G., Lamberty, G., Jenkins, R., McAdoo, H.P., Crnic, K., Wasik, B.H., Garcia, H.V. (1996). An integrative model for the study of development competencies in minority children. *Child Development, 67,* 1891–1914.

Cornell, E.H., Sénéchal, M., & Broda, L. (1988). Recall of picture books by three-year-old children: Testing and repetition effects in joint activities. *Journal of Educational Psychology, 80,* 537–542.

Delpit, L. D. (1990). Language diversity and learning. In S. Hynds & D. L. Rubin, (Eds.), *Perspectives on talk and learning* (pp. 274–266). Urbana, IL: National Council of Teachers of English.

DeTemple, J.E., & Snow, C.E. (1992, April). *Styles of parent-child book reading as related to mothers' views of literacy and children's literacy outcomes.* Paper presented at the Conference on Human Development, Atlanta, GA.

Dickinson, D.K. (1999). *Dimensions of reading style and pattern of book use in preschool.* Paper presented at the 49th annual meeting of the National Reading Conference, Orlando, FL.

Dickinson, D.K., & Smith, M.W. (1994). Long-term effects of preschool teachers' book readings on low-income children's vocabulary and story comprehension. *Reading Research Quarterly, 29,* 104–122.

Dickinson, D.K., & Snow, C.E. (1987). Interrelationships among pre-reading and oral language skills in kindergartners from two social classes. *Early Childhood Research Quarterly, 2,* 1–25.

Dickinson, D.K., & Tabors, P.O. (1991). Early literacy: Linkages between home, school, and literacy achievement at age five. *Journal of Research in Childhood Education, 6*, 30–46.

Dickinson, D.K., & Tabors, P.O. (2001). *Beginning literacy with language: Young children learning at home and school.* Baltimore, MD: Paul Brookes.

Dunn, L., & Dunn, L. (1981). *Peabody picture vocabulary test—revised.* Circle Pines, MN: American Guidance Services.

Fein, G.G., Ardila-Rey, A.E., & Groth, L.A. (2000). The narrative connection: Stories and literacy. In K.A. Roskos & J.K. Christie (Eds.), *Play and literacy in early childhood: Research from multiple connections* (pp. 27–43). Mahwah, NJ: Erlbaum.

Haden, C. A., Reese, E., & Fivush, R. (1996). Mothers' extratextual comments during storybook reading: Stylistic differences over time and across texts. *Discourse Processes, 21*, 135–169.

Hart, B., & Risley, T.R. (1995). *Meaningful differences in the everyday experience of young American children.* Baltimore: Paul H. Brookes.

Hart, B., & Risley, T.R. (1999). *The social world of children: Learning to talk.* Baltimore: Paul H. Brookes.

Heath, S.B. (1983). *Ways with words: Language, life and work in communities and classrooms.* New York: Cambridge University Press.

Jordan, G.E., Snow, C.E., & Porche, M.V. (2000). Project EASE: The effect of a family literacy project on kindergarten students' early literacy skills. *Reading Research Quarterly, 35*, 524–546.

Lonigan, C.J. (1994). Reading to preschoolers exposed: Is the emperor really naked? *Developmental Review, 14*, 303–323.

Lonigan, C.J., & Whitehurst, G.J. (1998). Relative efficacy of parent and teacher involvement in a shared-reading intervention for preschool children from low-income backgrounds. *Early Childhood Research Quarterly, 13*, 263–290.

Metsala, J.L., & Ehri, L.C. (Eds). (1998). *Word recognition in beginning literacy.* Mahwah, NJ: Erlbaum.

Michaels, S., (1986). Narrative presentations: An oral preparation for literacy with first grade. In J. Cook-Gumperz (Ed.), *The social construction of literacy* (pp. 94–116). New York: Cambridge University Press.

Morrow, L.M. (1988). Young children's responses to one-to-one readings in school settings. *Reading Research Quarterly, 23*, 89–107.

Morrow, L.M. (1990). Preparing the classroom environment to promote literacy during play. *Early Childhood Research Quarterly, 5*, 537–554.

Morrow, L.M., & Rand, M.K. (1991). Promoting literacy during play by designing early childhood classroom environments. *Reading Teacher, 44*, 396–402.

Morrow, L.M., & Smith, J.K. (1990). The effect of group size on interactive storybook reading. *Reading Research Quarterly, 25*, 213–231.

Neuman, S.B. (1999, December). *When teachers talk to children: Analyzing the quality of instructional conversations during storybook reading and activity time in preschools.* Paper presented at the National Reading Conference, Orlando, FL.

Newman, S.B., & Celano, D. (2001) Access to print in low-income and middle-income communities: An ecological study of four neighborhoods. *Reading Research Quarterly, 36*, 8–26.

Neuman, S.B., & Roskos, K.A. (1990). Play, print, and purpose: Enriching play environments for literacy development. *Reading Teacher, 44*, 214–221.

Neuman, S.B., & Roskos, K.A. (1991). Peers as literacy informants: A description of young children's literacy conversations in play. *Early Childhood Research Quarterly, 6*, 233–248.

Neuman, S.B., & Roskos, K.A. (1993). Access to print for children of poverty: Differential effects of adult mediation and literacy-enriched play settings on environmental and functional print tasks. *American Educational Research Journal, 30*(1), 95–102.

Neuman, S.B., & Roskos, K.A. (1994). Of scribbles, schemas, and storybooks: Using literacy albums to document young children's literacy growth. *Young Children, 49*, 78–85.

Ninio, A., & Bruner, J. (1978). The achievement and antecedents of labeling. *Child Language, 5*, 1–15.

Payne, A., Whitehurst, G.J., & Angell, A. (1994). The role of home literacy environment in the development of language ability in preschool children from low-income families. *Early Childhood Research Quarterly, 9*, 427–440.

Puma, M., Karweit, N., Price, C., Ricciuti, A., Thompson, W., & Vaden-Kiernan, M. (1997). *Prospects: Final report on student outcomes*. Washington, DC: U.S. Department of Education, Planning and Evaluation Services.

Robbins, C., & Ehri, L.C. (1994). Reading storybooks to kindergartners helps them learn new vocabulary words. *Journal of Educational Psychology, 86*, 54–64.

Roskos, K.A., & Christie, J.F. (Eds.). (2000). *Play and literacy in early childhood: Research from multiple perspectives*. Mahwah, NJ: Erlbaum.

Scarborough, H., & Dobrich, W. (1994). On the efficacy of reading to preschoolers. *Developmental Review, 14*, 245–302.

Sénéchal, M. (1997). The differential effect of storybook reading on preschoolers' acquisition of expressive and receptive vocabulary. *Journal of Child Language, 24*, 123–138.

Sénéchal, M., & Cornell, E.H. (1993). Vocabulary acquisition through shared reading experiences. *Reading Research Quarterly, 28*, 360–374.

Sénéchal, M., LeFevre, J., Thomas, E.M., & Daley, K.E. (1998). Differential effects of home literacy experiences on the development of oral and written language. *Reading Research Quarterly, 33*, 96–116.

Snow, C.E. (1983). Literacy and language: Relationships during the preschool years. *Harvard Educational Review, 53*, 165–189.

Snow, C.E., Burns, S., & Griffin, P. (Eds.). (1998). *Preventing reading difficulties in young children*. Washington, DC: National Academy Press.

Teale, W.H., & Sulzby, E. (Eds.). (1986). *Emergent literacy: Writing and reading*. Norwood, NJ: Ablex.

Valdez-Menchaca, M.C., & Whitehurst, G.J. (1992). Accelerating language development through picture book reading: A systematic extension to Mexican day care. *Developmental Psychology, 28*, 1106–1114.

Wasik, B.A., & Bond, M.A. (1999). Interactive book reading and vocabulary development. Paper presented at the National Reading Conference, Orlando, FL.

Wasik, B.A., & Bond, M.A. (2001). Beyond the pages of a book: Interactive book reading and language development in preschool classrooms. *Journal of Educational Psychology, 93*, 243–250.

Wells, G. (1986). *The meaning makers: Children learning language and using language to learn.* Portsmouth, NH: Heinemann.

Whitehurst, G.J., Arnold, D.S., Epstein, J.N., Angell, A.L., Smith, M., & Fischel, J.E. (1994). A picture book reading intervention in day care and home for children from low-income families. *Developmental Psychology, 30*, 679–689.

Whitehurst, G.J., Epstein, J.N., Angell, A.L., Payne, A.C., Crone, D.A., & Fischel, J.E. (1994). Outcomes of an emergent literacy intervention in Head Start. *Journal of Educational Psychology, 86*, 542–555.

Whitehurst, G.J., Falco, F.L., Lonigan, C.J., Fischel, J.E., DeBaryshe, B.D., Valdez-Menchaca, M.C., & Caufield, M.B. (1988). Accelerating language development through picture book reading. *Developmental Psychology, 24*, 552–559.

Whitehurst, G.J., & Lonigan, C.J. (1998). Child development and emergent literacy. *Child Development, 69*, 848–872.

CHAPTER 4

STORYBOOK READING:

What We Know and
What We Should Consider

Jon Shapiro, Jim Anderson, and Ann Anderson

INTRODUCTION

We are at an interesting point in the teaching and learning of literacy in North America. Influenced principally by the fields of linguistics and psychology, reading and writing have until recently been conceived of as a set of skills which, when mastered, are transferable from one context to another. However, the evolving work of ethnographers and sociolinguists in different social and cultural contexts has helped us to begin to understand literacy as social practice (Barton, Hamilton, & Ivanic, 2000; Gee, 1996; Street, 1995). For as Clay (1993) explained, the literacy practices engaged in by a particular cultural group, the meanings ascribed to literacy, and the ways in which literacy is mediated is determined by the values and beliefs of the group. We believe it is important to foreground the notion of literacy as social practice for several reasons. First, we want to recognize that what counts as literacy can differ markedly from one context to another. Second, because literacy practices differ across contexts, we believe that making universal assumptions about the importance of any particular literacy practice or event is unwise and can disadvantage some children. Third, because literacy practices are socially constructed, particular literacy events or activities or practices will be quite heterogeneous. It is in this light that we examine storybook reading in this chapter.

STORYBOOK READING: A BRIEF HISTORY

In the 1960s, a new concern for literacy skills, as measured by standardized test results, produced a focus on the preschool years as exemplified in Project Head Start and other early intervention projects that would "ready" children for academic experiences. The ensuing twenty years saw the focus of research on the home and preschool environments that would best lead to later school success. Longitudinal studies found links between oral language and emerging literacy behaviors (Chomsky, 1972). During these two decades, numerous researchers based their work on the premise, and then research findings, that children's knowledge of literacy and their literate behaviors begin to emerge in the preschool years (Ferreiro & Teberosky, 1982; Heibert, 1981; Lomax & McGhee, 1987). Teale's results (1986a,b) indicated that this developing knowledge and emerging abilities were constructed within the context of interactions in the home, rather than through direct instruction.

The last decade of the twenty-first century saw a renewed focus on events in the home that might influence later school performance. More specifically the role of parental storybook reading in children's later success in school-based literacy instruction came to the forefront of research and practice, particularly in family literacy studies and programs. Storybook reading would encompass a parent/guardian reading any appropriate text to their child, although the majority of what is read in the preschool years (and later assessed in the elementary school) tends to be narrative material (Doiron, 1994). It would be fair to characterize the types of practices being studied and promoted as those typical in Euro-American/Euro-Canadian middle- to upper-class homes. In this way, these programs are quite reminiscent of the preschool curricula developed during the early 1970s for children who were then categorized as lower SES and today might be thought of as "at-risk." The storybook reading style of the mainstream culture has become extolled so much that Pellegrini (1991) pointed out that it had become the literacy event "par excellence" (p. 380). Others have deemed it the "protypical form of literacy apprenticeship for young children" (Leseman & deJong, 1998, p. 298) and have claimed, "no other single activity is regarded as important" (Neuman, 1999, p. 286).

The roots of the belief that storybook reading has a significant impact on later school literacy achievement have a number of sources. One is from the work of Catherine Snow (1983) who suggested that the development of a child's literacy knowledge takes place as parents read to their children. Another source is the early work of Gordon Wells. Results of the large-scale Bristol Longitudinal Research Programme (Moon & Wells, 1979; Wells, 1985) in the United Kingdom indicated a strong relationship between early literacy knowledge and later school achievement in word identification and comprehension. The inference was that storybook reading played a large part in children's preparedness for literacy instruction. The reasoning seemed to be that since children's concepts of print were correlated with later achievement, and since concepts of print must be related to storybook reading, the latter was implicated in school achievement. However, what seemed to have been overlooked was that the researchers had pooled letter-name knowledge scores with concepts of print scores. This clouded the issue of the relationship of concepts of print, and therefore storybook reading, to later achievement especially since letter-name knowledge has been and remains one of the best predictors of later reading achievement (Durrell, 1958; Walsh, Price, & Gillingham, 1988). As well, Wells' (1985) study actually concluded that it was the act of listening to stories rather than book reading per se that was important. Other studies in the 1980s also call into question the direct link between storybook reading and later reading achievement. The studies carried out by David Yaden and his colleagues (Yaden & McGhee, 1984; Yaden, Smolkin, & Conlon, 1989) found that children actually attend to the illustrations of storybooks rather than print and print features and the questions children ask about storybooks deal with meaning rather than print.

Findings that call into question the significance or strength of the relationship between storybook reading and emerging literacy behaviors seem atheoretical to some and are often met with skepticism or downright hostility. A case in point is the narrative analysis of 31 studies of storybook reading conducted by Scarborough and Dobrich (1994). This analysis suggested that the relationship between storybook reading and later reading acquisition is far from robust. In fact, their results indicated that storybook reading accounted for only 8% of the variance in later reading achievement. Other researchers claimed that this meta-analysis was interpreted more negatively than it should have been and probably underestimated the relationship (Lonigan, 1994). One view was that the 8% relationship was, in fact, not negligible when compared to findings that SES only accounts for 5% of the variance in school achievement (Dunning, Mason, & Stewart, 1994). Finally, another meta-analysis conducted about the same time concluded that there was support for "the hypothesis that parent-preschooler book reading is related to outcome measures such as … reading achievement (Bus, van IJzendoorn, & Pellegrini, 1995, p. 15) and is "a necessary preparation for beginning reading instruction at school" (p. 17). Interestingly these researchers also found that storybook reading accounted for 8% of the variance in their outcome measures.

What becomes clear after reading the earlier literature on storybook reading is that there seems to be a discrepancy between the results of research and the insistence of advocates of storybook reading of the certainty of beneficial results. This insistence becomes more troublesome when there may be great divergence in storybook reading styles within homogenous groups (Shapiro, Anderson, & Anderson, 1997), yet a "typical" way to read to young children is usually advocated. The next section of this chapter will look at some of the literature since the meta-analyses of the mid-1990s before we deal with the major issues that confront researchers and practitioners.

STORYBOOK READING: THE LATEST

Access to Books

Since the two major meta-analyses of the mid-1990s, there have been more than 50 other published studies that in one way or another, have to do with storybook reading with preschool-age children. It is not our purpose here to do a thorough review of this literature. Rather we will try to highlight what seem to be new directions in the reported research on storybook reading.

There have been a number of studies that have concerned themselves with the amount of storybook reading in various socioeconomic groups. In a vein similar to the early work of Shirley Brice Heath and William Teale, Purcell-Gates (1996) described how print was used in a sample of low-income families. Following her sample (comprising diverse ethnic groups) for one year, she concluded that these families used print primarily when they pursued entertainment and in conducting daily life routines, findings that were very similar to Teale (1986b). She did find slightly more storybook reading than did Teale but it still was one of the least used literacy events. This work is consistent with the recent report of the National Center for Education Statistics (1999) that indicated that children in African-American and Hispanic households are less likely to be read to than children in Euro-American households.

The amount of independent reading that young children do or their seeking out of books may be related to how often they are engaged in storybook reading. Baker, Scher, and Mackler (1997) concluded that the affective dimensions of shared storybook reading promoted the motivation to read and they reported more middle-income parents indicating that their children interacted independently with books than did lower-income parents. What does one conclude from this type of data? These authors believe that their data "suggest that middle-income families tend to show greater endorsement of the cultural theme of literacy as a source of entertainment..." (p. 71). Apparently this was a result of positive experiences with storybook reading interactions. However, they caution their readers that research does not presently support the fact that this interest, a result of storybook reading, is related to later reading achievement as some claimed in earlier studies. About the only aspect of literacy achievement that has been found to be affected by early interest in books resulting from storybook reading is phonemic awareness (Lonigan, Dyer, & Anthony, 1996) and these results have not been confirmed by other studies. Certainly this research cannot support the conclusions of some that differences between cultural groups in reading achievement is due to deficient home experiences (Sonnenschein, Brody, & Munsterman, 1996; Rush, 1999).

This research or concern with differences in amount of storybook reading has spawned programs and research investigating what is known as "book floods." Susan Neuman is perhaps best known for investigating an increased access to storybooks. In 1996, studying access to books in low-income families, she found that all children, regardless of the reading proficiency of the parent, improved in measures of receptive language and concepts of print. In a follow-up study (1999), she found that "flooding" childcare centers with books resulted in the intervention group attaining significantly higher scores on some measures of emergent literacy but not on environmental print reading or receptive language. The latter result was contrary to her earlier finding, as well as findings of other studies that indicate that receptive language is one area that storybook reading tends to effect. Possibly confounding this study was the uneven distribution of 3- and 4-year-olds in the intervention and control groups.

Intervention

Along with the "book flood" intervention studies mentioned above have been others that attempt to teach parents "how to" read to their children. These studies have involved parents and children ranging in age from infancy to kindergarten, with varying levels of economic status, and with varying levels of language proficiency or other difficulties.

In a series of British studies, effects of intervention with parents of infants were examined. Hardman and Jones (1999) reported on the *Babies Into Books* project that involved forty parents of 7-month-old children who received book packs that included books, literacy information, and library cards. In addition, "baby book groups" were formed and met every two weeks for a two-month period. These sessions focused primarily on shared book reading and songs and rhymes. The researchers found that after the two-month period the children had more books, there was a significant increase in looking at books with their babies, and a higher incidence in baby reaching for book behaviors. These results were similar to the large-scale Birmingham Bookstart project (Wade & Moore, 1996) that reported significant results up to four years after the 9-month-olds participated, even without the benefit of parent support sessions.

Storybook reading intervention has also shown some success with children experiencing language (Dale, Crain-Thoreson, Notari-Syverson, & Cole, 1996) and/or developmental delays (Hockenberger, Goldstein, & Haas, 1999). In the former, thirty-three parents of mild-to-moderate language-delayed 3- to 6-year-olds were randomly assigned to a book reading or conversational program. Both groups "emphasized an interactive, responsive style of communication with children" (p. 217). Parents in the storybook reading group were found to have asked more who/what questions, more open-ended questions, and have elaborated more on their children's responses. The authors reported modest effects for children in this group in the areas of longer mean utterances, increased rate of verbal responses to questions, and in the use of different vocabulary.

Hockenberger et al. (1999) trained mothers of low-income parents of some mild-to-moderate developmentally delayed 4- and 5-year-olds in storybook reading with an emphasis on commenting on the story, especially with "how" and "when" questions. The training increased the number of parent comments during the four-week intervention but the level of comments returned to the baseline after the intervention program ended. Children demonstrated some gains in the areas of directionality, letter-name knowledge, and in their level of interaction during the storybook reading.

While not a study with preschool age children, a large-scale intervention with kindergarten children requires mention because even though the children attended Title 1 designated schools, the sample was not at "severe social or demographic risk, and the schools ... were generally successful by national standards" (Jordon, Snow, & Porche, 2000, pp. 528–529). Project Ease (Early Access to Success in Education) provided 177 parents with a year-long intervention program. Parents were exposed to five one-month units. Each unit consisted of a coaching session, practice time, and take-home guides that dealt with engaging their children in discussions about a book. For each of the three remaining weeks of the month parents received scripted, structured storybook reading activities. The children in the Project made a few statistically significant gains on the outcome measures as compared to a control group. The researchers reported a moderate effect on the composite language measure that included vocabulary, story comprehension, and story sequence. A slight effect was found for awareness of ending sounds, and virtually no effect was found on the print composite score except for concepts of print (reading). However the children who had scored lowest on the pretest measures made the greatest gains. The effect size of the intervention was considered significant by the authors because this was a "moderate-to-low risk sample of English-speaking European American families, with median family income above the poverty level and access to good schools..." thereby showing "...there is room for parental involvement to improve children's school performance" (p. 538). It should be pointed out here that these authors are equating results of kindergarten research outcome measures with actual school performance and there appears to be an assumption that if these types of programs are slightly successful with mainstream families they should be of huge benefit with non-mainstream, at-risk families.

Diverseness

This category of research deals with the diverseness in parental storybook reading. A series of studies on differences in various aspects of book reading have been conducted in the Netherlands and in Canada, as well as in the United States. We feel that these studies on what might be considered the uniqueness of parent storybook reading, especially in light of findings that within mainstream families there is great diversity in storybook reading styles (Haden, Reese, & Fivush, 1996; Shapiro et al., 1997), are important in that many family literacy programs are promoting "the way" to read with young children.

Adriana Bus has been one of the leading researchers in the area of mother-child attachment during storybook reading. Data from a number of studies indicates that emotional attachments impact on the storybook reading interaction with insecure mother-child relationships having a negative or inhibiting effect on both the frequency and quality of storybook reading interactions with infants and with older preschool-age children (Bus & van IJzendoorn, 1995, 1997). Findings indicated that insecure children are less attentive leading mothers to control the child physically, provide negative verbal feedback, and not allow book exploring behaviors or choose to read books at home. "Insecure-avoidant" mothers read to their children differently in that they tended to read the text with little elaboration, questions, or attention to illustrations (Bus, Belsky, van IJzendoorn, & Crnic, 1997). More recently this researcher has counseled that storybook reading "style is not a unidimensional phenomenon and that it is more fruitful to look at how an adult tailors his or her reading to the characteristics of the specific child. For now we would caution against a one-size-fits-all prescriptive book reading intervention..." (Bus & Sulzby, 2000, p. 35).

Monique Senechal and colleagues in Canada have examined the differences in parental reading style that are dependent upon the age of the child (Senechal, Cornell, & Broda, 1995). With younger children parents would attempt to maintain attention and to elaborate, while with older preschoolers they asked more questions and provided more feedback. In other words, parents expanded their storybook reading repertoire dependent upon age and their sensitivity to the child. The latter behavior does seem to impact on the child's language knowledge. Senechal (1997) studied 60 3- and 4-year-old primarily middle-class children and their parents' reading interactions in three experimental reading conditions. She discovered that different reading styles or didactic techniques impact differently on receptive and expressive language growth. Increased exposure to the same book enhanced both receptive and expressive language in the same manner but active responding affected expressive vocabulary more than receptive. Similar age-related findings have been found in studies conducted in the United States by Martin (1998) who studied differences in maternal reading to young children ranging in age from 6 months to 4 years, with mothers of younger children tending to simplify the text and use more strategies to engage their children.

Extending her work to school age children, Senechal examined the belief that storybook reading was related to success in early literacy. She and her colleagues examined the effects of storybook reading on both the oral and written language of 157 kindergarten and grade one children (Senechal, LeFevre, Thomas, & Daley, 1998). Using regression analyses and controlling for age and non-verbal intelligence, storybook reading was found to contribute to a statistically significant amount of variance in oral-language skills (vocabulary, listening comprehension, and phonological awareness) but not in the children's written language skills (print concepts, alphabet knowledge, invented spelling, and decoding). Two percent of the variance in kindergarten children's oral-language skills (effect size = .31) was attributed to storybook reading and 7% in grade one children's oral-language skills (effect size = .54).

Cross-curricular Literacies

The last decade or so has seen researchers expand what used to be an almost exclusive focus on print literacy to multiple literacies as we have come to see that meaning can be coded in different symbolic forms. Coupled with this movement (or perhaps because of it), researchers have begun to investigate the potentiality of storybook reading to support young children's developing knowledge in other disciplines.

For example, a series of case studies into children's early mathematics learning involving one of the current authors (Anderson, 1991, 1993; Phillips & Anderson, 1995) is beginning to point to bedtime reading as occasions when mathematics is shared. A case study of one child's early learning of mathematics through children's literature (Anderson & Anderson, 1995), documented how mathematics can constitute an integral part of shared book readings. Anderson (1997) reported parent-child interactions during storybook reading as one of the ways in which parents mediated their child's mathematics learning at home. Shapiro et al. (1997) found that while parents focused on print, illustrations, and the meaning of the story line in shared book reading, some parents and children also engaged in interactions which focused on mathematics while reading children's narratives not commonly thought of as having a focus on mathematics. Following up on this finding Anderson, Anderson, and Shapiro (1998) analyzed the types of mathematics-related interactions between parent and child while reading storybooks. They found that parent-child interactions during storybook reading show evidence of mathematics related talk, even when the storybooks would not be considered to have explicit mathematical content (e.g., "number or counting" books, "shape" books). However, the diversity of such interactions is striking considering the relative homogeneity of the sample.

Cultural Diversity

As pointed out elsewhere, much of the research in storybook reading has involved middle-class, Caucasian families. Recently, however researchers have begun to investigate these events with diverse populations.

For example, Janes and Kermani (2001) reported on a family literacy project intended to train low income, immigrant caregivers from Mexico and Central America to read with children in an interactive manner. Specifically, parents were trained to ask higher-order questions during the shared reading. Analyses showed that parents had great difficulty asking such questions and instead asked questions that required children to recall story events. The parents also reported that storybook reading, in the manner that they were trained, was a chore that neither they nor their children enjoyed. Modifications to the project that allowed parents to collaboratively write texts for sharing with their children and to share books, as they normally would resulted in more pleasurable shared reading episodes. However, Janes and Kermani caution, "...that storybook reading may not be the best route to literacy development..." (p. 465).

In a comparative study, Leseman and de Jong (1998) investigated storybook reading in immigrant Turkish and Surinamese families and native

Dutch families in the Netherlands. Differences in storybook reading behaviors were apparent with Turkish mothers pointing less frequently to illustrations or using them to help support children's understanding of the stories. Both Turkish and Surinamese mothers focused on literal understanding of the texts whereas higher level comments that involved explaining and elaborating were more prevalent with native Dutch mothers.

In summary then, the research literature since the mid-1990s has focused primarily on issues of access to books for low-income families and storybook reading interventions for this group. As well, researchers and educators have become interested in how storybook reading possibly contributes to children's developing knowledge in domains other than print literacy. However, the research results in any area cannot be said to be in agreement and differences in various aspects of storybook reading interactions, even in homogenous groups, are routinely found. At the same time, little attention has been focused on the role of storybook reading in young children's emerging knowledge in other curricular areas. Finally, as we consider the growing cultural diversity of Canada and the United States, views that there are multiple pathways to literacy and that storybook reading may not be the "literacy event par excellence" (Pellegrini, 1991 p. 380) for some cultural groups needs serious consideration (Bus & Sulzby, 2000: Anderson & Stokes, 1984). After all, in her foundational book *Family Literacy*, Denny Taylor (1983) documented a wide range of literacy events that children participated in as part of their daily life experiences other than storybook reading. Similar findings regarding the range of literacy events that occur daily in most homes in a literate society have been well documented (Taylor & Dorsey-Gaines, 1988; Teale, 1986).

STORYBOOK READING: WHAT SHOULD WE CONSIDER?

As the previous sections indicate, there are still lingering questions in the research community as to the role of storybook reading in children's early literacy (and language) development. This fact has not impeded the degree to which the phenomenon has been promoted as "the way" children acquire literacy (Shapiro et al., 1997). But as Pellegrini (1991) argued reading to children is not a universal practice and those children who entered schools having not been read to were seen as deficient in their early literacy development. Storybook reading has also been promoted as central to literacy development in many family literacy programs. Auerbach (1998) and others have reminded those who work in family literacy programs about the need for diversity in approaches to family literacy and the need to value and build on literacy practices in which families already engage. Purcell-Gates (2000) also acknowledges that storybook reading to children is among the practices commonly found in family literacy programs. As Purcell-Gates explains, many family literacy programs are targeted at specific (e.g., low income, immigrant) groups. Auerbach and others contend that many family literacy programs are based on deficit notions of the family, that there is something missing in the literacy lives of the family, and that families need fixing. It appears that the developers of many family literacy programs regard storybook reading as the key literacy practice that is missing.

We also believe that there are issues around gender in storybook reading that also need attention. Mace (1998), for example, contends that an assumption behind efforts to have young children read to at home is that the mother would do it. She argues:

> The evidence of a literacy "problem" in industrialized countries with mass schooling systems has revealed that schools alone cannot meet this need. Families must be recruited to do their bit too. This is where the spotlight falls on the mother. She it is who must ensure that the young child arrives at school ready for school literacy and preferably already literate. (p. 5)

Mace elaborates that mothers are expected to subjugate their own literacy needs so that all of their attention is focused on the child's literacy development. The mother's own literacy, she proposes, is viewed as "…a luxury and an indulgence" (p. 11).

However, there is also a body of research (Dwyer, 1974; Kagan, 1964; Shapiro, 1980, 1990) that indicates that many boys perceive reading as a feminine activity and that this is lessened when there are male reading role models. Some people suggest that this occurs because most of the reading role models in young children's lives are women and that boys make an association between being female and reading. There is speculation that some boys develop an aversion to reading because of this perception and that their reading ability lags because of this lack of engagement. If this is the case, the fact that mothers are the principle ones being enjoined to read to children at home could contribute to the feminization of reading for young boys.

There is also some emerging evidence that mothers may read differently to their daughters than they do to their sons. In examining the data from our earlier study (Shapiro et al., 1997), we discovered that the majority of parent initiated language events that related to print concepts or math concepts occurred with daughters rather than with sons (Shapiro, Anderson & Anderson, 1998). More recent work indicates that mothers and fathers differ in the language events they initiate when reading a narrative or expository/information storybook to their sons and daughters. Fathers initiated more events when reading expository/information books than did mothers and both initiated more events when reading narrative story-books to their daughters than to their sons. The opposite was the case when reading expository/information storybooks (Shapiro, Anderson, & Anderson, 2000).

A related problem identified by some educators is the propensity of teachers to use narratives almost exclusively when reading aloud to young children. Doiron (1994) points out that narratives are not the preferred genre of many young boys. Again, there is speculation that the pervasiveness of narrative texts in primary and early childhood classrooms contributes to the aversion to reading that many boys develop. Doiron (1994) calls for the inclusion of informational texts as a way of engaging young boys.

We also have concerns about the generalizability of the research in storybook reading to children. Most of the research, including much of that reviewed in this chapter, has been conducted in the United States where the educational and geopolitical contexts differ significantly from other countries. For example, a comparison of the United States and Canada—neighboring countries often assumed to be quite similar—reveals some of these major differences. Whereas the United States has one official language, Canada has two official languages and a significant number of other minority language groups. Second, whereas an ideology of assimilation of different cultural/linguistic groups pervades in the United States, Canada has an official policy of multiculturalism that encourages maintenance of first languages and cultural identity. Third, whereas three ethnic groups (African-American, Caucasian, and Hispanic) comprise the majority of the population of the United States (although there has been an increase in other groups over the past decade), Canada's population is made up of a large number of different cultural groups. For example, Gunderson and Clark (1998) found 158 languages groups from 128 countries represented in schools in Vancouver, Canada and immigrant children from 15 different language groups in some classrooms. As we indicated earlier, anthropological research is beginning to help us understand literacy as social practice, varying considerably across contexts. Furthermore, research in storybook reading with different cultural groups is beginning to indicate considerable variation in how parents and children share books. For example, Bus, Leseman, and Keultjes (2000), in a study of 57 parent-child dyads representing native Dutch, Turkish-Dutch, and Surinamese-Dutch backgrounds, found significant differences in parental paraphrasing of text and the themes initiated by the parents. Therefore, much caution is indicated with regard to generalizing research findings from specific populations across sociocultural contexts.

There are also issues of sample size and sample selection that impact on the generalizability of some studies of storybook reading. Some of the studies used in the Scarborough and Dobrich (1995) meta-analysis had very small sample sizes (e.g., 13). They point out that "...the socioeconomic range within most samples has been quite narrow" (Scarborough & Dobrich, 1995, p. 289). Furthermore, finding a truly random sample in these studies is highly problematic. These limitations, we believe, suggest the need for caution in how results are interpreted.

Illustrative of the problem of generalizing research in this area across contexts is Anderson and Matthews' (1999) replication of Sulzby's (1985) classic study of children's storybook reenactments. Whereas the Sulzby study involved children from middle class homes from the midwestern United States, the children in the Anderson and Matthews' study were from working class homes from a rural Canadian community. They found that these children did not show the same developmental progression as the children in Sulzby's study during the kindergarten year. Anderson and Matthews (1999) reported, "None of the [15] children in the current study advanced to the print governed categories: all were at the oral language like categories, whereas 17 of the 24 children in the Sulzby study were in the written language like or print governed categories by the year's end" (p. 296). And working with preschool-age children from Head Start classrooms in the United States and using Sulzby's developmental scheme, Elster (1994) had similar findings to those of Anderson and Matthews.

We also have concern about what we perceive to be the imposition of particular styles or stances imposed upon parents in home reading and family literacy programs. That is, we believe that there is an ideology that there is a "correct way" for parents to read to children. As was pointed out earlier, our own research (Shapiro et al., 1997) with well educated, middle/upper-middle class parents and their four-year-old children revealed tremendous diversity in the ways that books were shared. No real patterns emerged from our analyses of the shared readings of these dyads.

Furthermore, Heath and Mangiola (1991) remind us, "All cultural groups have some unique ways of transmitting background knowledge about the world and of asking about their world and of asking their children to display what they know" (p.14). As Anderson and Gunderson (2001) point out, research with Chinese-Canadian parents conducted in western Canada shows that these parents tend to see very little value in the highly interactive book reading which is often promoted as "the way" to share books. Instead, these parents tend to see the child's role as paying close attention and remembering the text being read and of being able to answer questions asked after the shared reading to demonstrate attention and understanding. We believe that instead of trying to impose particular behaviors on parents, we would be serving families much better if we were to provide resources for them through, for example, the book floods described by Neuman (1999). Furthermore, we have ethical concerns about imposing mainstream ways of thinking about literacy, no matter how well intentioned, upon marginalized groups whose literacy beliefs and practices are different.

There are also questions about imposing storybook reading on children who do not enjoy shared reading. Scarborough and Dobrich (1994) report that Wells (1985) "...found that 11% of the preschoolers were reported by their mothers to enjoy being read to "not at all" or "not that much" (p. 295). They continue:

> Because it has been made so clear to today's parents that reading to their young children is practically compulsory, many of our acquaintance appear to feel that failure to do so constitutes a serious lack of personal responsibility. Consequently, we have found that many parents dutifully incorporate book reading into the child's daily routine no matter what the response to it. (Scarborough & Dobrich, 1994, p. 295)

They draw an analogy between forcing a reluctant child to be read to and forcing a child who dislikes broccoli to eat it. They conclude that "Most of us know many instances in which insistence on a child's consuming a disliked substance, or engaging in a disliked activity has not had the desired effect" (p. 295). Based on our collective experiences as parents and as teachers of young children we strongly concur. We also believe the home reading programs promoted so heavily in schools in which parents are extolled to read regularly to their children, often with extrinsic rewards provided by large corporations, might be exacerbating this situation for some families.

As we have pointed out elsewhere in this chapter, there is ample evidence that parents can support their children in ways that are relatively unobtrusive, that fit more naturally into the daily routines of the family and that they and their children feel comfortable with. We believe that early childhood educators need to make a concerted effort to help parents understand this reality through information sessions, brochures, advertisements, and so forth. The research literature indicates that parents can support young children's early literacy development in myriad ways. Parents need to understand that there are multiple pathways into literacy

It is especially important that teachers who work with young children are aware of this diversity in early literacy development. We propose that there is increasing need for programs preparing teachers to work with young children to address in a comprehensive manner, issues of sociocultural diversity. This is especially so in terms of literacy development where, according to some (e.g., Auerbach, 1998) a "one size fits all" approach to early literacy development pervades.

In this chapter we have raised several issues about the perceived centrality of storybook reading in children's early literacy development. Despite the concerns we have raised, we still believe that storybook reading is valuable and important. As we have indicated, storybook reading seems to contribute to children's language development including vocabulary and the acquisition of the syntactic and discourse structures of written language. Not withstanding the earlier discussion of the "broccoli effect," we see the potentiality of parent-child storybook reading in helping children develop positive attitudes toward reading and thus, become more engaged and bring positive attitudes about books into school. As well, we acknowledge that storybook reading can be a very pleasurable social event promoting parental-child interaction and bonding. Of course, we also need to remember that storytelling can play similar roles in cultures with an oral tradition.

Our literature search revealed many articles promoting the use of storybook reading across the curriculum. However, we found a dearth of research to support this trend. For example, in studies of storybook reading and mathematics, there is little analysis of the storybook reading or the role(s) it plays. Rather, the emphasis seems to be on activities that emanate from the book sharing. Second, although there seems to be much intuitive and philosophical support for using storybooks to promote the learning of mathematics (and other disciplinary knowledge), there is very little empirical evidence to support this approach. Of particular concern is the lack of empirical evidence as to what happens with respect to young children and storybook reading and cross-curricular (multiple literacy) development, particularly how storybook reading is used by parents to support the early learning of multiple literacies. The curriculum materials encouraging the use of storybook reading in a cross curricular manner with school aged children generally follow a "springboard" model wherein the attention to particular concepts occurs within the follow-up activities rather than the book reading. This seems to contradict what happens with parents and children at home where it seems that engagement with ideas or concepts occurs within the storybook reading. Thus we are concerned that the school-like model of providing a book to read with suggested follow-up activities will start to be promoted for use by parents and young children.

We are also concerned that middle-class, Euro-centric practices seem to dominate both the events in many storybooks as well as the recommended practices around their use. That is, very few of the classroom-based examples we found incorporated multicultural literature and thus the books themselves portray a certain set of experiences that may or may not parallel those of other cultures. Furthermore, the recommendations for sharing books (i.e., surrounded with much interaction and questioning) in cross-curricular contexts may not reflect the diverse cultural ways of our children. In general, we fear that storybook reading has been uncritically adopted to promote multiple literacies and cross-curricular learning without evidence as to its suitability.

We also believe that there is a continued need for research in storybook reading with parents and children from different cultural groups to help determine how these groups share storybooks. If we have a better understanding of storybook reading amongst different cultural groups, perhaps teachers can begin to incorporate a variety of interaction patterns into storybook reading in their classrooms. In this regard, the work of Kathy Au (e.g., Au & Mason, 1983) with Hawaiian teachers and children is a model for what teachers can do to capitalize upon children's discourse patterns within the context of literacy lessons including storybook reading.

Case study research with young children reveals that children are aware of a variety of literacy genres and functions and that they reveal this knowledge as they engage in literacy events (Chapman, 1994; Dyson, 1994). Put differently, young children are quite capable of understanding and incorporating myriad forms and uses of literacy as they make sense of their world through print. Neuman and Roskos (1992) demonstrate how play centers containing appropriate literacy materials facilitate young children's utilization of a wide variety of literacy genres and functions. Again, their work can serve as a model for educators looking to expand upon the repertoire of literacy experiences they provide for preschoolers.

As we put it previously, it seems that educators have developed a "theoretical blind spot" with regards to the primacy which storybook reading has been afforded in early literacy development (Shapiro et al., 1997). We speculate that because children from middle-class, mainstream homes where storybook reading is often a daily ritual tend to be successful at acquiring literacy, educators have uncritically assumed that this particular literacy event is the key to success. We see this ethnocentric, middle-class bias as especially problematic in an increasingly diverse and global society where, in some cases, early childhood classrooms include children from an array of cultural and linguistic groups. We believe it is imperative that educators become cognizant of the multiple ways, in addition to storybook reading, that early literacy can be supported and enhanced. In our research and in our practice, we must be able to de-center our thinking and begin to recognize and value non-narrative literacy in our work with young children.

REFERENCES

Anderson, A. (1997). Families and mathematics: A study of parent-child interactions. *Journal for Research in Mathematics Education, 28,* 484–511.

Anderson, A. (1993). Wondering: One child's questions and mathematics learning. *Canadian Children, 18,* 26–30.

Anderson, A. (1991). Learning mathematics at home: A case study. *Canadian Children, 16*, 47–58.

Anderson, A., & Anderson, J. (1995). Learning mathematics through children's literature: A case study. *Canadian Journal of Research in Early Childhood Education, 4*, 1–9.

Anderson, A.B. & Stokes, S.J. (1984). Social and institutional influences on the development and practice of literacy. In. H. Goelman, A. Oberg, & F. Smith (Eds.) *Awakening to literacy* (pp. 24–37). Exeter, NH: Heinemann.

Anderson, J., & Gunderson, L. (2001). "You don't read a science book, you study it": Exploring cultural concepts of reading. *Reading Online, 4*. Available: http://www.readingonline.org/electronic/elec_index.asp?HREF=/electronic/anderson/index.html

Anderson, J., & Lynch, J. (In press). Family literacy in Canada: Issues and perspectives. In J. Spreadbury (Ed.). *Family literacies around the world.* Newark, NJ: International Reading Association.

Anderson, J., & Matthews, R. (1999). Emergent storybook reading revisited. *Journal of Research in Reading, 22*, 293–298.

Au, K., & Mason, J. (1983). Cultural congruence in classroom participation structures: Achieving a balance of rights. *Discourse Processes, 6*, 145–67.

Auerbach, E. (1998). Family Literacy. In V. Edwards & D. Corson (Eds.), *Encyclopedia of language and literacy education, Volume 2: Literacy* (pp. 153–161), Boston: Kulwer Academic Publishers.

Baker, L., Scher, D., & Mackler, K. (1997). Home and family influences on motivations for reading. *Educational Psychologist, 32*, 69–82.

Barton, D., Hamilton, M., & Ivanic, R. (Eds.). (2000). *Situated literacies: Reading and writing in context.* New York: Routledge.

Bus, A.G., Belsky, J., van IJzendoorn, M.H., & Crnic, K. (1997). Attachment and book reading patterns: A study of mothers, fathers, and their toddlers. *Early Childhood Research Quarterly, 12*, 81–98.

Bus, A., Leseman, P., & Keultjes, P. (2000). Joint storybook reading across cultures: A comparison of Surinamese, Turkish and Dutch parent-child dyads. *Journal of Literacy Research, 32*, 53–76.

Bus, A.G., & Sulzby, E. (2000). *Connections between characteristics of parent-child readings and characteristics of subsequent emergent readings.* Paper presented at the annual meeting of the National Reading Conference, Scottsdale, AZ.

Bus, A.G., & van IJzendoorn, M.H. (1997). Affective dimension of mother-infant picture book reading. *Journal of School Psychology, 35*, 47–60.

Bus, A.G., & van IJzendoorn, M.H. (1995). Mothers reading to their 3-year-olds: The role of mother-child attachment security in becoming literate. *Reading Research Quarterly, 30*, 998–1014.

Bus, A.G., van IJzendoorn, M.H., & Pellegrini, A.D. (1995). Joint book reading makes for success in learning to read: A meta-analysis on intergenerational transmission of literacy. *Review of Educational Research, 65*, 1–21.

Chapman, M.L. (1994). The emergence of genres: Some findings from an examination of first-grade writing. *Written Communication, 11*, 348–80.

Chomsky, C. (1972). Stages in language development and reading behavior. *Harvard Educational Review, 42*, 1–33.

Clay, M. (1993). Always a learner: A fable. *Reading Today, 3,* 10.

Dale, P.S., Crain-Thoreson, C., Notari-Syverson, A., & Cole, K. (1996). Parent-child book reading as an intervention technique for young children with language delays. *Topics in Early Childhood Special Education, 16,* 213–235.

Doiron, R. (1994). Using nonfiction in a read-aloud program. *The Reading Teacher, 47,* 616–624.

Dunning, D.B., Mason, J.M., & Stewart, J.P. (1994). Reading to preschoolers: A response to Scarborough and Dobrich (1994) and recommendations for future research. *Developmental Review, 14,* 324–339.

Durrell, D.D. (1958). Success in first grade reading. *Journal of Education, 140,* 1–48.

Dwyer, C.A. (1974). Influence of children's sex-role standards on reading and arithmetic achievement. *Journal of Educational Psychology, 66,* 811–816.

Dyson, A. (1994). The Ninjas, the X-Men, and the ladies: Playing with power and identity in an urban primary school. *Teachers College Record, 96,* 219–239.

Elster, C. (1994). Patterns within preschoolers' emergent reading. *Reading Research Quarterly, 29,* 402–418.

Ferreiro, E., & Teberosky, A. (1982). *Literacy before schooling.* Portsmouth, NH: Heinemann.

Gee, J. (1996). *Social linguistics and literacy: Ideology in discourses.* London: Taylor and Francis.

Gunderson, L., & Clarke, D. (1998). An exploration of the relationship between ESL students' backgrounds and their English and academic achievement. In T. Shanahan and F.V. Rodriguez-Brown (Eds.), *Yearbook of The National Reading Conference, 47* (pp. 264–273). Chicago: National Reading Conference.

Haden, C.A., Reese, E., & Fivush, R. (1996). Mothers' extratextual comments during storybook reading: Stylistic differences over time and across texts. *Discourse Processes, 21,* 135–169.

Hardman, M., & Jones, L. (1999). Sharing books with babies: evaluation of an early literacy intervention. *Educational Review, 51,* 221–229.

Heath, S.B., & Mangiola, L. (1991). *Children of promise: Literate activity in linguistically and culturally diverse classrooms.* Washington, DC: NEA Professional Library.

Heibert, E.H. (1981). Developmental patterns and interrelationships of preschool children's print awareness. *Reading Research Quarterly, 16,* 230–260.

Hockenberger, E.H., Goldstein, H., & Haas, S. (1999). Effects of commenting during joint book reading by mothers with low SES. *Topics in Early Childhood Special Education, 19,* 15–27.

Janes, H., & Kermani, H. (2001). Caregivers storyreading to young children in family literacy programs. Pleasure or punishment? *Journal of Adolescent and Adult Literacy, 44,* 458–466.

Jordon, G.E., Snow, C.E., & Porche, M.V. (2000). Project EASE: The effect of a family literacy project on kindergarten students' early literacy skills. *Reading Research Quarterly, 35,* 524–546.

Kagan, J. (1964). Acquisition and significance of sex typing and sex-role identity. In M.L. Hoffman & L.W. Hoffman (Eds.), *Review of child development research.* (pp. 151–160). New York: Russell Sage Foundation.

Leseman, P., & deJong, P. (1998). Home literacy: Opportunity, instruction, cooper-ation and social-emotional quality predicting early reading achievement. *Reading Research Quarterly, 33*, 294–318.

Lomax, R.G., & McGhee, L.M. (1987). Interrelationships among young children's concepts about print and reading: Toward a model of word recognition. *Reading Research Quarterly, 22*, 177–196.

Lonigan, C.J. (1994). Reading to preschoolers exposed: Is the emperor really naked? *Developmental Review, 14*, 303–323.

Lonigan, C.J., Dyer, S.M., & Anthony, J. (1996). *The influence of the home literacy environment on the development of literacy skills in children from diverse racial and economic backgrounds.* Paper presented at the annual meeting of the American Educational Research Association, New York.

Mace, J. (1998). *Playing with time: Mothers and the meaning of literacy.* London: UCL Press.

Martin, L. (1998). Early book reading: How mothers deviate from printed text for young children. *Reading Research and Instruction, 37*, 137–160.

Moon, C., & Wells, G. (1979). The influence of home on learning to read. *Journal of Research in Reading, 2*, 53–62.

National Center for the Study of Education Statistics. (1999). *Parental involvement in children's education: Efforts by public elementary schools.* Washington, DC: U.S. Department of Education.

Neuman, S.B. (1999). Books make a difference: A study of access to literacy. *Reading Research Quarterly, 34*, 286–310.

Neuman, S.B. (1996). Children engaging in storybook reading: The influence of access to print resources, opportunity, and parental interaction. *Early Childhood Research Quarterly, 11*, 495–513.

Neuman, S., & Roskos, K. (1992). Literacy objects as cultural tools: Effects on children's literacy behaviors in play. *Reading Research Quarterly, 27*, 202–225.

Pelligrini, A. (1991). A critique of the concept of at-risk as applied to emergent literacy. *Language Arts, 68*, 380–385.

Phillips, E., & Anderson, A. (1993). Developing mathematical power: A case study. *Early Child Development and Care, 96*, 135–146.

Purcell-Gates, V. (2000). Family literacy. In M. Kamil, P. Mosenthal, P.D. Pearson, & R. Barr (Eds.), *Handbook of reading research* (Vol. 3). Mahwah, NJ: Lawrence Erlbaum.

Purcell-Gates, V. (1996). Stories, coupons, and the TV guide: Relationships between home literacy experiences and emergent literacy knowledge. *Reading Research Quarterly, 31*, 406–428.

Rush, K.L. (1999). Caregiver-child interactions and early literacy development of preschool children from low-income environments. *Topics in Early Childhood Special Education, 19*, 3–14.

Scarborough, H.S., & Dobrich, W. (1994). On the efficacy of reading to preschoolers. *Developmental Review, 14*, 245–302.

Senechal, M. (1997). The differential effect of storybook reading on preschoolers' acquisition of expressive and receptive vocabulary. *Journal of Child Language, 24*, 123–138.

Senechal, M., Cornell, E.H., & Broda, L.S. (1995). Age-related differences in the organization of parent-infant interactions during picture-book reading. *Early Childhood Research Quarterly, 10,* 317–337.

Senechal, M., LeFevre, J., Thomas, E.M., & Daley, K.E. (1998). Differential effects of home literacy experiences on the development of oral and written language. *Reading Research Quarterly, 33,* 96–116.

Shapiro, J. (1990). Sex-role appropriateness of reading and reading instruction. *Reading Psychology, 11,* 241–269.

Shapiro, J. (1980). Primary children's attitudes toward reading in male and female teachers' classrooms. *Journal of Reading Behavior, 12,* 255–258.

Shapiro, J., Anderson, J., & Anderson, A. (2000). D*ifferences in mother/father storybook reading to daughters/sons.* Paper presented at the Annual Meeting of the College Reading Association, St. Petersburg, FLA.

Shapiro, J., Anderson, J., & Anderson, A. (1998). *Sex differences in mother/child book reading interactions.* Paper presented at the Annual Meeting of the College Reading Association, Charleston, SC.

Shapiro, J., Anderson, J., & Anderson, A. (1997). Diversity in parental storybook reading. *Early Child Development and Care, 127,* 47–59.

Snow, C. (1983). Literacy and language: Relationships during the preschool years. *Harvard Educational Review, 53,* 165–189.

Sonnenschein, S., Brody, G., & Munsterman, K. (1996). The influence of family beliefs and practices on children's early reading development. In L. Baker, P. Afflerbach, & D. Reinking (Eds.), *Developing engaged readers in school and home communities* (pp. 3–20). Mahwah, NJ: Erlbaum.

Sulzby, E. (1995). Children's emergent reading of favourite storybooks: A developmental study. *Reading Research Quarterly, 20,* 458–481.

Taylor, D. (1983). *Family literacy: Young children learning to read and write.* Exeter, NH: Heinemann.

Taylor, D., & Dorsey-Gaines, K. (1988). *Growing up literate: Learning from inner-city families.* Portsmouth, NH: Heinemann.

Teale, W.H. (1986a). The beginnings of reading and writing: Written language development during the preschool and kindergarten years. In M.R. Sampson (Ed.), *The pursuit of literacy: Early reading and writing.* Dubuque, IA: Kendall/Hunt.

Teale, W.H. (1986b). Home background and young children's literacy development. In W.H. Teale & E. Sulzby (Eds.), *Emergent literacy: Reading and writing* (pp. 173–205). Norwood, NJ: Ablex.

Wade, B., & Moore, M. (1996). Home activities: The advent of literacy. *European Early Childhood Research Journal, 4,* 63–76.

Walsh, D.J., Price, C.G., & Gillingham, M.G. (1988). The critical but transitory importance of letter naming. *Reading Research Quarterly, 23,* 108–122.

Wells, G. (1985). Preschool literacy related activities and success in school. In D. Olson, N. Torrance, & A. Hildyard (Eds.), *Literacy, language and learning.* Cambridge, MA: Cambridge University Press.

Yaden, D.B., & McGee, L. (1984). Reading as a meaning seeking activity: What children's questions reveal. In J.A. Niles & L.A. Harris (Eds.), *Changing perspectives on research in reading/language processing and instruction* (pp. 101–109). Rochester, NY: The National Reading Conference.

Yaden, D.B., Smolkin, L.B., & Conlon, C. (1993). Preschoolers' questions about pictures, print conventions, and story text during read aloud at home. *Reading Research Quarterly, 24*, 188–214.

CHAPTER 5

NEW DIRECTIONS IN FAMILY LITERACY:

Building Effective Partnerships Between Home and School[1]

Trevor H. Cairney

INTRODUCTION

Interest in the literacy of home is not new. Teachers and researchers have long recognized that the literacy children experience at home and in their communities has a significant impact on later literacy success at school and in the wider world. This recognition has been the driving force behind the many attempts to gain parent involvement in education from preschool to later high school. As well, we know that the literacy children experience outside early childhood education and school settings is varied and complex (Cairney, Lowe, & Sproats 1995; Freebody, Ludwig, & Gunn, 1995; Gutierrez, 1993). And yet, the impact of this known fact has been limited, with acknowledgment in curricula seemingly restricted in any widespread way to the use of environmental print in early childhood settings; the encouragement of children and families to share home literacy within the classroom context; and the sending of school books home to families to use as a stimulus to literacy learning. It is clear that while efforts to acknowledge family and community literacy are commendable, they have not gone far enough in recognizing the richness of literacy outside educational institutions and the need for genuine partnerships between educators and families. This chapter seeks to provide an overview of key literature that will inform readers' understanding of this area, and challenge educators to consider the implications of these findings for research and practice.

The focus of much discussion about building effective relationships between home, school and community has centered around discussions of "Family Literacy." Family Literacy is one of the "new" literacies that have been the focus of discussion, writing and research in the past decade. As a descriptive label it has emerged from a number of related, and at times overlapping terms, including Parent Literacy, Parent Involvement, Intergenerational Literacy, and Community Literacy. Taylor (1983) first used the term Family Literacy to describe the rich literacy practices that pervade home and community. The many initiatives that have been put in place tend to fall within three broad categories. The first, home/school programs, are initiatives that attempt to strengthen the relationship between home and school. The second, intergenerational programs, attempt to bring about change in families by strengthening the literacy of adults and children. The third covers attempts to devise a method for developing a more effective partnership between home and school.

HOME/SCHOOL PROGRAM INITIATIVES

The increasing realization that from birth family members contribute to children's literacy development has given rise to home/school literacy programs designed to support families' participation in their children's education. Such programs usually involve parents in literacy activities that support the goals of early childhood centers and schools. While many of these initiatives don't directly involve children, some do encourage their participation. Many examples of this type of program have been developed over the past decade.

The earliest attempts to recognize the relationship between home factors and school success were little more than parent education programs. Some of the most significant early initiatives in this area occurred in the United Kingdom. The Plowden report (Department of Education and Science, 1967) argued strongly for the concept of partnership between home and school and was a significant stimulus to a number of initiatives. Programs typically offered parents information about literacy, stressed the importance of reading to and with them, and suggested a range of strategies for supporting literacy learning.

Many of the early programs used specific literacy practices that were seen as useful for enhancing school literacy success as the core of programs. One of the most commonly used was the Paired Reading technique. This simple technique was first designed by Morgan (1976) and was later refined by Topping and McKnight (1984), and Topping and Wolfendale (1985). Its use was encouraged and parents were taught how to apply it. While such programs were effective at teaching these strategies, evidence of long term impact on children's literacy is limited.

A number of the most successful early British programs were designed for parents whose children had reading problems. While some of the programs showed encouraging outcomes, once again there was a degree of inconsistency (see Hannon, 1995).

In the United States there have been numerous attempts to design programs that aim to involve parents more fully in their children's early literacy learning. Funding for these programs has been provided from a variety of State and Federal government programs including *Head Start, Even Start,* and the *Family School Partnership Program.* However, as Nickse (1993) has argued, while considerable effort and money has been put into these programs, evidence concerning their effectiveness is limited and inconclusive. As well, most of the programs have been school centered and have done little to acknowledge the language, literacy and cultural diversity of communities.

In spite of the many and varied programs around the world, the benefits for children's literacy learning are difficult to confirm and the evidence, at best, mixed. In an Australian Federal Government-funded review of Family and Community literacy initiatives in Australia, Cairney, Ruge, Buchanan, Lowe, and Munsie (1995) found from the 261 programs examined that:

- there had been little evaluation of the effectiveness of family and community literacy initiatives;
- the majority of programs were initiated by schools and few took place in preschool settings;
- initiatives varied greatly in terms of content, process, participant control and purposes, but offered little recognition of the richness of literacy practices within the wider community;
- many initiatives were "tokenistic" (see Cairney & Munsie, 1995) and paid little attention to the needs of communities; focusing instead on the needs of the school;
- there was some limited evidence that some programs had the potential to support literacy learning and in a limited number of cases could lead to the development of significant partnerships between the home and school.

The Cairney et al. (1995) study confirmed that the programs were not well conceptualized, they were limited in their scope, and that few programs offered the potential to empower previously marginalized groups. Nor did these programs typically bring about significant changes in educational programs to make them more responsive to the diverse cultural and linguistic needs of students. This is not to deny that some programs are built on important findings from literacy research for which there is conclusive evidence. For example, typically, many of the above programs place great importance on parents reading with and to children at home because there is strong evidence in the research literature of a correlation between consistent home story reading and school success (see for example Anderson, Wilson, & Fielding, 1988).

One recent initiative that did involve an evaluation of student achievements is Project EASE (Jordan, Snow & Porche, 2000). This year-long project involved 248 kindergarten children in an experimental research program. In all 177 students and their parents received the intervention program that included parent education sessions, school based parent/child activities, and home based book-mediated activities. Children involved in the program were found to have made significant gains in vocabulary, story comprehension and story sequencing tasks. Interestingly, the researchers found that low-achieving students achieved the greatest gains. However, even the demonstrated success of this program must be viewed with caution because it relied heavily upon storybook reading and word recognition strategies. While its demonstration of success for low achieving students is encouraging, one is still left with many questions in relation to programs such as Project EASE. First, it needs to be noted that the literacy practices used and supported within this program were fairly restricted, and represented a limited range of school literacy practices. While at one level we cannot criticize this as the researchers did exactly what they set out to do, we are still left with questions about the extent to which such programs are representative of the world of literacy and whether this matters. Second, the study did not provide any insights in relation to the impact of such programs on minority groups. The participants in this study (like many family literacy initiatives) were predominantly European/American with a minority representation of less than 5%. Hence, it is impossible to know whether gains within a program of this type with such a non-representative group could be replicated with other more diverse groups.

INTERGENERATIONAL LITERACY PROGRAMS

Intergenerational literacy programs are designed to improve the literacy development of both adults and children. They focus on providing literacy instruction to adults while at the same time teaching parents how to help their children with literacy skills. Like home-school programs, intergenerational programs may or may not include children participating in literacy activities with their parents. A number of intergenerational programs have been developed to meet the diverse needs of different groups (e.g., Neuman, 1997; Paratore & Brisk, 1995).

Paratore (1993) studied the influence of an intergenerational approach to literacy on the literacy learning of adults and on the practice of shared literacy at home. This work differed from related studies in that the outcome studied was not academic achievement of children, but rather the influence of the project on adults and their resulting interactions with their children. The program was designed to show parents with lower levels of literacy how they might serve as role models for their children. Although the program had a significant impact on the reading practices of the parents, the researchers found little impact on writing.

Another interesting program is *Partnership for Family Reading* (Handel, 1992), which was designed to "help parents support the literacy development of their children and improve their own literacy in the process" (p. 118). A variety of evaluation measures showed that the program had positive outcomes for family relationships and reading practices. However, unlike some other home/school programs, the benefits were not confined simply to improvements in literacy. The researchers found that schools developed the expertise to strengthen and extend parent involvement, and parents were able to increase their knowledge of school functions and take a greater role in leadership and decision-making.

A number of programs have also attempted to acknowledge cultural and linguistic diversity by focusing on families from diverse backgrounds. One such program was the Family Initiative for English Literacy (FIEL) program described by Quintero and Huerta-Macias (1990). The program was designed to enhance the literacy and biliteracy development of parents and children through a series of intergenerational activities. It aimed to enhance parents' self-confidence, to contribute to their children's literacy development, and to empower parents to connect literacy activities to their own lives. Evaluation of the program concluded that "because Project FIEL stresses language use in meaningful context, the students' needs, wishes and past experiences naturally become the teaching methodology, and flexibility of the curriculum is a natural result (and) ... the experience of the project indicates that when social context is attended to in a positive way and the dignity of the learner is upheld, learning occurs" (p. 312).

Other attempts to focus on specific target groups include a study by Neuman and Daly (1996) that involved the development of an intergenerational literacy program for teenage mothers that "focused on the collaborative process between caregivers and children, as parents sought to transmit their newly developing skills and strengths to children in differing learning contexts" (p. 5). The program attempted to provide a range of experiences through which teenage mothers could enhance their communicative interactions with their children in ways that would support the children's move toward independence. The findings of the study indicated that a range of activities and practices are critical for literacy learning for both adult and child. Neuman and Daly concluded that literacy programs need to be reconceptualized to take account of a broad range of literacy contexts and practices.

Studies in this category have ambitiously attempted to transform family resources for the support of children by providing help for parents with limited literacy levels themselves. This type of initiative is not without its problems. First, they have been criticized because they make critical assumptions about the literacy practices to be privileged and the strategies that will support their development. Second, it has been suggested that there is the danger that this type of program might fail to acknowledge cultural differences and hence not meet the needs of all. Third, the programs have been criticized for imposing specific cultural practices on families that may be equally rich in other forms of language, literacy and textual traditions.

PARTNERSHIP PROGRAMS

While many of the above programs are fairly narrowly focused on the needs of a specific group of families, children or adults, other programs have sought to use home/school literacy initiatives to build more effective partnerships between schools, families and communities. Two Australian programs have attempted to do this are the TTALL and EPISLL programs. The *Talk to a Literacy Learner (TTALL)* program (Cairney & Munsie, 1992) was designed to focus on parents of children aged 0 to 12 years. In doing this it aimed to involve teachers and parents in a partnership that would help students cope more effectively with the literacy demands of schooling. The TTALL program involves a series of sixteen interactive workshops, each of which is integrated with observation of literacy learners, classroom visits, practice of strategies and a variety of home-tasks. It is designed to involve parents more closely in the literacy development of their preschool and elementary school children in order to support literacy learning while at the same time developing a more open and interactive relationship between home and school.

The *Effective Partners in Secondary Literacy Learning (EPISLL)* program (Cairney & Munsie, 1993) was an outgrowth of the TTALL program and is designed for parents of secondary aged students. It consists of eleven sessions that cover topics as diverse as reading and writing across the curriculum, learning, study, coping with teenagers, research work, and using resources. The program was developed at the request of parents who had been involved in the TTALL program but who wanted more help with the support of their secondary school children. Parents were involved at every stage of the development and implementation of the program. Like the TTALL program, it has been fully evaluated and has been shown to have positive outcomes for parents, students, teachers and schools (Cairney & Munsie, 1995a,b).

A number of notable U.S. programs have also attempted to focus on the creation of partnerships with families and communities. They include Project FLAME (Shanahan & Rodriguez-Brown, 1993; Shanahan, Mulhern & Rodriguez-Brown, 1995), the initiatives of the *Illinois Literacy Resource Development Center* (ILRDC, 1990), and *Schools Reaching Out, SRO* (Jackson, Krasnow & Seeley, 1994). In contrast with many of the early home/school and intergenerational programs, each of these has attempted to develop a sense of partnership with parents and families. In each case, efforts have been made to recognize the significant cultural differences between communities, and to adapt programs accordingly. For example, project FLAME was designed for Mexican American and Puerto Rican families, and involves components in "parents as teachers," adult learning, summer institutes and community experiences. An interesting feature of the program is its ability to adapt to the specific cultural and educational characteristics of the families. Programs like this have increasingly begun to recognize that relationships between home and school achievement are complex, and hence require initiatives that do more than simply offering parents information.

In spite of the many programs conducted over the last 20 or more years across all three of the above categories, there has been little progress in addressing a number of significant doubts about family literacy initiatives. First, to what extent are such programs simply replicating a specific set of cultural practices consistent mainly with European English-speaking culture? Second, how effectively do such initiatives meet the diverse needs of learners from many cultures and minority groups? Third, to what extent do such initiatives lead to genuine partnership between home, school and community that involve open communication, acceptance and willingness to engage with and respond to the needs of families and community members? These questions require further exploration by researchers and new directions identified for family literacy initiatives. They form the focus for the rest of this chapter.

THE NEED FOR NEW DIRECTIONS IN FAMILY LITERACY

All of the family literacy initiatives discussed above have contributed to our understanding of the ways in which families and communities construct literacy, and how family literacy practices impact on school success. However, Auerbach (1989) criticizes family literacy programs that do no more than teach parents to do school-like activities in the home and to assist children with homework. Her contention is that the theoretical stance of these programs is not based on sound current research. Furthermore, she argues that in practice these programs function under a new version of the "deficit hypothesis," which assume that the parents lack the essential skills to promote school success in their children. This view has also been echoed in the work of Taylor (e.g., 1997) and others (e.g., Cairney, 1997, 2000; Cairney & Ruge, 1998). Auerbach suggests that what is needed is a broader definition of family literacy that acknowledges the family's social reality and focuses on the family's strengths. As an alternative framework to program design, she has argued for a social-contextual approach in which community concerns and cultural practices inform curriculum development.

As the above discussion has shown, the use of the term "family literacy" has frequently been applied to school based programs that do little more than introduce parents to school literacy practices and strategies for supporting these practices (Cairney, Ruge, Buchanan, Lowe, & Munsie, 1995). This is a major weakness of the way much "family literacy" work has been conceptualized and strategies implemented. In short, many that have explored family literacy have failed to recognize three different inherent flaws in their use of the term:

- first, the term family has been used without considering the varied contexts within which the family leads its life, that is, they have failed to recognize that children use literacy with and without family in contexts other than their own home;
- second, the concern of the teachers and researchers has not been with family at all, but rather with the way literacy is supported by family members, particularly parents;
- third, the focus has been on how "school literacy" is privileged and supported, rather than with the richness of literacy practices in the varied contexts within which children spend their daily lives.

Like schools and classrooms, families can be understood as cultures in which participants (family members) construct particular ways of acting, believing and valuing through the interactions among family members. Thus, families[2] construct particular views of literacy, and what it means to be literate. However, a review of many initiatives in family literacy suggests that on the whole they are more narrowly defined.

More recently, Moje (2000) has also criticized the lack of definition of "community" in much of the work that has been done in this area. In a detailed analysis of a number of studies she points out that we need to "define and complicate community as a construct" otherwise she claims, researchers risk romanticizing what it means to engage in community-based literacy. She also argues that we need to clarify our purposes for community-based literacy projects, something others have also stressed (e.g., Cairney, 1994; Cairney & Ruge, 1996, 1998).

LITERACY AS SOCIAL PRACTICE

Of central importance to the discussion about family literacy is the conceptual framework that underpins or drives these efforts. Very few of the programs discussed in this chapter make explicit the definitions of literacy that underpins the work.

Literacy is not a unitary cognitive skill, it is a social practice with many manifestations (Cairney, 1995b; Gee, 1990; Luke, 1993; Welch & Freebody, 1993). While psychologists recognize that there are many forms of literacy, each with specific purposes and contexts in which they are used, such definitions often fail to recognize that literacy is a social practice as well as a psychological phenomenon. Literacy in all its forms, can only be understood when we also study the people who use it. Literacy is in essence a set of social practices situated in sociocultural contexts defined by members of a group through their actions with, through and about language. This view of literacy as "social accomplishment of a group" (Baker & Luke, 1991; Bloome, 1986; Cairney, 1987; Cairney & Langbien, 1989; Santa Barbara Classroom Discourse Group, 1992), suggests that teachers, students and parents construct their own models and definitions of literacy, and sanction particular understandings, norms, expectations, and roles that define what it means to be literate. Hence, to understand literacy in all its richness, we need to understand the groups and institutions that socialize us into specific literacy practices (Bruner, 1986; Gee, 1990).

Moll (1993) has suggested that we need "a shift away from a view of individual learners to a view of learning as participation in a community of practice." Such a move would change our focus from one preoccupied with how individual children learn to read and write, toward understanding why and how people learn through their social participation in the practices of specific groups and communities. This would also shift our concern away from a pragmatic preoccupation with how parents can help the preschool or school in its task, toward an attempt to understand differences between the literacy of home, school and community as a staring point for informed curriculum practices.

Children negotiate a world in which there are "multiliteracies" (Cope & Kalantzis, 2000). Each person's cultural identity both shapes and is shaped (at least in part) by their experiences of literacy education. A child who enters an early childhood or school setting will be confronted by social practices that may or may not be familiar to them. When there is a mismatch between the definition and significance of literacy as they are represented in a person's cultural identity and in the learning situation, the individual is faced with a choice. They either adopt the perspective of the school and risk undermining their cultural identity, or resist the externally imposed activities at the risk of becoming alienated from the school (Au, 1993; Cummins, 1986; Ferdman, 1990). This is the "cutting edge" of all discussions concerning family literacy. Understanding this issue and responding to it is critical for the school success of many children.

Ferdman (1990) has argued that "cultural identity mediates the process of becoming literate as well as the types of literate behavior in which a person subsequently engages" (p. 197). At the group level, cultural identity involves the beliefs, values and ways of thinking and behaving that help to characterize the group and distinguish it from the dominant group. At the individual level, cultural identity has to do with the person's sense of what it means to be a member of a particular cultural group, as well as what their image is of the features that characterize the group's culture.

Like schools and classrooms, families can be understood as cultures in which participants (family members) construct particular ways of acting, believing and valuing through the interactions among family members. Thus, families construct particular views of literacy, and what it means to be literate. As Hannon (1995) points out, "The family's literacy values and practices will shape the course of the child's literacy development in terms of the opportunities, recognition, interaction and models available to them" (p. 104). That is, families share ways of participating in literate behavior that may be defined as the opportunities for literacy learning that family members have through the provision of resources and experiences. As well, families recognize and value members' achievements, the interactions surrounding literacy events, and the models of literacy demonstrated by family members (Hannon, 1995). Furthermore, how educational institutions recognize and respond to the complexity of the literacy worlds that children experience has a significant impact on children's school success.

It needs to be stated that how we deal with cultural difference in our schools is a very big issue that extends well beyond concerns with literacy alone. There are social, educational and political issues to balance when examining this issue, hence the response of educators and community members is never neutral. McCarthey and Dressman (2000) suggest two different metaphors for dealing with difference, the multicultural "quilt" or the "pyramid." The horizontal quilt implies the creation of a society from the diverse experiences and backgrounds of all children, parents and teachers, "stitched together by their contacts with one another." The vertical pyramid implies "increased stratification, increased competition, and hegemonic relationships" (p. 548). At the heart of the concern expressed above and more generally in this chapter, is the belief that educators must respond and build on difference in order that all students receive a just education.

SOCIAL AND CULTURAL DIFFERENCES AND THEIR IMPACT ON SCHOOL SUCCESS

The observation of difference between the language, literacy and culture of our early childhood centers and communities has led to study of the nature of such differences and what, if anything, this means for teachers and the students they teach. The juxtaposition of this reality against the observation that not all students succeed at school, and that specific groups (particularly minorities) appear to be educationally disadvantaged, has led to many explanations for this phenomenon and a myriad of potential theories and solutions. While we know that achievement gaps widen between children as they grow and move from early childhood settings to later elementary schooling, the foundations of disadvantage are laid within the early childhood years. Two major theories have been suggested as explanations for our persistent failure to ensure high levels of educational success for students from minority backgrounds. The first is the theory of *cultural discontinuity*, while the second can be termed the theory of *structural inequality* (Au, 1993). These theories have each contributed different approaches to the study of educational disadvantage.

The theory of cultural discontinuity, or cultural difference, suggests that cultural mismatches between teachers and students may result in difficulties in communication and interaction in the classroom (Erickson, 1993). These differences, or mismatches, work against the literacy learning of students whose home culture does not reflect that of the school. Studies that adopt a cultural discontinuity perspective tend to focus less on broad issues of social and economic power, and more on the day-to-day patterning of specific activities (e.g., Delgado-Gaitan, 1992; Deyhle &

LeCompte, 1994; Heath, 1993; Malin, 1994; Mulhern, 1995). Au (1995) points out that a key assumption of cultural difference analyses "is that there are systematic, identifiable differences in cultural values, knowledge, and practices, and that these differences are related to students' chances for school success" (p. 90).

The theory of structural inequality looks beyond mismatches between the culture of the home and the educational institution. It suggests that the lack of educational success of students from minority backgrounds reflects structural inequalities in the broader social, political and economic spheres (Au, 1993; Ogbu, 1993). This theory takes into account the power relationships between groups, and argues that educational institutions function to maintain the status quo. Critical analyses of social and cultural differences and the impact of these on school success tend to adopt a "structural inequality" perspective (e.g., Luke, 1993; May, 1995; Ogbu, 1992, 1993). This perspective attributes educational disadvantage to "oppressive social structures that create vast inequalities in power and opportunity favoring the dominant group" (Au, 1995, p. 87). As Luke (1995) argues, schools "naturalize particular interactional patterns and textual practices in ways that systematically exclude those students from economically marginal and culturally different backgrounds" (p. 16).

STUDIES OF CULTURAL DIFFERENCE AND THEIR SIGNIFICANCE FOR LITERACY EDUCATION

Recent Australian studies (Breen, Louden, Barrat-Pugh, Rivalland, Rohl, Rhydwen, Lloyd, & Carr, 1994; Cairney, Ruge, Buchanan, Lowe, & Munsie, 1995; Cairney, 2000; Cairney, Lowe, & Sproats, 1995; Cairney & Ruge, 1998; Freebody, Ludwig, & Gunn, 1995) have shown that there are differences between the language and literacy practices of school and community. In contrast, evidence exists which suggests that diversity of literacy practices within and between schools is far less evident (Breen et al., 1994; Cairney, Lowe, & Sproats, 1995; Freebody, Ludwig, & Gunn, 1995) than might be expected. This evidence is consistent with other research that has identified the difference between the language and literacy of school and that of homes and communities as a significant factor in the achievement or non achievement of students at school (e.g., Heath, 1983; Scribner & Cole, 1981). Louden and Rivalland (1995) noted that:

> although the family literacy practices associated with middle-class families are the most powerful predictor of school success, correlations between social class location and school performance do not capture the complexities of educational inequality. Families are not fixed in a static class location, but

they actively construct and negotiate their futures. One of the key sites for this negotiation is the educational system. (Louden & Rivalland, 1995, p. 30)

A study of differences in the educational achievement of students from urban, rural and remote schools in Western Australia (Breen et al., 1994) found that location of the school did not significantly affect student performance. The two factors which were found to have most influence on students' school success were whether the student was from Aboriginal or Torres Strait Islander background, and the socioeconomic status of the school.

Of even greater concern were findings of Barratt-Pugh and Rohl (1994) in their study of three minority-language families in Western Australia, that the children in each family consistently rejected use of the home language, in favor of English. It would appear that the decision to reject home language was complicated by the parents' use of nonstandard English. Other issues that were evident from observations of the families' experiences included: the status of the home language in the eyes of school personnel; a different hierarchy of values accorded to various literacy and cultural practices by the families and their schools; and the prerequisite of English language proficiency for parents wishing to help their children with homework or research. As a result of these observations Barratt-Pugh and Rohl suggested that schools should promote "building on multiple literacies that children bring to school," and equip children to understand the "ways in which literacy practices are socially constructed and differentially valued" (p. 324).

A special case in point in the Australian context is the education of indigenous people. The differences between Aboriginal and European world views are vast. According to Harris (1990), "To say remote Aboriginal culture and Western culture are on two different thought paths is more accurate than to say they are at different ends of some kind of values continuum" (p. 21). Moreover, Aboriginal education is not a politically neutral issue. "Decision makers of the past used education as a tool for assimilation … Schooling was the means by which they separated the children from their heritage" (Valadian, 1991, p. 5). Highlighting a lack of intercultural understanding in schools, Valadian (1991) laments the concentration in Aboriginal studies on cultural manifestations, such as the arts, to the exclusion of less visible cultural elements. With specific reference to literacy, Christie (1985) observes that, "These children have … little familiarity with the language attitudes and behaviours which are fundamental to school success" (p. 51).

In considering literacy mismatches from home to school for minority groups like Indigenous Australians, one needs also to recognize that at times there are fundamental language differences across these contexts. For example, Eagleson, Kaldor, and Malcolm (1982) demonstrated that

Aboriginal languages are grammatically complex, making distinctions unknown in English. The status and use of Aboriginal English and Aboriginal languages also reflects and shapes attitudes to Aboriginal culture. In Aboriginal society, verbal indications such as promises, or saying please and thank you are deemed unnecessary, as it is assumed that one will accommodate the demands of others, including those of children. As a result, Aboriginal children do not find themselves under the special obligations of their Western counterparts (Baarda, 1990). This relative autonomy can be disconcerting for some teachers. Added to this is the Aboriginal belief that doing or saying something wrong can affect moral or spiritual consequences. Because of these expectations (compliance and consequences for mistakes), children are rarely asked to attempt tasks they are unlikely to accomplish. In general, though, social gaffes, especially those of children, are overlooked (Hughes, 1987). The differences between expectations of Aboriginal society and Western schools are strident, and may serve to explain the fear many Aboriginal children have of making mistakes or taking risks. Such basic cultural differences have profound relevance for classroom pedagogy.

Foster (1992) has suggested that research over the past two decades or so "has found that many of the difficulties African-American students encounter in becoming literate result in part from the misunderstandings that occur when the speaking and communication styles of their community vary from those expected and valued in the school setting" (p. 303). However, she laments that such research has "done little to advance our ability to use knowledge about cultural and linguistic differences to improve classroom learning" (p. 304) and, in particular, has had little impact on creating classroom environments, pedagogy, or curricula "specifically designed to improve the literacy learning of African-American children" (p. 308). Foster suggests that part of the reason for this is that researchers have concentrated on explaining cultural discontinuities and differences in linguistic codes, and have devoted little attention to differences in interactional styles and ways of using language at home and at school.

Willis (1995) has also argued that children from cultural and linguistic minority groups continue to have difficulty in achieving school success because the dominant pedagogical approaches are based on "a narrow understanding of school knowledge and literacy, which are defined and defended as what one needs to know and how one needs to know it in order to be successful in school and society" (p. 34).

Several researchers have investigated the impact of differences between the cultural beliefs and expectations of Native Americans, and those of the dominant cultural groups (Deyhle & LeCompte, 1994; Locust, 1988; McCarty, 1987). For example, Locust (1988) examined traditional native American belief systems, including their holistic approach to life and death, their emphasis on nonverbal communication, and their valuing of visual, motor and memory skills over verbal skills. She investigated the ways in which these beliefs conflict with the education system, and argued that traditional psychological education tests reflect the dominant culture resulting in native American children achieving low scores and being treated as learning disabled.

Like Locust, Deyhle and LeCompte (1994) argued that cultural differences in expectations and approaches result in the low school achievement of native American children in middle schools. Through an in-depth case study of one middle school, they showed how some features of the educational structure and pedagogy were congruent with Navajo culture, while many were not. They argued that "Navajo children face conflict not only because their parents' conceptions of proper ways to raise children are different from those of Anglos, but also because of a related set of differences in attitudes and beliefs about stages in child development" (p. 157). They found that although many educators at the school were genuinely interested in good teaching, cultural differences other than language were ignored, rendered invisible, or considered to be irrelevant. As a consequence, few teachers made any alterations to their teaching to accommodate their predominantly Navajo population, and the school encouraged parental involvement only so that it could impose school sanctioned expectations and practices.

Language minority students also experience significant challenges in moving across home, school and community literacy contexts. Bilingual studies of school literacy achievement have provided insights into our growing understanding of the impact of home/school differences. Au (1993, p.94) has argued that bilingual analyses show "how linguistic diversity may influence the acquisition and practice of literacy ... (and) may offer more guidance to educators and policymakers concerned with improving the literacy achievement of students of diverse backgrounds than do critical and cultural difference analyses."

For many years there was widespread belief that one of the major causes of educational difficulty for students from minority language backgrounds was the task of code-switching from the language of the home to the language of the school. While students have long since been shown to be quite capable of effective code-switching, the assumption has led to the development of bilingual programs aimed at providing students with instruction in their home language (L1) in the hope of improving educational outcomes in the school language (L2). However, research into the effectiveness of bilingual programs has produced conflicting results (Cummins, 1986).

Bilingual programs have generated much debate among educators and policymakers. On the one hand, supporters of bilingual education argue that children cannot learn effectively in a language in which they have limited proficiency, and that instruction in their first language is necessary to sustain academic progress while learning a second language. In this way, it is argued that the effects of the mismatch between home and school languages can be minimized. Cummins (1986) termed this the "linguistic mismatch" hypothesis. On the other hand, those who oppose bilingual programs argue that less exposure to L2, which is seen as a consequence of bilingual instruction, cannot lead to increased achievement in L2. What is needed, they argue, is increased exposure to L2. This has been called the "insufficient exposure" hypothesis. However, he argued that neither of these hypotheses can adequately account for what research tells us about bilingual learners.

An insightful bilingual study completed by Jimenez, Garcia, and Pearson (1995), attempted to identify what characteristics distinguish a proficient bilingual reader from a marginally proficient bilingual reader and a proficient monolingual reader. These researchers suggested that too much attention has been given to language minority students who are unsuccessful at school, and that "a more constructive research approach involves the search for enabling, rather than disabling, attributes of non-mainstream populations" (p. 68). Through qualitative analysis of a range of types of responses to reading tasks, they found that proficient bilingual readers demonstrate a "flexible, multi-strategic approach to reading (including) strategies that are unique to biliterate individuals" (p. 88). Furthermore, their analyses of the responses and experiences of a marginally proficient bilingual reader indicated that "bilingualism can be debilitating if a student possesses a faulty conception of reading, a fragmented deployment of reading strategies, and, most important, a failure to appreciate the advantages of bilingualism" (p. 88).

Cummins (1986) has argued that the educational success or failure of minority students is "a function of the extent to which schools reflect or counteract the power relations that exist within the broader society" (p. 32). His work provides a useful framework for evaluating the efforts of the schools. Cummins concluded that language-minority students' educational progress is strongly influenced by the extent to which individual educators become: "advocates for the promotion of students' linguistic talents; actively encourage community participation in developing students' academic and cultural resources; and implement pedagogical approaches that succeed in liberating students from instructional dependence" (p. 32).

DEVELOPING CULTURALLY RESPONSIVE CURRICULUM

There is a fine line separating the acknowledgment of a community's diversity and attempts to conform families to school expectations of what it is to be literate. The initiators of any family or home/school literacy initiative put themselves in a position of unequal power when initiating such programs. Hence they invariably begin to shape the agenda to reflect their personal agendas (Cairney & Ruge, 1998). Since schools have typically been responsible for initiating many family and intergenerational initiatives it is not surprising that many have been dominated by concerns with school literacy. However, as Delgado-Gaitan (1992) argues, we need to find ways to help schools recognize the cultural practices of the home and community and build effective communication between these parties that will lead to genuine partnerships.

Au (1993) suggests that "the culture of the classroom can be seen as a dynamic system of values, beliefs, and standards, developed through understandings which the teacher and the students have come to share" (Au, 1993, p. 9). Recognizing classrooms as cultures entails acknowledging that literacy in classrooms is more than reading and writing, that "it also involves the communicative processes through which it is constructed" (Santa Barbara Classroom Discourse Group, 1992, p. 121). When viewed in this way, we are challenged to move beyond superficial discussions of teaching strategies and patronizing training programs for parents. Instead, we begin to consider ways to understand mismatches between the literacy of home, school and community and the means to build more effective relationships and partnerships across and between these varied contexts.

Foundational to understanding some of these relationships is an ability to understand how people define what it is to be literate, and construct the literacy practices of daily life. Using the methodology of interactional sociolinguistics, the Santa Barbara Classroom Discourse Group (1992) has shown how literate actions and what counts as literacy, are constructed through the actions and interactions with and about text that occur in everyday classroom situations. They point out that students construct a model of literacy based on the literate actions in which they engage, and that the model or models that are constructed reflect school literacy and may support or constrain students' use of literacy in contexts outside the classroom. Thus, "student actions and statements [are] a patterned way of acting or communicating that students have learned from the opportunities afforded them in ... classrooms" (p. 145) and do not necessarily reflect students' ability.

In attempting to understand how literate action is constructed in classrooms, the Santa Barbara Classroom Discourse Group acknowledge a range of sources of influence both inside and outside the group (eg., family, community, peer group, education system). They suggest that studies of classroom interaction cannot, of themselves, illuminate the ways in which literacy is defined and used by individuals and groups (Santa Barbara Classroom Discourse Group, 1992, p. 137). What is required is a more sophisticated understanding of how varied sociolinguistic contexts impact on literacy learning in and out of school.

One such study attempted to discover the essential features of effective schooling for language minority students. The researchers, Lucas, Henze and Donato (1990), conducted an exploratory investigation of six high schools recognized as achieving excellence with Latino students. Their in-depth case studies and cross-case analysis revealed eight features which seemed to underpin the schools' success. In each of the six schools, value was placed on students' languages and cultures; high expectations of language-minority students were made concrete; school leaders made the education of language-minority students a priority; staff development was explicitly designed to help teachers and other staff serve language-minority students more effectively; a variety of programs for language-minority students were offered; counseling programs gave special attention to language-minority students; parents were encouraged to become involved in their children's education; and staff members shared a strong commitment to empowering students through education. The researchers concluded that their findings could form the basis of a framework against which to compare other schools or programs, or to guide the efforts of educators wishing to develop more effective school environments for language-minority students.

Similar findings were obtained by Cairney and Ruge (1998) who conducted detailed cases studies of four culturally and linguistically diverse Australian schools (3 elementary and 1 secondary) over a period of 3 months. Once again these schools that had been identified as effective in acknowledging the cultural diversity of their communities were driven by five key principles. First, all children can achieve school success. Second, reading and writing develop simultaneously with speaking and listening. Third, children's literacy development benefits from the maintenance of first language competence. Fourth, children need opportunities to succeed as they learn new skills. Finally, parents play an important role in children's educational success.

As Ladson-Billings (1995a) has pointed out, much of the existing work on linking students' home and school cultures has been limited to small scale communities and concentrated on "improving achievement in relation to White middle-class norms" (p.150). Many of the existing studies, she noted (1995b), attribute poor school achievement of minority children to differences in interaction patterns between teachers and students. She argued that the terms *culturally appropriate, culturally congruent and culturally compatible*, which are commonly used in the research literature, all suggest that mainstream school culture should merely accommodate students' home culture, rather than respond to it. Ladson-Billings suggested that:

> A next step for positing effective pedagogical practice is a theoretical model that not only addresses student achievement but also helps students to accept and affirm their cultural identity while developing critical perspectives that challenge inequities that schools (and other institutions) perpetuate.

Ladson-Billings (1995b, p. 469) has termed this *culturally relevant pedagogy*. Having proposed the use of the term *culturally relevant pedagogy*, Ladson-Billings defined its features in this way:

> . . . culturally relevant teaching must meet three criteria: an ability to develop students academically, a willingness to nurture and support cultural competence, and the development of a sociopolitical or critical consciousness. (Ladson-Billings, 1995b, p. 483).

Closely related to Ladson-Billings' concept of culturally relevant pedagogy is Cummins' (1986) framework for empowering students of diverse backgrounds. Cummins argues that previous attempts at education reform have been unsuccessful because the relationships between teachers and students and between schools and communities have remained essentially unchanged. To reverse the pattern of minority student failure, Cummins suggests that there needs to be a redefinition of the classroom interactions between teachers and students; relationships between schools and minority groups; and intergroup power relations within society as a whole. He insists that students from dominated communities will be empowered in the school context to the extent that the communities themselves are empowered through their interactions with the school. He points out that when educators involve minority parents as partners in their children's education, parents appear to develop a sense of efficacy that communicates itself to children, with positive academic consequences.

In the Australian context, Howard (1994) presents a model of culturally responsive pedagogy for Aboriginal children, which takes advantage of the "social relationships with which they are familiar" (p. 41). He describes two processes of successful programs: teaching in ways which attempt to maximize Aboriginal student learning, while apprenticing them to the processes and assumptions of Western learning. In particular, he advocates the establishment of positive student-teacher relationships, application of peer learning opportunities, recognition and use of Aboriginal children's real-life skills, as well as tolerance and understanding of their autonomy. Also recommended is a different approach to the use of time, which may range from allowing longer pauses for Aboriginal children to consider their answers to questions, to the provision of a more flexible timetable.

Cummins proposes a framework for empowering students, which encompasses many of the essential ideas and arguments of other proponents of culturally responsive curricula. His framework includes four areas of reform which need to be attended to: the incorporation of students' language and culture into the school curriculum; community participation in students' education; pedagogical assumptions and practices which reflect constructivist rather than transmission models of instruction; and advocacy-oriented assessment practices.

One group of researchers that has attempted to genuinely empower parents and communities is led by Luis Moll. Working primarily with Mexican American working-class families, Moll and his colleagues have explored the notion of the "funds of knowledge" (Moll, Amanti, Neff, & Gonzalez, 1992; Moll, 1993) that communities and their members possess. Through their analysis of how households and families function as part of broader social and economic networks, they demonstrated that the families they worked with had important cultural and cognitive resources that sustained them through changing, and often difficult, social and economic circumstances. Through working with groups of classroom teachers, they explored ways in which these "funds of knowledge" could become pedagogically useful in linking students' home and school cultures. Teachers and researchers visited the homes of their students to develop greater knowledge and understanding of the students' home backgrounds. Teachers then developed learning modules based on information gathered from the households, with the result that students became more active in their learning and were able to draw on their own "funds of knowledge."

> It is our contention that existing classroom practices not only underestimate and constrain what children display intellectually, but help distort explanations of school performance. It is also our contention that the strategic application of cultural resources in instruction is one important way of obtaining change in academic performance and of demonstrating that there is nothing about the children's language, culture, or intellectual capacities that should handicap their schooling. (Moll & Diaz, 1991, p. 67)

Moll and Diaz (1991), in drawing on the work of Heath to explain their work, argue that schools often privilege "a single developmental model of learning" which results in minority students being "stuck in the lower levels of the curriculum" (p. 69). They argue that research shows that when instruction is modified to capitalize fully on students' "talents, resources, and skills" (p. 69), minority children can succeed. Consistent with this view is May's (1995) description of one school principal's attempts to develop a culturally responsive school:

Laughton was concerned with developing at Richmond Road both *cultural maintenance*—the fostering of identity and self-esteem through the affirmation of cultural difference, and *access to power*—equipping minority children with the skills necessary to live in the wider society. Both aspects are necessary, he believed, if dominant discourses in society are to be effectively contested. In implementing these ideas, he saw certain values as prerequisite: difference is never equated with deficiency; co-operation is fostered not competition; cultural respect is seen as essential to developing a pluralistic society; and the school's function is directed towards increasing a child's options rather than changing them (May, 1995, p. 6).

Foster (1992) points out that while radical reform of curriculum might be necessary, there are some educational strategies that may be culturally and linguistically responsive, even though they not specifically designed to address problems of discontinuities between home and school. For example, she cites Cooperative Learning Groups, which focus on the group rather than the individual (and are marked by social equality), as one educational strategy that may be more compatible with the values and cultural norms of certain groups of disadvantaged children. Furthermore, she argues that they "...may actually confer an advantage by providing them with a familiar social context" (p. 308).

Adopting a similar line of reasoning Ferdman (1990) also encourages teachers to carefully consider the methods and content of existing classroom literacy practices from the perspective of specific groups' cultural identities. Ferdman argues that "rather than aim[ing] for a curriculum that avoids discussions of ethnicity, the goal should be to facilitate the process by which students are permitted to discover and explore ethnic connections" (Ferdman, 1990, p. 200). Both Ferdman and Cummins (1986) suggest that such opportunities create an environment that can empower members of minority groups.

What is common to all these studies is a desire to understand the differences between the language, literacy and culture of children's families in order to acknowledge and build on this diversity. This is in contrast to many initiatives that appear to be built on the assumption that such differences represent problems or deficits to be overcome. One assumption leads teachers and researchers to seek to conform families to the literacy practices of schooling. The other seeks to draw on the richness of community knowledge, language, literacy and experience to develop more inclusive and responsive curricula.

CONCLUSION

As the above discussion has argued, one of the great challenges for early childhood educators in multicultural societies is how to cater for the needs of all students and acknowledge and build on the rich cultural diversity present within any early childhood or school setting. One of the imperatives for teachers in the last two decades has been the need to understand the language and cultural diversity of the children who enter early childhood education. Children live in a world of diverse opportunities for learning, in which literacy is an important vehicle for this to occur. They experience language and literacy in many forms, and are enculturated into literacy practices, which may or may not match those of their teachers or care givers.

Research from a broad range of disciplines and perspectives has contributed a great deal to our understanding of the interrelationships between culture, language, literacy and school success. No longer should the failure of children from minority backgrounds be attributed to deficits in their family environments, linguistic codes, or the children themselves. However, the difficulties associated with applying these understandings to the development of culturally responsive classroom environments and pedagogy has meant that the richness of research findings is not reflected widely in family literacy and home/school initiatives. As Foster (1992) has warned:

> If this line of research is to have a significant impact on practice, researchers must explain and practitioners must understand the cultural, linguistic, and sociolinguistic principles undergirding (culturally responsive) practices. If teachers are going to become reflective practitioners, they need to possess both theoretical and practical knowledge of how to use cultural, linguistic, and sociolinguistic information to develop ways of teaching that not only respect cultural diversity but insure high levels of literacy. (p. 309)

Gee (1990) has suggested that "short of radical social change" there is "no access to power in society without control over the social practices in thought, speech and writing essay-text literacy and its attendant world view" (p. 67). As I have suggested elsewhere (Cairney, 1994) we need to ask constantly, what does this mean for the way literacy is defined and used at school, the programs we initiate with and for families, and the relationships that exist between schools and communities?

At a more practical level there appear to be a number of specific implications for researchers, policy makers and practitioners. In brief these are:

1. There is an urgent need for greater clarity about what educators and researchers mean by the terms literacy, family, community, and family literacy. While many researchers and writers have called for

the problematizing of these terms, the literature is still reporting a majority of home/school and family literacy initiatives that fail to grapple with exactly what they mean by each of these terms. As a result, most programs are built on restricted and impoverished definitions of what it means to be literate, what families and communities are, and what the relationship between home, school and community is and could become.

2. Schools and early childhood centers also need to examine what they currently do in the name of family literacy or home/school initiatives. Such an examination needs to focus on the assumptions that drive such initiatives (see Cairney et al., 1995 for a discussion of one framework for conducting such an analysis) and the extent to which a collaborative partnership between home, school and community is being fostered.

3. There is a need to focus more fully on how initiatives of the type discussed in this chapter meet the diverse needs of all students. In particular, researchers need to move beyond designing and evaluating initiatives that reproduce a limited range of school literacy practices.

4. Teachers and researchers need to ask themselves some more difficult questions about their own research as a form of self evaluation. For example, to what extent does the initiative developed reinforce existing power relationships between educational institutions and families? Could this program be guilty of a new form of cultural imperialism in transforming the literacy practices of homes to be more like those of school? And, if so, what is the long term impact of such outcomes?

5. Finally, teachers and researchers need to examine more closely the differences between the literacy practices of early childhood centers and schools and those of families and communities and consider the implications that such matches and mismatches have for children's educational success.

The match and mismatch in language and literacy between home/community and school is of vital importance in addressing the specific needs of all students, but in particular, those who experience difficulties with literacy and schooling. However, there is still much to be learned about this topic. What we do know is that classrooms are not simple places; they are dynamic interactional spaces where individuals come together for the purpose of schooling to construct situated definitions of teacher, student, knowledge, values and so on (Fernie et al., 1988; Green, Kantor & Rogers, 1991). In the words of Bruner (1986), they are a forum for negotiating culture. But as I have asked elsewhere, whose culture, and on what (and whose) terms is this culture negotiated? Furthermore, what impact do such practices have on the achievement of all students? (Cairney, 1994).

There is little doubt that the teachers and researchers who have been responsible for the many family literacy initiatives developed and implemented have had sound motives. The desire in implementing these programs has been to help children to succeed at school. However, what the above review shows is that there are many unanswered questions about the initiatives planned and the research that has evaluated them. We need to ask many hard questions about these initiatives to ensure that the very practices that have been implemented to help children, do no inadvertently ensure a continuation of inequitable outcomes for specific students and their families.

NOTES

1.   A version of this chapter has been previously published in *Early Child Development and Care, 172*(2), 153–172.

2.   When using the term family it is important to recognize that families take many forms. Even the nuclear family does not simply consist of two parents and their biological children. A child's immediate nuclear family may contain one or both of their biological parents, or at times other non-related caregivers and children with varied relationships to their biological parent(s). As well, children experience vastly different forms of extended families, with some living in households that contain grandparents, uncles, aunts, boarders and so on. In short, there are immense differences in the make of the families that children experience.

REFERENCES

Anderson, R.C., Wilson, P.T., & Fielding, L.C. (1988). Growth in reading and how children spend their time outside of school. *Reading Research Quarterly, 23,* 285–303.

Au, K. (1993). *Literacy instruction in multicultural settings.* Fort Worth, TX: Harcourt Brace Jovanovich.

Au, K. (1995). Multicultural perspectives on literacy research. *Journal of Reading Behaviour, 27*(1), 85–100.

Auerbach, E. (1989). Toward a social-contextual approach to family literacy. *Harvard Educational Review, 59,* 165–181.

Baarda, W. (1990). Cultural differences in schools. In C. Walton & C. Eggington (Eds.), *Language: Maintenance, power and education in Australian Aboriginal contexts.* Darwin: Northern Territory University Press.

Baker, C., & Luke, A. (1991). *Toward a critical sociology of reading pedagogy.* Philadelphia: John Benjamins.

Barratt-Pugh, C., & Rohl, M. (1994). A question of either or: Must fluency in English be Achieved at the expense of home languages. *The Australian Journal of Language and Literacy, 17,* 313–326.

Breen, M.P., Louden, W., Barrat-Pugh, C., Rivalland, J., Rohl, M., Rhydwen, M., Lloyd, S., & Carr, T. (1994). *Literacy in its place: Literacy practices in urban and rural communities* (Vols 1 & 2). Canberra: Department of Education, Training and Employment.

Bloome, D. (1986). *Literacy and schooling.* Norwood, NJ: Ablex.

Bruner, J. (1986). *Actual minds, possible worlds.* Cambridge, MA: Harvard University Press.

Cairney, T.H. (1987). Supporting the independent learner: Negotiating change in the classroom. In J. Hancock & B. Comber (Eds), *Independent learners at school* (pp. 78–96). Sydney: Methuen.

Cairney, T.H. (1994). Family literacy: Moving towards new partnerships in education. *Australian Journal of Language and Literacy, 17,* 262–275.

Cairney, T.H. (1995a). Developing parent partnerships in secondary literacy learning. *Journal of Reading, 38,* 520–527.

Cairney, T.H. (1995b). *Pathways to literacy.* London: Cassell.

Cairney, T.H. (1997). Reconstructing teacher views on parent involvement in children's literacy. In D. Taylor (Ed.), *Many families many literacies: Developing family literacy programs based on an international declaration of principles.* Portsmouth, NH: Heinemann.

Cairney, T.H. (2000). The home-school connection in literacy and language development. In R. Campbell & D. Green (Eds.), *Literacies and learners* (pp. 91–104). Melbourne: Prentice-Hall.

Cairney, T.H., & Langbien, S. (1989). Building communities of readers and writers. *The Reading Teacher, 42,* 560–567.

Cairney, T.H., Lowe, K. & Sproats, E. (1995). *Literacy in transition: An investigation of the literacy practices of upper primary and junior secondary schools* (Vols 1–3). Canberra: DEET.

Cairney, T.H., & Munsie, L. (1992). *Talk to a literacy learner.* Sydney: UWS Press.

Cairney, T.H., & Munsie, L. (1993). *Effective partners in secondary literacy learning program.* Sydney: UWS Press.

Cairney, T.H., & Munsie, L. (1995a). *Beyond tokenism: Parents as partners in literacy learning.* Portsmouth (NH): Heineman.

Cairney, T.H., & Munsie, L. (1995b). Parent participation in literacy learning. *The Reading Teacher, 48,* 393–403.

Cairney, T.H., & Ruge, J. (1996, April). *Examining the impact of cultural mismatches between home and school: Coping with diversity in classrooms.* Paper presented to the American Educational Research Association Conference, New York.

Cairney, T.H., & Ruge, J. (1998). *Community literacy practices and schooling: Towards effective support for students.* Canberra: Department of Employment, Education, Training & Youth Affairs (DEETYA).

Cairney, T.H., Ruge, J., Buchanan, J., Lowe, K., & Munsie, L. (1995). *Developing partnerships: The home, school and community interface* (Vols 1–3). Canberra: Department of Education, Employment and Youth Affairs.

Christie, M. (1985). *Aboriginal perspectives on experience and learning; The role of language in Aboriginal education.* Geelong: Deakin University Press.

Cope, B., & Kalantzis, M. (Eds) (2000). *Multiliteracies: Literacy learning and the design of social futures.* Melbourne: Macmillan.

Cummins, J. (1986). Empowering minority students: A framework for intervention. *Harvard Educational Review, 56,* 18–36.

Delgado-Gaitan, C. (1992). School matters in the Mexican-American home: Socialising children to education. *American Educational Research Journal , 29,* 495–516.

Department of Education and Science. (1967). *Children and their primary schools: A report of the Central Advisory Council for Education (England) Vol.1: Report & Vol 2: Research and Surveys (Plowden Report).* London: HMSO.

Deyhle, D., & LeCompte, M. (1994). Cultural differences in child development: Navajo adolescents in middle schools. *Theory Into Practice, 33,* 156–166.

Eagleson, R., Kaldor, S., & Malcolm, I. (1982). *English and the Aboriginal child.* Dickson, ACT: Curriculum Development Centre.

Ferdman, B. (1990). Literacy and Cultural Identity. *Harvard Educational Review, 60,* 181–204.

Fernie, D., Kantor, R., & Klein, E. (1988). Becoming students and becoming ethnographers in a preschool. *Journal of Childhood Research in Education. 3,* 95–110.

Foster, M. (1992). Sociolinguistics and the African-American community: Implications for literacy. *Theory Into Practice, 31,* 303–310.

Freebody, P., Ludwig, C., & Gunn, S. (1995). *Everyday literacy practices in and out of schools in low socio-economic status urban communities: A descriptive and interpretive research program.* Canberra: DEETYA.

Gee, J. (1990). *Social linguistics and literacies: Ideology in discourses.* London: The Falmer Press.

Green, J., Kantor, R., & Rogers, T. (1991). Exploring the complexity of language and learning in the classroom. In B. Jones & L. Idol (Eds.), *Educational values and cognitive instruction: Implications for reform* (Vol. 2, pp. 333–364). Hillsdale, NJ: Erlbaum.

Gutierrez, K.D. (1993). How talk, context, and script shape contexts for learning: A cross-case comparison of journal sharing. *Linguistics and Education, 5,* 335–365.

Handel, R.D. (1992). The partnership for family reading: Benefits for families and schools. *The Reading Teacher, 46,* 116–126.

Hannon, P. (1995). *Literacy, Home and School: Research and practice in teaching literacy with parents.* London: The Falmer Press.

Harris, S. (1990). *Two way Aboriginal schooling: Education and cultural survival.* Canberra: Aboriginal Studies Press.

Heath, S.B. (1983). *Ways with words: Language , life and work in community and classrooms.* Cambridge: Cambridge University Press.

Howard, D. (1994). Culturally responsive classrooms: A way to assist Aboriginal students with hearing loss in urban schools. In S. Harris & M. Malin (Eds.), *Aboriginal kids in urban classrooms.* Wentworth Falls, NSW: Social Science Press.

Hughes, P. (1987). *Aboriginal culture and learning styles—A challenge for academics in higher education institutions.* Canberra: National Library of Australia.

Illinois Literacy Resource Development Center. (1990). *The mechanics of success for families.* Rantoul: Illinois Literacy Resource Development Center.

Jackson, B.L., Krasnow, J., & Seeley, D. (1994, April 4–8). *The league of schools reaching out: A New York City cluster building family-school-community partnership.* Paper presented to the American Educational Research Association Conference, New Orleans.

Jimenez, R., Garcia, G., & Pearson, P.D. (1995). Three children, two languages, and strategic reading: Case studies in bilingual/monolingual reading. *American Educational Research Journal, 32,* 67–97.

Jordan, G.E., Snow, C.E., & Porche, M.V. (2000). Project EASE: The effect of a family literacy project on kindergarten students' early literacy skills. *Reading Research Quarterly, 35,* 524–546.

Ladson-Billings, G. (1995a). Introduction to themed issue on culturally relevant teaching. *Theory Into Practice, 34,* 150–151.

Ladson-Billings, G. (1995b). Toward a theory of culturally relevant pedagogy. *American Educational Research Journal, 32,* 465–491.

Locust, C. (1988). Wounding the spirit: Discrimination and traditional American belief systems. *Harvard Educational Review, 55,* 315–330.

Louden, W., & Rivalland, J. (1995). *Literacy at a distance: Language and learning in distance education.* Perth, WA: Edith Cowan University.

Lucas, T., Henze, R., & Donato, R. (1990). Promoting the success of Latino language-minority students: An exploratory study of six high schools. *Harvard Educational Review, 60,* 315–340.

Luke, A. (1993) Stories of social regulation: The micropolitics of classroom narrative. In B. Green (Ed.), *The insistence of the letter: Literacy studies and curriculum theorising* (pp. 137–153). London: Falmer Press.

Luke, A. (1995, April). *When literacy might/not make a difference: Textual practice and capital.* Paper presented at the American Educational Research Association Conference, San Francisco.

McCarty, T.L. (1987). School as community: The rough rock demonstration. *Harvard Educational Review, 59,* 484–503.

Malin, M. (1994). Make or break factors in Aboriginal students learning to read in urban classrooms: A socio-cultural perspective. In S. Harris & M. Malin (Eds.), *Aboriginal kids in urban classrooms* (pp. 155–169). Wentworth Falls, NSW: Social Science Press.

May, S. (1995). Deconstructing traditional discourses of schooling: An example of school reform. *Language and Education, 9,* 1, 1–29.

Moje, E.R. (2000). Critical issues: Circles of kinship, friendship, position, and power: Examining the community in community—based literacy research. *Journal of Literacy Research, 32*(1), 77–112.

Moll, L. (1993, April 12–16). *Community-mediated educational practices.* Paper presented at the American Educational Research Association Conference, Atlanta, GA.

Moll, L., Amanti, C., Neff, D., & Gonzalez, N. (1992). Funds of knowledge for teaching: Using a qualitative approach to connect homes and classrooms. *Theory Into Practice, 31,* 132–141.

Morgan, R.T.T. (1976). "Paired reading" tuition: A preliminary report on a technique for cases of reading deficit. *Child Care, Health and Development, 2,* 13–28.

Mulhern, M. (1995, April). A *Mexican-American child's home life and literacy learning from Kindergarten through second grade*. Paper presented at the American Educational Research Association Annual Meeting, San Francisco.

Neuman, S. (1997). Guiding young children's participation in early literacy development: A family literacy program for adolescent mothers. *Early Child Development and Care, 127–128*, 119–29.

Neuman, S.B., & Daly, P. (1996). *Guiding young children: A family literacy approach*. Unpublished report.

Nickse, R. (1993). A typology of family and intergenerational literacy programmes; Implications for evaluation. *Viewpoints, 15*, 34–40.

Ogbu, J. (1992). Adaptation to minority status and impact on school success. *Theory Into Practice, 21*, 287–295.

Ogbu, J. (1993). Frameworks—Variability in minority school performance: A problem in search of an explanation. In E. Jacob & C. Jordan (Eds.), *Minority education: Anthropological perspectives* (pp. 186–204). Norwood, NJ: Ablex.

Paratore, J.R., & Brisk, M. (1995). *Teaching literacy to bilingual children: Effective practices for use by monolingual and bilingual teachers*. ERIC, #ED390249.

Quintero, E., & Huerta-Macias, A. (1990). All in the family: Bilingualism and biliteracy. *The Reading Teacher, 44*, 306–312.

Santa Barbara Classroom Discourse Group. (1992). Constructing literacy in classrooms: Literate action as social accomplishment. In H. Marshall (Ed.), *Redefining student learning: Roots of educational change* (pp. 119–151). Norwood, NJ: Ablex.

Shanahan, T., Mulhern, M., & Rodriguez-Brown, F. (1995). Project FLAME: Lessons learned from a family literacy program for linguistic minority families. *The Reading Teacher, 48*, 586–593.

Shanahan, T., & Rodriguez-Brown, F. (1993, April 12–16). *The theory and structure of a family literacy program for the Latino community*. Paper presented at the American Educational Research Association Conference, Atlanta, GA.

Scribner, S., & Cole, M. (1981). *The psychology of literacy*. Cambridge, MA: Harvard University Press.

Taylor, D. (1983). *Family literacy: Young children learning to read and write*. Exeter, NH: Heinemann.

Taylor, D. (1997). *Many families many literacies: Developing family literacy programs based on an international declaration of principles*. Portsmouth , NH: Heinemann.

Topping, K., & McKnight, G. (1984). Paired reading—and parent power. *Special Education-Forward Trends, 11*, 12–15.

Topping, K., & Wolfendale, S. (Eds) (1985). *Parental involvement in children's reading*. Beckenham, UK: Croom Helm.

Valadian, M. (1991) *Aboriginal education—Development or destruction. The issues and challenges that have to be recognised*. Unpublished report.

Welch, A.R., & Freebody, P. (1993). Introduction: Explanations of the current international "Literacy Crises." In P. Freebody & A. Welch (Eds.), *Knowledge, culture & power: international perspectives on literacy as policy and practice*. London: Falmer Press.

Willis, A.I. (1995). Reading the world of school literacy: Contextualising the experience of a young African American male. *Harvard Educational Review, 65*, 1, 30–48.

CHAPTER 6

ENGAGING CHILDREN IN THE APPROPRIATION OF LITERACY:

The Importance of Parental Beliefs and Practices

Susan Sonnenschein

INTRODUCTION

Becoming literate is a process of appropriation. The young child must acquire both a set of skills and knowledge of when and how to utilize these skills. Becoming a reader requires the development of phonological analysis skills, letter knowledge, sound-letter correspondence, and comprehension skills (Snow, Burns, & Griffin, 1998). Although formal schooling plays an important role in a child's acquisition of these skills, children begin the process of literacy appropriation before ever setting foot through a school door (Adams, 1990; Baker, Serpell, & Sonnenschein, 1995). The experiences that a child has at home, such as being read stories, learning about the world through outings, having dinnertime conversations, help the child acquire early literacy skills such as learning about story structure, analyzing sound patterns in words, learning letters, even before formal school-based instruction starts (Baker et al., 1995). These early literacy-related skills, in turn, foster later literacy development. The process of learning to read goes fairly smoothly for many children in our society, particularly middle income children; however, it does not work quite as well for many low income children (Snow et al., 1998).

Earlier accounts of systematic group-based differences in literacy outcomes relied upon social address models, such as ethnicity and/or low income, as explanations for the differences. Such approaches failed to disentangle income/ethnicity from confounding factors, such as possible limited literacy skills of the parents, poor quality schools, and language differences between home and school. Such approaches neglected to sufficiently consider the importance of the child as an agent in his or her learning. More important, using social address as an explanation failed to explicate the processes involved in literacy acquisition. In addition, a social address approach neglected to account for variability among members of a particular group. Moreover, such an approach did not lead to effective programs to facilitate literacy acquisition for all children.

In the past 15 or so years we have made some headway moving away from a social address model explanation of differences among children's literacy skills to one more likely to result in effective educational practices for all children. Attention has been given to the importance of a match between the worlds of home and school which has enabled us to increase our understanding of the range of literacy-related activities available in the homes of all children. Researchers also have begun to focus on the processes involved in literacy appropriation by considering the child an agent in his or her socialization and by expanding our understanding of the importance of social context.

Implicit in the concept of literacy appropriation is the notion that in order to learn to read the child must want to acquire the necessary knowledge and skills (Snow et al., 1998). Thus, any review of how children learn to read must address how it is that children become engaged in the process. In this chapter I will review the role that a child's home environment plays in literacy appropriation by considering parents' beliefs about the importance of literacy and how literacy skills are acquired as well as the nature of literacy-relevant activities that a child experiences at home. In discussing each issue I will review sociocultural differences, when there are known differences. It is important to realize, however, that although there are some differences in children's literacy development related to sociocultural group, research showing relations between parental beliefs, practices and children's development are independent of a sociocultural group.

The theoretical orientation that informs this review reflects several contemporary developmental perspectives. Development occurs in a context of overlapping and interdependent contexts or systems (Bronfenbrenner, 1979). In order to understand a child's literacy development one needs to examine the interrelations among the contexts in which a child spends time (e.g., home and school). Children's development is influenced by their sociocultural background (Vygotsky, 1978). Children appropriate literacy knowledge in a social context through their interactions with others (Rogoff, 1990).

This chapter focuses only on parental beliefs and what goes on at home. In order to fully understand how children learn to read, however, one must consider both what occurs at home and what occurs at school as congruence between a child's home experiences and what is expected of that child at school is very important (Sonnenschein & Schmidt, 2000). In fact, a mismatch between home and school is thought by many to account for certain children's failure to acquire literacy skills. However, there is much controversy in opinion as to how to bridge the gap between home and school; some researchers advocate training programs to improve parents' literacy skills and teach them how to read with their children; other researchers specifying a need for schools to better reflect the desires, goals and experiences of children in their community (see Purcell-Gates, 2000, for a review).

The thesis to be presented in this chapter is that a key element in helping a young child learn to read is engaging the child's interest. One way to engage a child's interest is by fostering a sense that literacy is a source of pleasure. Helping a young child find reading pleasurable is at least partially a function of parental beliefs about literacy and its acquisition as well as the nature of activities that children engage in. The beliefs that parents have about reading and learning to read may influence the activities they make available to their children and how they interact with their children while engaging in these activities. Children themselves play a role in the process by selecting certain activities over others.

The thesis that serves as an organizational tool for this chapter is consistent with a burgeoning body of research on influences on children's motivations for learning (see Baker, Scher, & Mackler, 1997 for a review of this literature). For example, Gottfried, Fleming, and Gottfried (1998) have shown the positive long-term impact of a cognitively stimulating home environment on children's intrinsic interest in learning to read. Parents of 8-year-olds completed questionnaires about the type and amount of cognitive stimulation available at home. Children of these parents were given a battery of tests assessing their interest in learning math and reading when they were 9, 10, and 13 years old. Growing up in a stimulating environment positively predicted children's motivation at each age, regardless of socioeconomic status of the family.

There appear to be some systematic differences in the approaches taken by parents for helping their children learn to read which may play some role in these children's subsequent literacy development. The differences in approaches may reflect systematic differences in parental beliefs about the nature of literacy and how to facilitate its development. Differences in beliefs about literacy, in turn, may influence the choice of activities made available to children and how one engages in the activities.

As will be reviewed in more detail in subsequent sections, a consideration of activities relevant for literacy acquisition needs to move beyond just the nature of an activity. One also needs to consider the child's interest in an activity. Storybook reading is currently thought to be one of the better ways to facilitate young children's reading development. Discussion of the efficacy of storybook reading has typically focused on the skills it can foster. However, as will be discussed in this chapter, some of the efficacy of storybook reading may be due to fostering a child's interest in the reading process rather than direct skill inculcation (Baker, Mackler, Sonnenschein, & Serpell, 2001).

PARENTAL BELIEFS

Parental beliefs are considered an important topic because parental beliefs are thought to influence parental practices which in turn influence children's developmental outcomes (Miller, 1988). The nature of the activities that parents engage in with their children and the patterns of interaction may reflect, at least in part, parental beliefs about education and children's learning. Thus, parental beliefs about how children learn may influence both the nature of the activities made available to children as well as the form of the interaction while engaging in an activity (Goodnow & Collins, 1990; Super & Harkness, 1986). Parental beliefs initially may stem from a parent's cultural background and history (Ninio, 1980; Sonnenschein, Brody, & Munsterman, 1996) but over time can come to reflect aspects of the individual child (e.g., child's perceived needs and strengths; Hastings & Rubin, 1999).

Inquiry into parental beliefs about literacy development is limited. Instead research has focused on parental practices with beliefs, at times, inferred from practices. Research on parental beliefs often attempts to document sociocultural patterns of beliefs. However, the extant research often conflates ethnicity, income and parental literacy level. There has also been insufficient attention devoted to intergroup variability.

Three types of parental beliefs that may be especially important for children's succeeding in school, particularly in the area of reading, are: ideas about the importance of education, notions of how children learn, and expectations for parental involvement in the schooling process (Sonnenschein & Schmidt, 2000). Although almost all parents stress the importance of education, there appear to be differences related to sociocultural background in how parents socialize their young children for school (Baker, 1999; Baker et al., 1995). These differences among parents appear to continue once their children enter school (see Sonnenschein & Schmidt, 2000).

Importance of Education

Almost all parents stress the importance of their children receiving a good education (Sonnenschein et al., 1997). Thus, a difference in the emphasis placed upon an education cannot account for systematic group-based differences in how children succeed in school. In fact, there is some evidence that parents of children at-risk for not succeeding in school place greater emphasis on the importance of an education than do other parents. For example, several researchers have found that many African American or Hispanic parents have high educational aspirations for their children and are supportive of any attempts made by schools to teach their children, even ones considered by many to be developmentally inappropriate (see Sonnenschein, Brody et al., 1996).

Despite emphasizing the importance of their children's getting an education, there are differences related to sociocultural identity in how parents view the utility of certain educational skills and ways to foster these skills. Sonnenschein et al. (1997) report data from the Early Childhood Project, a 5-year longitudinal study of young children's reading development which started when the children were in prekindergarten. Participating families were selected from neighborhood public schools in Baltimore City serving either low income or middle income African American or European American families. Parents participated in several in-depth structured and semi-structured interviews. Children's early literacy and literacy skills were assessed annually. Parents and children were also observed completing several literacy activities. As part of a series of ongoing interviews, parents were asked when their children were in preschool or kindergarten, "What do you believe is the most important reason for learning to read? Other reasons?" The most common categories of responses given were daily living activities, getting an education, employment, empowerment. Middle income families were significantly more likely than low income families to mention that reading was important for learning.

Support for findings of some group-based differences in parents' views on the importance of literacy comes from ethnographic observations of different types of literacy activities engaged in by families. For example, Teale (1986) observed literacy activities in the homes of 22 low income families. Focal children in the families were between 2.5 and 3.5 years. Although families participated in a wide array of literacy-related activities, the most common was daily living routines. Shared storybook reading was a far less common occurrence.

Sonnenschein et al.'s (1997) findings are also consistent in some ways with Fox's (1990) explanation of one possible cause of low income children's difficulties learning to read. She suggested that parents of these children may view literacy in a different manner than parents of children more likely to succeed in school, "Even though literacy is an integral part of everyday household routines ... the parents frequently do not associate reading and writing with work-related or leisure-time activities" (p. 6). According to Fox, the children in such families may come to view literacy as the domain of school and not something engaged in outside of school.

Other research has shown that despite having high aspirations for their children's learning, certain groups of parents are less likely to foster what many teachers consider necessary foundational skills prior to their children's entering school (Goldenberg & Gallimore, 1995; Sonnenschein et al., 1996; Whitehurst & Lonigan, 1998). Although these parents think school is important and want their children to get a good education, they also are less likely than others to believe their children will necessarily attain educational success. In fact, many of these parents' children do have difficulty learning to read once they start school.

Findings that children are entering school lacking skills viewed as important by teachers convey an implicit message that the child and his or her home is deficient in certain ways. Such a notion does not seem the best basis for establishing a positive working relationship between home and school. In contrast, certain theorists and researchers argue that as most children do have exposure at home to a broad array of literacy-relevant activities, the onus is on schools to devise programs that capitalize upon the knowledge children bring with them when they enter school (Auerbach, 1995; Taylor & Dorsey Gaines, 1988). Clearly, additional research is needed to better understand what skills children do have upon entry to school and how to build upon them as well as how the attitude that parents have about literacy influences what is learned.

How Children Learn

There appear to be some systematic differences related to sociocultural background in how parents think learning to read should be facilitated. Although there are individual differences, it appears that low income parents espouse a more traditional didactic approach to fostering literacy acquisition than do middle income parents. Note that it is income, and those factors correlated with income, more than ethnicity that seems to be the relevant factor across the various studies.

Early research on children's learning often focused on the age at which children were expected to acquire certain cognitive or social skills. Expected milestones are of interest because parents who expect earlier attainment of skills report introducing activities which can foster skill development at an earlier age than those who do not expect such early attainment (Ninio, 1979). In contrast, parents who underestimate their children's cognitive capabilities may not provide appropriate experiences for their children which in turn can hinder the children's development (Ninio, 1980). Middle income parents generally reported that cognitive skills develop earlier than did low income families (Ninio, 1979).

DeBaryshe (1993) found a positive relation between maternal beliefs, age of child when activities were introduced and children's language development. She explored the nature and frequency of reading activities engaged in by mothers and their 2-year-old children and these children's oral language skills. DeBaryshe concluded that mothers' beliefs about how children learn and their goals for their children were the best predictors of how old children were when their mothers first started reading to them. The age of the child when a mother began reading to him or her was the best predictor of the child's subsequent receptive language skills.

More recent research on parents' beliefs about the approach that should be taken when helping children learn to read has shown systematic group-based differences in the emphasis given to traditional didactic approaches. Holloway, Rambaud, Fuller, and Eggers-Pierola (1995) interviewed 14 low income single mothers of different ethnicities repeatedly over a three-year period about their socialization goals for their preschool children. A key objective for these mothers was getting their children ready to enter school. The mothers expected the daycare providers at their children's day care centers to engage in didactic lessons emphasizing basic literacy and numeracy skills. Unlike many middle income mothers and educators who favor a more child-centered approach, these mothers reported not seeing any relation between play and learning. Neuman, Hagedorn, Celano, and Daly (1995) reported that the majority of their adolescent African American low income mothers espoused a similar view of literacy learning for their preschool children. These mothers reported reading to their children in order to teach them letters, numbers and knowing right from wrong. Learning letters was viewed by many of these mothers as an important benchmark of development. Most of the mothers, although not all, stressed the importance of an emphasis on skill instruction in preschool to foster children's acquiring knowledge of letters.

Stipek, Milburn, Clements, and Daniels (1992) asked parents of children in late preschool or kindergarten to complete a questionnaire about appropriate ways to teach basic skills to their children. They also asked parents what activities the children engaged in at home. The sample of 551 parents was fairly diverse in terms of income and ethnicity. In addition to interviewing parents, children were observed in their classrooms. The findings showed that parents expressed a coherent set of beliefs about how to teach this age group. Some parents emphasized skills instruction within a traditional teacher-controlled classroom. Other parents emphasized a more child-centered approach. The set of beliefs expressed by parents was related to their educational level with less educated parents emphasizing more of a skills-based approach than better educated parents. Parents espousing more of a skills-based approach were more likely than other parents to report having their children use flash cards and workbooks to learn relevant skills. The approach to education espoused by the parents was related to the type of school chosen by these parents for their children, when such choice was available.

A similar set of findings comes from the work of Fitzgerald, Spiegel, and Cunningham (1991) who interviewed 181 parents of beginning kindergartners about what parents can do to help their children learn in school. As part of the interview each parent was given a literacy test. Although most parents thought that literacy learning can begin in preschool, the nature of instruction advocated varied according to the parents' literacy level. Parents whose own literacy skills were low were more likely than those with higher literacy skills to emphasize the use of flash cards and similar types of materials for teaching reading. Parents with higher literacy skills tended to disavow the use of such tools. Parents whose reading skills were low emphasized direct teaching of literacy skills to their children whereas parents whose reading skills were higher tended to reject a skills-based approach but were more likely to discuss nurturing their children's literacy development. Parents with higher literacy skills also talked about the importance of being role models for their children. Parents whose reading skills were low never mentioned this, perhaps because they felt they did not know how to be good role models or perhaps because they themselves did not find reading rewarding. The authors concluded that parents with higher reading skills tended to view literacy as a cultural practice not just simply something learned in school, a view that was not shared by the parents with low literacy skills.

An emphasis on direct inculcation of skills also was noted by Delpit (1986) in discussing her experience as a new teacher in an inner-city school. Parents of Delpit's African American students wanted her to teach their children how to read using a traditional approach that emphasized skills. In fact, it was not until Delpit switched from an approach which emphasized whole language and authentic texts to a more traditional didactic model that her students started showing progress. This suggests that the skills-based approach advocated by many low income parents may reflect, at least in part, a correct assessment of their children's learning needs.

Goldenberg (2001) explained the skills inculcation approach practiced by low income Latino parents in his research as reflecting what the parents believed learning to read meant. The parents in the Goldenberg, Reese, and Gallimore (1992) study interacted in a similar manner with their children regardless of whether they read storybooks or completed workbooks. Goldenberg suggested that these parents viewed learning to read as mastering decoding skills rather than appropriating meaning from text and that a skills inculcation approach was consistent with such a viewpoint.

A recent line of research has considered what could be viewed as the opposite of a skills-based approach, one focusing on a child's engagement and interest as a basis for early literacy development. As part of the Early Childhood Project described in an earlier section, parents were asked a series of questions tapping their beliefs about how preschool or kindergarten-aged children learn to read. One of the questions asked, "What is the most effective way of helping your child learn to read?" Responses were scored as reflecting either an entertainment or a skills orientation. An entertainment orientation focused on children's engagement in and enjoyment of literacy activities. Parents emphasizing an entertainment orientation discussed the importance of reading with children and making the interaction enjoyable. A skills orientation stressed the deliberate cultivation of skills, often through the use of flash cards or workbooks. Parents also kept a diary for a period of a week listing all the activities children did over the course of that week. Activities were coded as emphasizing an entertainment or skills orientation. Another coding category, daily living, is not considered in this paper. Additional information about the parents' orientations toward fostering literacy in their children was collected when the children were in second grade. Parents rated the importance of various activities for children's learning to read. Activities included those more in keeping with an entertainment orientation and those more in keeping with a skills orientation. The major difference between parents from the four sociocultural groups occurred in their emphasis on direct inculcation of skills as a means of fostering literacy in their children. Although there was some variability across findings from the three measures, middle income European American families were significantly less likely than low income families of either European American or African American ethnicity to favor a skills orientation. Middle income African American families generally also emphasized a skills orientation, although not always as much as the two low income groups (Sonnenschein, Baker et al., 1997; Sonnenschein, Baker, Serpell, & Schmidt, 2000). As will be discussed in a subsequent section, an orientation toward literacy learning that emphasized a child's engagement and interest was positively related to later literacy development, an orientation that focused on skills inculcation was not.

Parental Beliefs about Their Involvement in Their Children's Schooling

Parents are considered to play an important role in facilitating their children's appropriation of literacy by providing relevant experiences before children start school and by reinforcing school-based learning activities at home once children are in school. According to Sonnenschein and Schmidt (2000), parental involvement in children's schooling is important beyond just increasing children's exposure to literacy-relevant activities. Parental involvement also conveys a message to the child about the importance of school and conveys a message to the teacher that this parent cares about how her child does in school. If teachers think that parents do not care about how their children are succeeding in school or think that parents are not supporting and reinforcing what is learned at school, the nature of instruction or amount of attention given to the child may suffer (Snow, Barnes, Chandler, Goodman, & Hemphill, 1991).

Middle income parents tend to spend many hours reading with their preschool children and engaging in other experiences such as taking children to the library that both foster a notion of literacy as entertaining and help the child develop literacy-related skills. As the child transitions into elementary school, middle income parents continue to be involved in their children's schooling by helping with homework and by supporting the school. Although there are differences depending upon ethnicity, many low income parents seem less outwardly involved in their children's schooling than do their middle income counterparts (Sonnenschein & Schmidt, 2000). Group-based differences in parental involvement can be due to differences in parental beliefs about their role in their children's education, differences in a sense of self-efficacy to teach pertinent skills to children and differences in the schools' push for involvement (Hoover-Dempsey & Sandler, 1997). As reviewed in Sonnenschein and Schmidt (2000), there is a fairly large research literature showing some differences across sociocultural groups in parents' beliefs about their role in their children's schooling. Even when parents believe they should play a role, whether they do can be a function of their sense of self-efficacy as instructors for their children.

The research reviewed here shows that parents have a coherent set of beliefs about the importance of education, especially reading, and how to help children learn to read. There are some differences related to sociocultural group, however, in the approach advocated by parents. Parents from low income groups are more likely than those from middle income groups to endorse an approach to learning that stresses direct skill inculcation. This difference in approach may reflect parental beliefs about the role of and importance of literacy in their lives.

THE TYPES AND NATURE OF LITERACY-RELEVANT
ACTIVITIES AVAILABLE AT HOME

Much research has been conducted showing the impact of various literacy-related activities on young children's reading development (e.g., see Baker, 1999; Snow et al., 1998; Whitehurst & Lonigan, 1998 for reviews). Most studies on this topic have focused on the frequency with which a child engages in an activity, either alone or with others. Recently, however, theorists have acknowledged that in order to fully understand the impact of an activity on a child's literacy development, we also need to consider affective elements of interactions with others as well as the child's interest in the activity (Baker et al., 2001). Considering the nature of interactions is especially relevant given that most children do have exposure at home to some literacy-relevant activities suggesting that frequency alone is probably not the correct explanation of differences in literacy development. The research presented in this section focuses mainly on the social/affective aspects.

Storybook reading is probably the activity most often recommended by researchers and teachers as important for facilitating children's reading (Purcell-Gates, 2000). In fact, Marilyn Adams (1990) suggested, in her discussion of how children learn to read, that without the many hours that children spend reading with their parents even before starting school, young children would flounder once they do enter school. Frequency of storybook reading has been shown to increase children's early literacy knowledge (Baker, 1999) and indirectly predict later reading activity and literacy development (Baker et al., 2001). However, the exact magnitude of the effect as well as what aspects of storybook reading foster what aspects of early literacy knowledge are still debatable (Bus, van IJzendoorn, & Pellegrini, 1995; Scarborough & Dobrich, 1994; Whitehurst & Lonigan, 1998).

Although storybook reading is considered important for literacy development, the frequency of engagement in this activity varies by sociocultural group (Whitehurst & Lonigan, 1998). These differences in reported frequencies are often used to explain differences in literacy skills among children when they enter school. Just as children vary in how frequently they read, the parents of these children may vary in how frequently they themselves read. Fox (1990) suggested that parents of at-risk children, in particular low income parents, may not engage in reading activities and thus not provide their children with strong literacy role models. On the other hand, research by Purcell-Gates, L'Allier, and Smith (1995) and Taylor and Dorsey-Gaines (1988) shows that there is much variability across families within a group in the frequency with which they engage in reading activities.

It is not only storybooks that are important to literacy acquisition. As Baker (1999) and others (e.g., Purcell-Gates, 1996; Snow et al., 1998) have noted, there are many other activities that may be relevant for early literacy or later reading skills. For example, playing certain word games can foster phonological awareness. Using various forms of printed matter may foster an awareness of the uses and meanings of print. Certain forms of oral language usage, such as dinner time conversation, may familiarize a child with the narrative structure found in books. Even television shows can both increase one's world knowledge and improve narrative understanding.

Research on the nature of storybook reading interactions has focused mainly on the type of discussion about a book that occurs while reading. In general, researchers have found that the type of talk, particularly talk that goes beyond the immediate text, fosters later comprehension skills (Snow et al., 1998). However, reading a book with someone is a social interaction and social-affective aspects of the interaction should be considered as well as cognitive aspects. In fact, in trying to understand the impact of different literacy-related activities on children's reading development, Sonnenschein et al. (2000) suggested that one should consider (1) the nature of an activity and the cultural artifacts used when engaging in the activity; (2) the affective quality of an interaction; and (3) whether an activity is child- or parent-initiated.

Sonnenschein et al. (2000) noted that all the children in their study had frequent opportunities to engage in activities relevant for literacy acquisition based upon parental reports when children were in kindergarten and first grade. The data revealed few, if any, sociocultural differences in the frequency with which children engaged in various activities. However, a qualitative analysis of the data indicated differences in all three of the previously mentioned factors between children who became good readers and those that did not. Children who became good readers in first, second and third grades where more likely to use printed matter as part of their play in kindergarten than children who did not. Similarly, positive affective interactions with printed matter when children were in kindergarten were more characteristic of the interactions for those children who would become the better readers. Children who became better readers were more likely to have initiated interactions involving print when they were in kindergarten whereas those who did not become as good readers were more likely to have those activities initiated by adults. Thus, it was differences in the nature of interactions rather than differences due to sociocultural group that predicted later reading development.

In a somewhat similar vein, Fritjers, Barron, and Brunello (2000) investigated the relation between home literacy, children's interest in engaging in literacy activities and children's early language and literacy skills. Children were in kindergarten but not yet independent readers at the time the study was conducted. Of interest here is that children's reported interest in engaging in reading activities was positively related to their ability to identify letters and know the sounds of the letters. It was not related to phonological awareness or to frequency of engagement in literacy activities at home, as reported by these children's parents.

Other research from the Early Childhood Project has considered the cognitive and affective nature of reading interactions between mothers and their preschool or first grade children (Sonnenschein & Munsterman, 2002; Baker et al., 2001). Sonnenschein and Munsterman found that the affective quality of a dyadic reading interaction when children were in preschool predicted children's subsequent motivations or interest in reading when they were in first grade. Baker et al., (2001) showed that the affective nature of dyadic reading interactions when children were in first grade predicted the frequency with which these children read chapter books in third grade. Frequency of reading chapter books predicted third grade reading skills. Relatedly, the type of discussion between the mother and her first grade child that occurred during the reading interaction was related to affective quality of the interaction which in turn predicted the frequency with which the child later engaged in reading activities. The affective quality of the reading interactions did not directly predict subsequent reading skills. Baker et al. (2001) concluded that the impact of affective quality on reading is indirect; that is, it fosters an interest in reading more often which in turn can lead to improved skills (see also Bus, 2001). Similarly, Leseman and de Jong (1998), in a broad-based longitudinal study of multiethnic Dutch families and their children which started when the children were 4 years and continued until they were 7, found that a positive social-emotional climate was related to the number of literacy opportunities available in the home and to the amount of talk during book reading about non-immediate story content. The social-emotional climate during reading interactions observed when children were between 4 and 6 years of age was not related, however, to children's reading skills assessed at age 7.

Elliott and Hewison (1994) also focused on the importance of reading interactions that foster children's interest. They investigated how families from different sociocultural backgrounds help their children with reading and which style of interaction is most beneficial. They interviewed the families about the types of literacy-related activities their child engaged in and observed parent/child storybook reading interactions when the children were 7 years old. The child's success in reading, based on the number of mistakes the child made when reading with the parent, was positively related to a parental helping style which emphasized comprehension and interest. According to Elliott and Hewison, middle income parents displayed an interactional reading style that emphasized the meaning of the story rather than just focused on their child's acquiring reading skills. "Middle class children generally had access to a range of interesting storybooks and this was likely to increase their motivation to read and foster understanding of the principle that it is possible to read for pleasure" (p. 216). In contrast, "Many of the working class had little exposure to literacy in the home ... For many of the lower income families the overall orientation tended to be on reading as an exercise rather than reading for meaning. The emphasis was on accuracy rather than comprehension and interest" (p. 217).

Goldenberg et al.'s (1992) findings with low income Latino parents were similar to those of Elliott and Hewison. As previously mentioned, the families in the Goldenberg et al. study read Spanish storybooks to their children as if they were completing a workbook.

On the other hand, Taylor and Dorsey-Gaines' (1988) ethnographic findings with low income families containing children successfully learning to read shows the need to consider intragroup variability. The children in these families were exposed to a wide range of activities including storybook reading. Descriptions of the nature of these events clearly indicated that interactions went beyond an emphasis on skills inculcation to include appropriating meaning from text.

Before concluding this section on literacy activities, one note is in order. Many researchers, in considering activities that children engage in at home, survey the number of books or other forms of literacy-relevant artifacts in the house. For example, Elliott and Hewison (1994) talked about the number of storybooks found in the homes of middle income children. Presumably, people in a home with literacy-relevant artifacts will be more actively engaged in literacy activities than those in a home with few or no literacy-relevant artifacts. It is important, however, to distinguish between artifacts found in the home and the child's actual engagement with the artifact or observation of someone else's engagement with an artifact (Purcell-Gates, 2000). In a study based on observations of children and families from 20 low income homes, Purcell-Gates (1996) found a positive relation between children observing parents engaged with printed matter and having parents orient their children to print while so engaged and the children's scores on measures of early literacy, such as a Concepts of Print task.

THE RELATION BETWEEN PARENTAL BELIEFS, AVAILABLE LITERACY ACTIVITIES AND CHILDREN'S LITERACY APPROPRIATION

This section is further subdivided into one on the relation between parental beliefs and available activities and one on the relation between parental beliefs and children's literacy appropriation. The research to be reviewed demonstrates a relation between parental beliefs and both available activities and children's literacy appropriation.

Parental Beliefs and Available Activities

Although there is not much research on this topic, what has been done reveals a positive relation between the approach to literacy endorsed by parents and the activities their children engage in. Parents who emphasize children's engagement and enjoyment as important for fostering early literacy acquisition seem to provide their children access to activities consistent with such an approach. Sonnenschein et al. (1997), based on data from the Early Childhood Project, found a positive relation between parents' endorsement of an entertainment approach to early literacy and the reported frequency with which they and their kindergarten-aged children read storybooks together. Parents having an entertainment perspective also spontaneously reported in a diary that their child engaged in more activities consistent with such an orientation.

Sonnenschein et al. (2000), also working with data from the Early Childhood Project, found positive correlations between parents' endorsement of an orientation toward literacy that focused on engaging or entertaining the child and the frequency with which their children engaged in activities that could be considered consistent with such an approach (e.g., playing word games, board games). In contrast, there was a negative correlation between parents who emphasized a skills-based orientation toward reading acquisition and engagement in "entertainment-type" activities or in storybook reading. There was a positive relation between parents endorsing a skills orientation and their children's using workbooks, reviewing flash cards and partaking in related activities.

DeBaryshe's (1995) findings also illustrate the relation between parental beliefs and engagement in literacy activities. Her findings are based on a series of studies conducted using mothers and their preschoolers. The families came from different income and ethnic groups. Mothers completed questionnaires about their reading activities, beliefs about how reading is learned, and their self-efficacy as their children's teachers. Mothers were also asked about their children's interest in reading. Reading interactions were taped and subsequently coded for the affective quality and the type of direct reading instruction used. Mothers' literacy orientation was related to their educational background and their sociocultural group. Mothers with a stronger literacy orientation reported providing their children with a broader range of and more frequent reading experiences. Mothers with a stronger literacy orientation also tended to engage in more discussion with their children during reading interactions.

Parental Beliefs and Children's Literacy Appropriation

Research on this topic also has been limited. What has been done has either focused on children's early literacy skills (e.g., phonological awareness, orientation toward print), reading skills (word recognition, reading comprehension) or motivation.

Sonnenschein et al. (1997) found that parents' endorsement of an approach toward literacy focusing on entertainment and engagement was positively related to children's scores on measures of early literacy when these children were in prekindergarten and kindergarten. More specifically, an entertainment approach was significantly and positively related to children's phonological awareness and knowledge about printed matter. A skills approach was either negatively or not at all related.

Sonnenschein et al. (2000) extended the previously reported findings by considering the relation between parents' orientation toward fostering young children's literacy development, the nature of activities children engaged in when in kindergarten and children's early literacy and reading scores. Children's reading skills were assessed when the children were in the spring of first, second and third grades. Word recognition was assessed with the Woodcock Johnson Test of Achievement Revised (1989) in first, second and third grade. Reading comprehension was assessed with the Passage Comprehension task from the Woodcock during the spring of third grade. Also considered were the frequency of reported engagement in activities consistent with either an entertainment approach (reading storybooks, playing rhyming hand clap games, etc.) or a skills approach (completing work books, reviewing flash cards, etc.) when children were in kindergarten and first grade. Zero order correlations revealed significant positive relations between parents' endorsement of an entertainment perspective and children's early literacy and later reading skills. Similarly, there was a significant, positive relation between the frequency of engagement in activities consistent with an entertainment approach and children's subsequent reading development. Multiple regression analyses were conducted on children's early literacy and later reading skills to determine whether any unique variance was predicted by parents' orientation towards literacy and by the type of activities children engaged in. An orientation towards literacy consistent with the notion of literacy as a source of entertainment and engagement in activities consistent with such an orientation were significantly and positively related to both early literacy and later reading development. A skills-based approach to helping children learn to read was not. Relatedly, Sonnenschein et al. (1997) found that an emphasis on literacy as a source of entertainment for children's appropriation of reading skills facilitated the development of children's early literacy skills, assessed in kindergarten, which in turn fostered word recognition skills in second grade.

Other research on this topic has considered the relation between parental beliefs and children's motivations for reading. The results from the De Baryshe (1995) study, described in the previous section, revealed a positive relation between maternal beliefs and children's interest in reading. She suggested that mothers who have a strong literacy orientation may make the reading interaction more interesting and thus positively affect their children's motivation for reading.

CONCLUSION

Most research on children's reading development has addressed the type of activity children engage in and the frequency with which the children engage in an activity. The research reviewed in this chapter shows the importance of moving beyond just the type of activity to consider parental beliefs about literacy and the nature of children's engagement with an activity.

Parents' ideas about their children's education need to be considered as an important element in children's school success because the beliefs or ideas that parents have will play a role in the nature of activities they provide at home before the child even enters school. These beliefs also will influence how parents continue to interact with their children once they start school. Research presented in this chapter considered parental beliefs about the importance of education, how children learn and parental involvement in the learning process.

All parents want their children to do well in school. Reading is a key determinant of how well a child will do in school. Despite an almost universal desire for their children's success, there appear to be differences in parental beliefs about how to help their children. Many of the differences are related to differences in sociocultural group.

Perhaps the most interesting beliefs are those focusing on the approach taken by parents to help their children learn to read. Research from different investigators has shown that low income parents are more likely to view literacy as something necessary to learn in order to succeed in school and to use in various daily living functions, including jobs. In contrast, more middle income parents are likely to view literacy as something pleasurable and important for entertainment and learning about one's world. It is unclear from the available literature whether these differences are due to actual cultural differences or instead reflect the parents' different successes when they were in school. Income and education are often conflated with many low income parents reporting less education and more limited literacy skills. If one has difficulty reading, it is probably hard to view it as pleasurable or to make it so for one's own children.

Research on parental beliefs about literacy and learning to read suggests a relation between the nature of activities made available to children, affective elements during interactions and children's development. Although there is not yet much available research on the topic, it appears that parents who view literacy as pleasurable tend to provide activities for their children consistent with such an orientation. Children of these parents show higher performance on measures of early literacy and later reading.

It is also important to consider the affective quality of literacy-related interactions. Summarizing over the findings from several studies, it seems that a pleasant interaction increases a child's interest in reading and is related to the frequency with which the child chooses similar activities in the future. More frequent engagement with literacy-relevant activities, in turn, facilitates the child's reading development.

The remainder of this section deals with areas for future research and educational implications of the findings. Inquiry into parental beliefs about children's literacy is a fairly new topic and the research on it is limited. More is needed to confirm findings and broaden the scope of inquiry.

Most of the research has been done with parents of preschoolers and children in early elementary school. What is the nature of parental beliefs as children get older? Do parents' beliefs change as children succeed or struggle in school? Both Lee and Groninger (1994) and Sonnenschein and Schmidt (2000) suggest that the impact of parents' own educational background becomes increasingly important as children progress through school. A parent who struggled in school might feel competent to assist her child when the child was a preschooler but not when the child was in sixth grade.

There is a tendency when reviewing research showing differences in performance across sociocultural groups to assume that within group variability is negligible. Research conducted with low income families (e.g., Neuman et al., 1995; Purcell-Gates et al., 1995; Taylor & Dorsey-Gaines, 1988) shows that there is significant diversity within such groups that needs to be considered in order to understand how children learn to read. Thus, it seems important to understand both between and within group similarities and differences. Although there are some differences in beliefs related to sociocultural group, relations between beliefs, practices and children's development are independent of sociocultural group.

Another topic that needs additional inquiry is the influence of role models on children's learning. As several researchers have suggested, if parents themselves do not read, children may come to view literacy as something that occurs at school but that is not relevant at home. Additional research is necessary to investigate the accuracy of this notion. If parents serve as important role models of reading for their children, does it matter what type of printed matter the parents read or why they are reading? If children see their parents get enjoyment from reading the newspaper, will that spark children's interest in reading newspapers as well as other types of text? What level of active involvement with literate artifacts is necessary, if any, for children to benefit?

Let us turn now to educational implications of the research presented here. Almost every school teacher tells parents to read with their children. Such recommendations also can be found in the writings of theorists and researchers (e.g., Adams, 1990; Snow et al., 1998). Nevertheless, from the available data on parental beliefs and related practices, it seems certain cautions are in order.

Recommendations from teachers will be followed by parents only if they are consistent with parental beliefs. For example, teachers should be somewhat cautious in recommending storybook reading to parents with more limited literacy skills or less interest in reading. What appears most beneficial about reading storybooks with children is discussion about the meaning of the story, especially if the discussion occurs in a pleasant affective atmosphere. If parents lack time to read or have difficulty reading, this may impact on the quality of the discussion or interaction which in turn will not have the desired effect on the child (Baker et al., 2001). Instead of recommending that parents read storybooks to children, teachers might suggest other forms of text that can be read in addition to or instead of storybooks. For example, Pellegrini, Galda, and Brody (1990) have shown that low income mothers are less likely to talk to their children in a manner consistent with current pedagogical recommendations when reading storybooks than when reading expository text. Alternatively, teachers might make use of volunteers in the community who can read with children when parents are less available (Sonnenschein & Schmidt, 2000). Teachers also can seek out ways to help parents, if they are interested, in improving their own literacy skills.

It is important that teachers dialogue with parents in order to understand what strengths the children come to school with. Teachers need to be sensitive to the beliefs and attitudes of the parents in order to be successful with their children (Auerbach, 1995).

The research in this chapter has addressed home-based influences on children's literacy. It is as important, however, to consider the role of the school in children's learning and to understand relations between parents and teachers. A shared understanding between parents and teachers about what occurs at home and at school seems the foundation of children's school success (Sonnenschein & Schmidt, 2000). Such a shared understanding will need to be negotiated between each teacher and parent for each child.

REFERENCES

Adams, M. (1990). *Beginning to read: Thinking and learning about print.* Cambridge, MA: MIT Press.

Auerbach, E.R. (1995). Which way for family literacy: Intervention or empowerment? In L.M. Morrow (Ed.), *Family literacy: Connections in schools and communities* (pp. 11–28). Newark, DE: International Reading Association.

Baker, L. (1999). Opportunities at home and in the community that foster reading engagement. In D.E. Alvermann & J.T. Guthrie (Eds.), *Engaged reading: Processes, practices, and policy implications* (pp. 105–133). New York: Teachers College Press.

Baker, L., Mackler, K., Sonnenschein, S., & Serpell, R. (2001). Parents' interactions with their first grade children during storybook reading and relations with subsequent home reading activity and reading achievement. *Journal of School Psychology, 38,* 1–24.

Baker, L., Scher, D., & Mackler, K. (1997). Home and family influences on motivations for reading. *Educational Psychologist, 32,* 69–82.

Baker, L., Serpell, R., & Sonnenschein, S. (1995). Opportunities for literacy-related learning in the homes of urban preschoolers. In L. Morrow (Ed.), *Family literacy: Multiple perspectives to enhance literacy development* (pp. 236–252). Newark, DE: International Reading Association.

Bronfenbrenner, U. (1979). *The ecology of human development.* Cambridge, MA: Harvard University Press.

Bus, A.G. (2001). Joint caregiver-child storybook reading: A route to literacy development. In S. Neuman & D.K. Dickinson (Eds.), *Handbook of literacy research* (pp.179–191). New York: Guilford.

Bus, A.G., Van IJzendoorn, M.H., & Pellegrini, A.D. (1995). Joint book reading makes for success in learning to read: A meta-analysis on intergenerational transmission of literacy. *Review of Educational Research, 65,* 1–21.

DeBaryshe, B.D. (1993). Joint picture-book reading correlates of early oral language skill. *Journal of Child Language, 20,* 455–461.

DeBaryshe, B.D. (1995). Maternal belief systems: Linchpin in the home reading process. *Journal of Applied Developmental Psychology, 16,* 1–20.

Delpit, L.D. (1986). Skills and other dilemmas of a progressive black educator. *Harvard Educational Review, 56,* 379–385.

Elliott, J.A., & Hewison, J. (1994). Comprehension and interest in home reading. *British Journal of Educational Psychology, 64,* 203–220.

Fitzergerald, J., Spiegel, D.L., & Cunningham, J.W. (1991). The relationship between parental literacy level and perceptions of emergent literacy. *Journal of Reading Behavior, 23,* 191–213.

Fox, B. (1990). Antecedents of illiteracy. *Social Policy Report: Society for Research in Child Development, IV*(4).

Fritjers, J.C., Barron, R.W., & Brunello, M. (2000). Direct and mediated influences of home literacy and literacy interest on prereaders' oral vocabulary and early written language skill. *Journal of Educational Psychology, 92*, 466–477.

Goldenberg, C. (2001). Home and communities. In S. Neuman & D.K. Dickinson (Eds.), *Handbook of literacy research* (pp. 211–231). New York: Guilford.

Goldenberg, C., & Gallimore, R. (1995). Immigrant Latino parents' values and beliefs about their children's education: Continuities and discontinuities across cultures and generations. In P.R. Pintrich & M. Maehr (Eds.), *Advances in motivation and achievement: Culture, ethnicity, and motivation* (Vol. 9, pp. 183–228). Greenwich, CT: JAI Press.

Goldenberg, C., Reese, L., & Gallimore, R. (1992). Effects of school literacy materials on Latino children's home experiences and early reading achievement. *American Journal of Education, 100*, 497–536.

Goodnow, J.J., & Collins, W.A. (1990). *Development according to parents: The nature, sources, and consequences of parents' ideas*. Hillsdale, NJ: Erlbaum.

Gottfried, A.E., Fleming, J.S., & Gottfried, A.W. (1998). Role of cognitively stimulating home environment on children's academic intrinsic motivation: A longitudinal study. *Child Development, 69*, 1448–1460.

Hastings, P.D. & Rubin, K.H. (1999). Predicting mothers' beliefs about preschool-aged children's social behavior: Evidence for maternal attitudes moderating child effects. *Child Development, 70*, 722–741.

Holloway, S.D., Rambaud, M.F., Fuller, B., & Eggers-Pierola, C. (1995). What is "appropriate practice" at home and in child-care?: Low-income mothers' views on preparing their children for school. *Early Childhood Research Quarterly, 10*, 451–473.

Hoover-Dempsey, K.V., & Sandler, H.M. (1997). Why do parents become involved in their children's education? *Review of Educational Research, 67*, 3–42.

Lee, V.E., & Groninger, R.G. (1994). The relative importance of home and school in the development of literacy skills for middle-grade students. *American Journal of Education, 102*, 286–329.

Leseman, P.P.M., & de Jong, P.F. (1998). Home literacy: Opportunity, instruction, cooperation, and social emotional quality predicting early reading achievement. *Reading Research Quarterly, 33*, 294–313.

Miller, S.A. (1988). Parents' beliefs about their children's cognitive development. *Child Development, 59*, 259–285.

Neuman, S.B., Hagedorn, T., Celano, D., & Daly, P. (1995). Toward a collaborative approach to parent involvement in early education: A study of teenage mothers in an African-American community. *American Educational Research Journal, 32*, 801–827.

Ninio, A. (1979). The naive theory of the infant and other maternal attitudes in two subgroups in Israel. *Child Development, 50*, 976–980.

Ninio, A. (1980). The effects of cultural background, sex, and parenthood on beliefs about the timetable of cognitive development in infancy. *Merrill-Palmer Quarterly, 34*, 369–388.

Pellegrini, A.D., Galda, L., & Brody, G.H. (1990). Joint reading between Black Head Start children and their mothers. *Child Development, 61*, 443–453.

Purcell-Gates, V. (1996). Stories, coupons, and the TV guide: Relationships between home literacy experiences and emergent literacy knowledge. *Reading Research Quarterly, 31,* 406–428.

Purcell-Gates, V. (2000). Family literacy. In M.L. Kamil, P.B. Mosenthal, P.D. Pearson, & R. Barr (Eds.), *Handbook of reading research* (Vol. III, pp. 853–870). Mahwah, NJ: Erlbaum.

Purcell-Gates, V., L'Allier, S., & Smith, D. (1995). Literacy at the Harts' and the Larsons': Diversity among poor innercity families. *The Reading Teacher, 48,* 571–578.

Rogoff, B. (1990). *Apprenticeship in thinking: Cognitive development in social context.* New York: Oxford University Press.

Scarborough, H.S., & Dobrich, W. (1994). On the efficacy of reading to preschoolers. *Developmental Review, 14,* 245–302.

Sonnenschein, S., Baker, L., Serpell, R., Scher, D., Goddard Truitt, V., & Munsterman, K. (1997). Parental beliefs about ways to help children learn to read: The impact of an entertainment or a skills perspective. *Early Child Development and Care, 127–128,* 111–118.

Sonnenschein, S., Baker, L., Serpell, R., & Schmidt, D. (2000). Reading is a source of entertainment: The importance of the home perspective for children's literacy development. In K. Roskos & J. Christie (Eds.), *Literacy and play in the early years: Cognitive, ecological, and sociocultural perspectives* (pp. 107–124). Mahwah, NJ: Erlbaum.

Sonnenschein, S., Brody, G., & Munsterman, K. (1996). The influence of family beliefs and practices on children's early reading development. In L. Baker, P. Afflerbach, & D. Reinking (Eds.), *Developing engaged readers in school and home communities* (pp. 3–20). Mahwah, NJ: Erlbaum.

Sonnenschein, S., & Munsterman, K. (2002). The influence of home-based reading interactions on kindergartners' reading motivations and early literacy development. *Early Childhood Research Quarterly.*

Sonnenschein, S., & Schmidt, D. (2000). Home and community support for children's reading. In L. Baker, M.J. Dreher, & J.T. Guthrie (Eds.), *Engaging young readers: Promoting achievement and motivation* (pp. 264–284). New York: Guilford Press.

Snow, C.E., Barnes, W.S. , Chandler, J., Goodman, I.F., & Hemphill, L. (1991). *Unfulfilled expectations: Home and school influences on literacy.* Cambridge, MA: Harvard University Press.

Snow, C.E., Burns, M.S., & Griffin, P. (Eds.). (1998), *Preventing reading difficulties in young children.* Washington, DC: National Academy Press.

Stipek, D., Milburn, S., Clements, D., & Daniels, D.H. (1992). Parents' beliefs about appropriate education for young children. *Journal of Applied Developmental Psychology, 13,* 293–310.

Super, C., & Harkness, S. (1986). The developmental niche: A conceptualization at the interface of child and culture. *International Journal of Behavioral Development, 9,* 545–569.

Taylor, D., & Dorsey-Gaines, C. (1988). *Growing up literate: Learning from inner-city families.* Portsmouth, NH: Heinemann.

Teale, W. (1986). Home background and young children's literacy development. In W.H. Teale & E. Sulzby (Eds.), *Emergent literacy: Writing and reading* (pp. 173–206). Norwood, NJ: Ablex.

Vygotsky, L. (1978). *Mind in society: The development of higher psychological process.* Cambridge, MA: MIT Press.

Whitehurst, G.J., & Lonigan, C. J. (1998). Child development and emergent literacy. *Child Development, 69,* 848–872.

Woodcock, R.W., & Johnson, M. B. (1989, 1990). *Woodcock-Johnson Psycho-Educational Battery-Revised.* Allan, TX: DLM Teaching Resources.

CHAPTER 7

FAMILY LITERACY:

Promising Perspectives and Practices in the New Millennium

Olivia N. Saracho

HISTORICAL FOCUS

One of the eight goals introduced in the United States Department of Education's (1993) *Goals 2000: Educate America* is the composition of partnerships with parents. Family literacy is an educational and public policy attempt to align early childhood and adult literacy education. The fundamental assumption of the family literacy treatment is that "Parents are the first teachers their children have, and they are the teachers that children have for the longest time" (Morrow, 1995, p. 6). According to Durkin (1974), "...the family's role in teaching reading has a long history. In fact, the descriptions of the earliest education in the United States indicated that beginning reading was once taught more often in a kitchen than in a classroom" (p. 136). In 1862, Tolstoy (1967) wrote that reading as a mother would read with her child "will always remain the best and only one for teaching people to read and read fluently" (p. 264). Later Huey (1908) wrote that "the secret of it all [literacy] lies in the parents reading aloud to and with their children" (p. 332). In the 1950s Sheldon and Carrillo (1952) showed that the percentage of good readers increases with the addition in the number of books in the home. Durkin (1966) examined the children's home experiences for indexes of literacy acquisition. She showed that being read to stimulates an interest in reading. In addition, she reported that children who learn to read before first grade are the ones who are read to by siblings, parents, or other caring adults. In the later 1970s and early 1980s the academic community initiated a sustained interest in story reading in school and at home (Wan, 2000). Nickse (1993) calculated that more than 500 family literacy programs existed in the 1990s and this number continues to increase rapidly. Several state and federal government programs (e.g., Head Start, the Family School Partnership Program (PACE), Even Start) stimulated these initiatives (Cairney, 2000). Evidently, the importance of parents reading to children has been recognized for more than two centuries. The importance of reading to children at home was actually acknowledged by Congress in 1998 when it passed the Reading Excellence Act which guarantees that all children are able to read well and independently by the end of third grade, and the Workforce Investment Act substitutes the National Adult Literacy Act of 1991 by providing family literacy, adult basic education, and ESL programs.

Family literacy programs have grown extensively over the past 15 years, attaining support from legislation in 1998. This funding has motivated researchers to conduct studies to explore the benefits of these programs. The results of these studies provide suggestions for promising practices to help families promote their children's literacy development. Family literacy has been transformed into a new and popular word in literacy. It has acquired support from the federal government and private foundations (e.g., Barbara Bush Foundation for Family Literacy, National Center for Family Literacy/Kenan Trust, Coors Family Literacy Foundation).

Barbara Bush, the former first lady, spearheaded family literacy into a high profile national campaign that contributed to its wide interest by scholars and practitioners. Former President Clinton promoted the America Reads Challenge, providing an important federal intervention for early literacy and in 1990 initiating a trend for the Even Start Family Literacy Program and the federal Head Start Family Literacy Centers. In addition to these national early childhood/family literacy programs, many local family literacy programs have evolved throughout the nation. For example, the St. Louis, Missouri, Parents as Teachers(PAT) Program, the Arkansas Home Instruction Program for Preschool Youngsters (HIPPY), and the Pajaro Valley (California) School District's Bilingual Program were founded (Hendrix, 1999/2000). Federal funding for family literacy programs has risen from 14.8 million in 1989 to more than 135 million in 1999 (Amstutz, 2000).

Four federal laws that govern family literacy programs (the Reading Excellence Act, Workforce Investment Act, Elementary and Secondary Act, and Head Start Act Family Literacy) have jointly defined family literacy as literacy programs that provide services to families with sufficient intensity in terms of hours and of sufficient duration to make sustainable changes in a family. Such programs combine services in early childhood education, adult basic skills education, and parental education. Family literacy programs integrate all of the following activities:

- Interactive literacy activities between parents and children.
- Training for parents regarding how to be the primary teachers for their children and how to be full partners in the education of their children.
- Parent literacy training that leads to economic self-sufficiency.
- An age-appropriateness education to prepare children for success in school and life experiences (Amstutz, 2000, p. 207).

Family literacy programs try to offer help to those families who have the most need of educational services. The aim is mainly to provide preschool activities and to enhance the children's kindergarten to second grade academic development.

For approximately 15 years the focus in family literacy has concentrated on family support initiatives within school and home contexts. Legislative efforts (e.g., Family Support Act of 1988) require that family literacy include child to adult development in the integration of services for children and families and modification of the role of school in providing assistance to families and communities (Gadsden, 1994; U.S. Department of Education and U.S. Department of Human Services, 1993). Such efforts embody the intergenerational nature of literacy and life-span development of individual family members (Coleman, 1987; Smith, 1991).

ROLES OF FAMILY MEMBERS

Over the past 40 years literacy researchers have attempted to identify the home factors that influence young children's acquisition of literacy. Many researchers, professional organizations, and eminent educators emphasize the significance of family involvement and stress the key role that parental interest and support that influences the children's school achievement (Barbour, 2000). Countless studies pinpoint the importance of family members as literacy role models, but their role in developing their children's literacy learning becomes challenging for family members who did not have the opportunity to observe role models in their families. Dzama and Gilstrap (1985) explored the way parents were able to establish role models to develop children's literacy learning in three preschool and child care centers. Parents in their study rely on their past experiences as children and use intuition to establish their ideas about reading and about interacting with their child. The U.S. Department of Education (2000) believes that parents can help their children establish a base for literacy skills when they coo, sing lullabies, associate sounds with letters, or read to the children.

According to Cairney (2000), from birth parents are basically attentive to their children's learning. The parents' role in language and learning the communication process is enhanced by becoming a listener, prompter, information giver, asker of questions, and fellow meaning maker. When children of different cultures discuss the way their families help them in relation to school, they fail to perceive them in a teaching role. They perceive their parents' affection, loyalty, and support, and their role in motivating them by expressing high expectations and making sacrifices— activities that are important (Janes & Kermani, 2001). Nistler and Maiers' (2000) family literacy program built a system where parents participated in the children's development as readers and writers. Barillas (2000) believe that when the parent-student interactions in written homework assignments are used, the parent's voices can be shared in the classroom. These writing assignments can also attest to, honor, and appreciate the experiences, culture, and language of students and their families. Families can assume the important role of becoming literacy models for their children. Family members develop role models (Auerbach, 1989, 1995) to convey to their children the merit of literacy (Saracho, 1997a, 1999a). Lancy (1994) shows how adults adopt a critical mediating role when they direct the children to pay attention to text and print details, the association between the text and their past experiences, and searching for the meaning in a text. Tett (2000) had families develop a log of their own reading and writing practices. Such a log documents their role as readers in the family literacy practices as they regularly engage in such as communication, reading, and writing. Families need to perceive that they are real partners in their children's education where they share power, responsibility, and ownership.

Family members recurrently read to children, model reading to children, make reading and writing materials accessible to children, and stimulate children to raise and respond to questions. For example, fathers' responses have an impact on their young children's knowledge of literacy (Hiebert &Adams, 1987).

Family members carry out various roles in facilitating and focusing their children's literacy development and learning. They become role models (Auerbach, 1989) in conveying to their children the importance of literacy. The families' attitudes and expectations for their children's performances can be a good predictor of children's attitudes toward learning, effort in school, and classroom performance. It seems as if families are able to accept new roles in helping their children in their literacy learning (Wigfield & Asher, 1984). Delgado-Gaitan (1990) conclude that parents who participate in family literacy programs understand the importance of their role in their children's education. The children's language and literacy experiences in the home can broaden their literacy learning. Rasinski, Bruneau, and Ambrose (1990) confirm that family members carry out parallel applications at home that teachers apply in the classroom settings that contribute to the acquisition of young children's language and literacy. Young children can attain literacy skills when they (1) explore their environment, (2) socialize with others, (3) express themselves, (4) authenticate events, and (5) interact with the text (Neuman & Roskos, 1989) in both the home and school settings. Nistler and Maiers (2000) describe what can occur when parents and children engage in literacy activities during the school day. They believe that working closely with families helps teachers to understand the parents' beliefs, attitudes, and concepts of the roles they assume in their children's literacy development. This also provides parents with the opportunity to give voice, through their actions, to the allegiance they feel for their children to succeed. The family's role in promoting their children's literacy development is complimented by a rich literate environment.

HOME ENVIRONMENT

For over 40 years researchers (e.g., Durkin, 1974–1975; Goldenberg, Reese & Gallimore, 1992; Heath, 1983; Labov, 1965; Saracho, 1997a,b, 1999a,b, 2000, 2001) in reading, linguistics, psychology, and sociology have investigated the relationship between the home environment and children's success and failure in school. Durkin's (1974–1975) study revealed that the home environment of low-income parents from Chicago affects Black children's reading development, performance, and behaviors. Labov (1965) explained that the language of Black children from urban homes and communities influences their literacy development. Goldenberg, Reese and Gallimore (1992) described the way low-income parents support their children in reading, such as focusing on letter naming and spelling-sound correspondences. Baker, Serpell, and Sonnenschein (1995) described the possibilities for literacy learning in the homes of urban preschoolers including singing songs heard on the radio or television and chanting nursery rhymes and other rhyming games. Parents can help young children to establish a base for literacy skills when they coo, sing lullabies, associate sounds with letters, or read to the children (U.S. Department of Education, 2000). Saracho (1997a) showed a relationship between family's involvement in a home literacy and children's literacy development. Significantly higher scores were observed for children whose parents provide literacy activities and materials than for those whose parents did not. Apparently research studies support a clear relationship between the literacy experiences in the home environment and children's school-based literacy development.

Children's daily family life experiences allow them to understand the uses of literacy. Children are able to learn these uses in their family setting, even though each family setting differs (Taylor & Dorsey-Gaines, 1988). Literacy learning develops when children understand the practical uses of literacy that they use in their daily family life experiences. Children use their experiences in the home environment to account for narratives in the course of their everyday lives, directing them to understand the structural organization of stories (Heath, 1983). While a family's discourse occurs, children integrate knowledge about narratives and recognize the language and communication family members talk about their day's activities (Snow & Tabors, 1993). Family members can contribute to the children's literacy learning with developmentally appropriate activities and materials such as reading to children often, allowing them to see others read, providing them with reading and writing materials, and encouraging them to ask and answer questions (Teale & Sulzby, 1986). Family members can motivate children to acquire, develop, and utilize literacy. The family's home environment can have an influential impact on the literacy components, including (a) print awareness, concepts, and functions; (b) knowledge of narratives structure; (c) literacy as a source of enjoyment; and (d) vocabulary and discourse patterns (Snow & Tabors, 1996). Goodman (1986) believes that children become aware of print when print items (e.g., newspapers, books, magnetic refrigerator letters, posters, writing materials for making lists and memoranda) are displayed in their home environment and family-child interactions center on environmental print. Children engage in literacy activities when they interact with print (a) during make believe reading periods, (b) attempt to identify words and letters on T-shirts and cereal boxes, and (c) play with educational toys.

Studies demonstrate young children's language and literacy learning can be promoted in the home environment when literacy activities and materials are used. An abundant selection of literacy activities and materials in different contexts are the richest resource for literacy development and a reinforcement of real-life literacy learning. Families can provide several experiences to promote their children's literacy development. Ortiz (1997) recommends that families:

1. Choose reading and writing materials to share with their children.

2. Introduce informal and simple activities where a family member and child read together comic strips or television commercials.
3. Engage in extemporaneous reading experiences (e.g., reading letters, notes, labels).
4. Focus on environmental print (e.g., familiar signs, logos, billboards).
5. Provide children a comfortable environment that is infused with print.
6. Answer the children's countless questions.

Children can be helped to develop their literacy skills in a variety of contexts and situations. The home environment can contribute to the children's literacy learning when families provide literacy experiences in a multitude of settings and contexts. Literacy experiences can include access to books, shared reading experiences, having print materials available, and developing positive attitudes toward literacy (Saracho & Dayton, 1991, 1989). Clearly, the home environment affects the family members' contributions to their children's literacy learning.

INTERVENTION PROGRAMS

Literacy intervention approaches can equip parents with strategies to develop literacy learning in their children (Saracho, 1997a,b, 1999a,b, 2000, 2001). Effective interventions demand a multipurpose program with families, concentrating on clearly motivating the child by ameliorating the quality of parent-child interactions and the home environment. Interventions need to concentrate on the (a) parents' strengths instead of their "deficits," (b) development of more "desirable" values (Delgado-Gaitan, 1990), and (c) understanding of culturally and economically diverse families, which means that interventions must consider both that the (1) objects and materials in the home environment manifest the child's interests and emerging skills (Tomasello & Farrar, 1986) and (2) strategies to support communication and broaden the children's understanding of new information (Anastasiow, 1982). For example, Saracho (2001) describes a five-month intervention where families learn to use the children's interests and skills to select strategies, activities, and materials to develop the children's language and literacy learning. She describes a workshop approach, activities, demonstrations, and stories that assist parents in developing their children's literacy skills and understandings by designing a supportive literacy environment in their home. She also explains how families can use a pattern of resources in and outside the school context.

Saracho (1997b) demonstrates the importance of providing children with a supportive home environment for the development of children's emergent literacy. She examines the home literacy experiences of 15 families who participate in a parent program. She describes activities that are used in a workshop approach to assist parents in developing skills and understandings that create a supportive literacy environment in their home. Her analyses suggest that families use a pattern of resources consisting of nonliteracy, literacy, library, and human resources. Douville (2000) discusses ways on how parents can prevent school failure by engaging in effective home literacy instruction for their children. Language experience approach and scaffolded writing are promising practices that parents can use for home literacy instruction with their young children. These practices encourage children to assume more responsibility in literacy activities. Saracho (1997a) identifies significant differences in the outcomes between children whose parents participate in a parent program and those whose parents do not. She reports significantly higher scores for the children whose parents participate in the parent program. Stainthorp and Hughes (2000) reveal the effects of the literacy activities of parents of young earl readers and non early readers. Although there were nonsignificant differences among the reading tests (e.g., *Concepts about Print Test, British Ability Scales Word* Reading test, *Neale Analysis of Reading -Revised*) for the two groups of parents, observations of the home environment suggest that it provides in nurturing toward these children's literacy development. Apparently, families can offer children a rich learning environment for success in literacy that will continue in school (Anderson, 2000).

Jordan, Snow, and Porche (2000) support these results with a study of a larger population of kindergarten children showing that parents are happy to receive training and that their efforts improve the children's language and language analysis skills (e.g., vocabulary knowledge, story comprehension, story sequencing). The kindergarten children in this study who scored low on language measures at the beginning of kindergarten achieved gains after the intervention. In addition, Jones, Franco, Metcalf, Popp, and Thomas (2000) determine whether anticipatory guidance at well-child visits (WCV) that includes early literacy development and the provision of books. Additionally, the treatment group receives an age-appropriate book at each visit. Two years after enrollment, mother-child pairs who received guidance and a book were two times more likely to report enjoyment in reading together than the control group who received guidance but not a book. The researchers conclude that anticipatory guidance that includes early literacy development and distribution of books at WCV results in increased family literacy.

Elley (1992) reports that access to books is a critical factor in early literacy development. Saracho (1999c) documents the participation of 48 families in a family literacy program. Family members use an array of strategies and skills to generate literacy experiences (e.g., reading stories, telling stories, discussing stories, interacting about stories, teaching vocabulary, dramatizing stories, writing experiences) that can enhance their children's literacy development. They engage in planning and implementing literacy activities for their young children to learn literacy practices and behaviors. They use strategies and skills that foster the children's language and literacy learning. Literacy teaching in this meaningful situation can reinforce interpersonal communication between children and family members. Saracho (2001) explores a literacy program for families of five-year-old kindergarten children. Family members learn to effectively use dramatizations, discussions, stories, children's books (e.g., *Caps for Sale, The Grouchy Ladybug, Larry the Lion*), and puppets. Saracho and Spodek (1998) investigate the potential effects of a family literacy intervention program. Parents learn to use appropriate strategies and activities for use in the home. The parents demonstrate in a variety of activities that they can promote their children's literacy learning in their home. These activities consist of reading stories, telling stories, listening to children's stories, engaging children in predicting sequencing in stories, expanding the children's vocabulary based on the stories, using puppets to retell stories, reading poetry, dramatizing stories, discussing stories, writing stories, and interacting about stories. Reading stories with family members (e.g., parents, older siblings, grandparents, aunts, uncles) is very critical. The repetition of specific stories and responses to questions relating to the reading of the stories prompt young children to infer the meaning of print. The quality of family-children interactions contribute extensively to the children's literacy development (Vacca & Vacca, 2000). Saracho (1999b) studies a family literacy program for families of five-year-old kindergarten children. Families learn strategies, activities, and materials that include Conversations, Reading Children's Books, Browsing through Books, Borrowing Books, Dramatizing and Improvising Stories, Relating Stuffed Animals or Dolls to a Story, Reciting and Dramatizing Nursery Rhymes, Writing Stories, and Writing Recipes for Cooking Experiences, which develop the children's language and literacy learning as they engage in family literacy. Barbour (2000) describes the use of home literacy bags, which contain books and activities that promote literacy, for children to take home. She believes this family literacy project was successful in encouraging family cooperation, because literacy bags:

1. reach all families;
2. encourage family/school partnerships that promoted children's learning;
3. allow all families to become directly involved in their children's learning and improved parental attitudes and behaviors;
4. encourage parental interest and support.

Martin (2000) describes a full service school program which provides an array of services and opportunities with the goal of strengthening families. The program includes parent involvement and parent literacy. The birth to five programs provides children with early quality interventions including literacy programs for parents, play groups for parents with their infants and toddlers, home visits, a lending library, and a preschool. Nistler and Maiers (2000) provide a home-school family literacy program that can assist parents to envision the importance of their role is in their child's literacy development. In this program parents learned to (a) cherish their own skills, (b) use new skills, (c) acquire confidence in extending their children's literacy growth, (d) foster their children's literacy development, (e) value this development, and (f) share responsibility between home and school. Interest in and commitment to family literacy programs persists in their expansion. Klassen-Endrizzi (2000) describes a parent participation program in their four-week University Summer Reading Program. Parents become active members of the program's learning community, work with other parents in the family literacy workshops each Monday, inquire about literacy events each day with their child at home, read and react to a parent literacy book, keep a parent-teacher journal, and attend a parent conference one week before the beginning of the program. She concludes that at the end of the program (1) the readers together with their family members lack time to explore literacy experiences that concentrate on reading as something more than a visual act and (2) parents experience an alternative model of reading that emphasizes the establishment of a literate environment where the reader's strengths are dominant.

Jones et al. (2000) show that parents are more impressionable when the examining physician gives them a book. However, parents need more than just having a book. They need instruction to become their child's first teacher at an early age. Jones et al. (2000) also indicate that the mother/child pairs who receive books and a demonstration of sharing or reading books are more likely to enjoy reading together. Supposedly, the book can be presented immediately after the discussions on literacy development to intensify its importance. Tice (2000) presents findings from a family literacy program for Appalachians who have multiple needs. The program provides weekly activities consisting of parenting skills, life skills, nutrition, easy to understand information about children's developmental stages, and early childhood education. The parent-educator makes monthly home visits to explain how to use the parent-as-teacher curriculum. The instructor teaches parents the early childhood education component on the site, while parents spend two hours per week attending adult education (basic skills) and interacting with their children at the Head Start Center. The data indicate that 22% of the parents can succeed at 100% of the program's stated goals, 45% can fulfill a 75% goal attainment, and 15% can accomplish 50% of their goals. The leftover 18% of the parents can acquire between 15% and 45% goal attainment. Tice (2000) concludes that a family literacy program should contain several features: (1) services need to be individualized to help parents who have extremely limited literacy skills to get more intensive social, educational, and training services and (2) social services should be provided based on an interdisciplinary model that appraises the characteristics that might affect the parents. It is important for service providers to address ways to transcend organizational and professional boundaries to better work with families who have limited literacy skills and to engage in a range of family, work, and social activities.

CULTURAL DIFFERENCES

Families and communities have their own rich cultural resources and practices that researchers and practitioners need to understand to develop family literacy programs that are appropriate for these unique families and communities. Janes and Kermani (2001) describe a three-year Family Literacy Tutorial project in southern California serving low-income families, most of them recent immigrants from rural areas of Mexico and Central America. Tutors teach families how to read storybooks by creating text-based questions of increasing complexity such as identification questions, description questions, closed-ended questions, and open-ended questions about stories. High order thinking questions consist of prediction, reasoning, or conjecture about the texts. Posttest and videotapes reveal that about 30% of the families can successfully learn to talk with their children about storybooks using questioning strategies. However, the families, on their own, initiated, collaborated, and culminated their family literacy program with a parent-organized Literacy Fair. It becomes evident that the stories that are initially presented by the project organizers are simply not part of the family's culture. Parents read the stories differently and substitute them with what they know is successful in their relationships with their children. The transmission of text that is conveyed from parents to children may differ from the methods of school literacy. Pursuing to duplicate in the home what children do in school seems to be an error, futile, head to an empty concept of literacy as unidimensional, and antagonize some families and children.

Douville (2000) discusses how parents can prevent school failure by engaging in effective home literacy instruction for their children. The language experience approach and scaffolded writing are promising practices that parents can use for home literacy instruction with their young children. These practices encourage children to assume more responsibility in literacy activities. Barillas (2000) describes a parent home work program for Spanish-speaking students. She sends home writing assignments with writing prompts and directions for both children and parents to share their writing with one another. Two weeks later the assignment is returned and permission is requested to include their work in a classroom publication. Each student receives a copy of the published book, while additional copies are placed in the classroom library. Writing responses reflect the parents and children's preoccupations and concerns.

Packard (2001) explores the bidirectional benefits of family literacy practices involving a Chinese immigrant mother and her daughter who use and discuss culturally appropriate literature to develop reciprocity in family literacy practices. Tett (2000) discusses a family literacy project for working-class Scottish communities. Literacy practices of everyday life are used to value the home and community life of the parents. A critical language awareness is included to facilitate the learners' understanding that the language and reading of texts is problematic. Participants accumulate texts from a range of genres (e.g., advertisements, newspapers, letters from school, bills, cereal packets, "junk mail," family photographs). Families also take a problematic focus to reading and writing practices. They learn that a variety of literacies exist other than the one at school. They engage in investigations including taking photographs of a range of public writing (e.g., graffiti, public notes, shop signs, posters) and discuss these pictures by focusing on the concerns of the community and the messages that these photographs communicate. Both of these approaches make families aware of modes in which literacy occurs in different contexts and for different functions as well how their life style differs from society. Recording the informal literacy practices of a diverse set of families and communities can provide a better understanding on ways to design and facilitate novel family literacy programs. It is essential to become cognizant of the rich cultural resources and practices that families and communities use to know the factors that encourage the success of family literacy programs.

Analysis of incidents in a child's day indicates that learning occurs beyond the classrooms. In calculating a year's average, including vacations and weekends, Klassen-Endrizzi (2000) estimates that children spend only 14% of their time each day in school. This small portion of time suggests that literacy learning occurs in a variety of contexts. Klassen-Endrizzi (2000) uses Hill's (1989) concept of environmental print and reports that parents reconsider and value reading through their daily lives. Parents are aware that reading occurs everywhere ranging from reading road signs to labels in a grocery store. Children's literacy learning occurs in an assortment of contexts and situations. Families can extend their children's acquisition of literacy within these contexts and situations. Saracho (2000) shows how family members engage their children in literary activities in both inside and outside the home including trips to the library. They apply informational reading in the home when they participate in activities that offer general information(e.g., storybooks, recipes, cooking instructions), advertising information (e.g., newspapers, catalogs or advertisements, telephone book), and school/home information (e.g., personal letters, personal notes or messages left by family members in the home, student homework assignments, notes sent home by school or teachers, school cafeteria menu), where families build a bridge to communicate between the school and the home. Family members also provide other literacy activities in the home (e.g., writing activities, board games, educational television programs) and literacy activities outside the home (e.g., road/street signs, billboard signs, video boxes at the video store, menus at restaurants, books and magazines in stores). These also offer information in education and advertising.

The studies by Tett (2000) and Stainthorp and Hughes (2000) show similar results. Tett (2000) indicates families use literacy practices that they previously know and do in the home and community. Such practices are composed of scanning the TV pages, checking their horoscopes, reading signs and symbols in their local environment, writing sketch notes to family members, making an inventory of shopping lists, inscribing family photographs, maintaining a log of family birthdays and anniversaries, disseminating greeting cards and immersing in adult -child conversations. Stainthorp and Hughes (2000) show that families participate in reading and writing experiences including visits to the library or bookshops; reading newspapers, magazines, comic books, or children's books; using the computer, playing games, writing activities (letters, cards, lists, diary); and reading to the child. Other researchers describe different contexts where reading occurs. Bloome, Katz, Solsken, Willett, and Wilson-Keenan (2000) provide a review and extend family literacy to the community such as neighborhoods and religious settings. Talan (2001) describes California's Families for Literacy Program (FFL) which is provided by a funded public library. It is conceived as a full family literacy drive consisting of four basic family literacy components:

1. Literacy improvement and enrichment for the adult, as needed;
2. Emerging literacy activities and opportunities for the child, with emphasis on, but not limited to, the preschool and primary child;
3. Interactive/intergenerational activities for the adult(s) and child(ren);
4. Parenting development and discussion opportunities (p. 13).

During the 1998/1999 fiscal year, more than 5,000 families and their children were enrolled in the FFL. Minimum requirements in providing services with FFL funding, a public library must:

1. Provide free gift books for the families to build home libraries (over 35,000 books were distributed in FY 1998/1999);
2. Hold meetings in libraries (and other sites convenient to the families) and introduce the families to the resources and services available in the library (over 850 held in FY 1998/1999);
3. Provide storytelling, word games, and other enjoyable reading-oriented activities for families to engage in together;
4. Encourage the use of children's books in adult literacy tutoring and use of language experience stories from the family programs as adult literacy instructional materials;
5. Teach parents how to select appropriate children's books and how and why to read aloud to their children;
6. Provide services that enhance full family participation and that foster a family environment for reading;
7. Help parents gain access to information on parenting, childcare, health, nutrition, family-life education, etc. Since many parenting materials are written at a level too difficult for an adult literacy learner to handle, much information is shared with parents through discussion groups and presentations (p. 14).

FFL is considered a joint effort of Children's Services and Adult Literacy Services in the local public library. Local programs are advised to create partnerships with other agencies or/and organizations in their communities to provide better services for these families. Partners frequently consist of Head Start, Even Start, Healthy Start, low income child care providers, elementary schools, adult schools, detention facilities, homeless shelters, rehabilitation centers, and health care providers.

Research shows a strong relationship between the home experiences and children's literacy development. Literacy interventions can aid family members to learn strategies, select materials, and use activities that foster young children's literacy learning (Saracho, 1997a,b, 1999a,b, 2000, 2001). Studies demonstrate that literacy intervention programs can assist families to learn how to promote their children's literacy learning. Saracho and Spodek (1998) demonstrate that family members can immerse themselves in playful explorations with literacy materials in their homes abased on the children's interests and skills. They can also enhance the quality of parent-child interactions in the home environment (Saracho, 1997a,b, 1999a,b, 2000, 2001). Literacy interventions can teach family members how to enrich the quality of parent-child interactions in the home environment. Saracho (2001) suggests that family members can learn how to promote literacy. A predominant factor in family literacy reveals a combination of models and procedures that family members employ in helping their children to acquire literacy skills (Packard, 2001).

Early intervention programs can focus on approaches that teach parents to develop their children's literacy learning (Saracho, 1997a,b, 1999a,b, 2000, 2001) and use their home environment and resources (Saracho, 1997a,b, 1999a,b, 2000, 2001). They can learn to select objects and materials in the home environment that parallel the child's interests and emerging skills (Saracho, 1997a,b, 1999a,b, 2000, 2001; Tomasello & Farrar, 1986) and strategies that encourage communication and that aid children to refine new information (Anastasiow, 1982).

EDUCATIONAL IMPLICATIONS

Parents serve as both teachers and role models in reading. The U.S. Department of Education (2000) provide the following suggestions for families to assist young children become readers:

1. Provide them with rich language experiences throughout the day beginning when they are infants. These experiences include talking with them frequently, naming things, telling stories, singing songs, reciting nursery rhymes or poems, and describing the world around them.
2. Read aloud to them daily for 30 minutes.
3. Maintain reading materials visible and available throughout the home.
4. Assign a special place a home for reading and writing activities and make available many good books and writing materials.
5. Visiting the public library often.
6. Have their vision and hearing tested early and annually.
7. Restrict the time children watch television and encourage educational television programs or videos that lend themselves to discussion.
8. Request that child care providers spend time talking with and reading to children, take children to the library, and assign a special children's reading area.

SUMMARY

For more than ten years, research has demonstrated the importance of parent-child interactions in the development of children's literacy. Language and literacy theories have been observed, tested, and enriched. Evidence confirms that parent literacy programs are effective in the children's literacy development. Research on the value of extensive interventions can suggest how to improve the parents' interactions with their children during literacy experiences.

Quality parent-child interactions can develop the children's literacy abilities. Evidently these interactions require more than simply reading to children and making books available to them. Studies indicate that the parents' background influences the way parents read to their child. They also show that how parents speak with their children and the quality of time they spend reading to their children affects their later reading achievement.

The studies on family literacy need to be taken seriously, because they suggest strategies that assist parents to focus on literacy instruction that can help them to have more control over their world. It is important for parents to know successful strategies that can be used to promote their children's literacy development. Family literacy programs need to have a balanced, concrete focus on literacy, parenting, and child development. They need to improve literacy skills of both parents and children. Data are also needed on the effects of the different programs in developing a curriculum for parents to help them cope with their daily social situations.

Family literacy programs should be an extension of the family itself rather than an extension of the school. They must be involved with and coordinated with support services. Research advises that programs help instructors to become more sensitive to parents and teach them how to promote their children's literacy development in their own unique teaching style. Parents must participate in making decisions concerning the process of the program and their expressed needs must guide the delivery and instruction of the program. It has been found that when participants are involved in planing, retention rates in the family literacy program are higher.

REFERENCES

Amstutz, D.D. (2000). Family literacy: Implications for public school practice. *Education and Urban Society, 32*(2), 207–221.

Anastasiow, N. (1982). *The adolescent parent.* Baltimore, MD: Brookes.

Anderson, S.A. (2000). How parental involvement makes a difference in reading achievement. *Reading Improvement, 37*(2), 61–86.

Auerbach, E.R. (1989). Toward a socio-contextual approach to family literacy. *Harvard Educational Review, 59*, 165–187.

Auerbach, E.R. (1995). Which way for family literacy: Intervention or empowerment. In L. Morrow (Ed.), *Family literacy connection in schools and communities* (pp. 11–28). Newark, DE: International Reading Association.

Baker, L., Serpell, R., & Sonnenschein, S. (1995). Opportunities for literacy learning in the homes of urban preschoolers. In L.M. Morrow (Ed.), *Family literacy:*

Connections in schools and communities (pp. 236–252). Newark, DE: International Reading Association.

Barbour, A.C. (1998/1999). Home literacy bags promote family involvement. *Childhood Education, 75*(2), 71–75.

Barillas, M.D. R. (2000). Literacy at home: Honoring parent voices through writing. *The Reading Teacher, 53*(3), 302–308.

Bloome, D., Katz, L., Solsken, J., Willett, J., & Wilson-Keenan, J. (2000) Interpellations of family/community and classroom literacy practices. *The Journal of Educational Research, 93*(3), 155–162.

Cairney, T.H. (2000). Beyond the classroom walls: The rediscovery of the family and community as partners in education. *Educational Review, 52*(2), 163–172.

Douville, P. (2000). Helping parents develop literacy at home. *Preventing School Failure, 44*(4), 179–181.

Delgado-Gaitan, C. (1990). *Literacy for empowerment: The role of parents in children's education.* Nnew York: The Falmer Press.

Durkin, D. (1966). *Children who read early.* New York: Teachers College Press.

Durkin, D. (1974). *Teaching them to read.* Boston: Allyn & Bacon.

Durkin, D. (1974–1975). A six year study of children who learned to read in school at the age of four. *Reading Research Quarterly, 10*, 9–61.

Dzama, M., & Gilstrap, R.L. (1985, November). *How parents prepare their children for a formal reading program.* Paper presented at the annual meeting of the Association for Children Education International, Omaha, NE.

Elley, W.B. (1992) *How in the world do students read?* Hamburg: International Association for the Evaluation of Educational Achievement.

Goldenberg, C., Reese, L., & Gallimore, R. (1992). Effects of literacy materials from school on Latino children's home experiences and early reading achievement. *American Journal of Education, 100*, 497–537.

Goodman, Y.M. (1986). Children coming to know literacy. In W.H. Teale & E. Sulzby (Eds.), *Emergent literacy: Writing and reading.* Norwood, NJ: Ablex.

Heath, S.B. (1983). *Ways with words.* Cambridge: Cambridge University Press.

Hendrix, S. (1999/2000). Family literacy education—Panacea or False Promise? *Journal of Adolescent and Adult Literacy, 43* (4), 338–346.

Janes, H., & Kermani, H. (2001). Caregivers' story reading to young children in family literacy programs: Pleasure or punishment? *Journal of Adolescent and Adult Literacy, 44*(5), 455–464.

Jones, V.F., Franco, S.M., Metcalf, S.C., Popp, R., & Thomas, A.E. (2000). The value of book distribution in a clinic-based literacy intervention program. *Clinical Pediatrics, 39*(9), 535–542.

Jordan, G.E., Snow, C.E., & Porche, M.V. (2000). Project EASE: The effect of a family literacy project on kindergarten students' early literacy skills. *Reading Research Quarterly, 35*(4), 524–546.

Klassen-Endrizzi, C. (2000). Exploring our literacy beliefs with families. *Language Arts, 78*(1), 62–70.

Labov, W.A. (1965, June). *Linguistic research on nonstandard English of Negro children.* Paper presented to the New York Society for the Experimental Study of Education, New York, June.

Lancy, D. (Ed.). (1994). *Children's emergent literacy: From research to practice.* Westport, CT: Praeger.

Martin, L.E. (1999). Mothers' prosodic features: Strategies to guide young children's understanding of book language. *Reading Horizons, 40*(2), 127–146.

Morrow, L.M. (1995). Family literacy: New perspective, new practices. In L. Morrow (Ed.), *Family literacy connection in schools and communities* (pp. 5–10). Newark, DE: International Reading Association.

Nickse, R. (1993). A typology of family and intergenerational literacy programmes; Implications for evaluation. *Viewpoints, 15*, 34–40.

Nistler, R.J., & Maiers, A. (2000). Stopping the silence: Hearing parents' voices in an urban first-grade family literacy program. *The Reading Teacher, 53*, 670–680.

Ortiz, B. (1997, Winter). Fathers assisting in their young children's early literacy development. *Families as Educators Newsletter, 1* & 5–8.

Packard, B.W. (2001). When your mother asks for another book: Fostering intergenerational exchange of culturally relevant books. *Journal of Adolescent and Adult Literacy, 44*, 626–633.

Rasinski, T., Bruneau, B., & Ambrose, R. (1990, November). *Home literacy practices of parents whose children are enrolled in a whole language kindergarten.* Paper presented at the annual conference of the College Reading Association, Nashville, TN.

Saracho, O.N. (2001). Enhancing young children's home literacy experiences, *International Journal of Early Childhood Education, 5*, 135–141.

Saracho, O.N. (2000). Literacy development in the family context, *Early Child Development and Care, 165*, 107–114.

Saracho, O.N. (1999a). Families' involvement in their children's literacy development, *Early Child Development and Care, 153*, 121–126.

Saracho, O.N. (1999b). Helping families develop emergent literacy strategies, *International Journal of Early Childhood, 31*(2), 25–36.

Saracho, O. N. (1999c). Promoting Literacy Development Through School-Home Partnerships, *International Journal of Early Childhood Education, 4*, 51–70.

Saracho, O.N. (1997a). The influence of a home literacy program on the children's literacy development. *Perceptual and Motor Skills, 85*, 185–186.

Saracho, O.N. (1997b). Using the home environment for emergent literacy. *Early Child Development and Care, 127–128*, 201–216.

Saracho, O.N., & Dayton, C.M. (1991). Age related changes in reading attitudes of young children: A cross-cultural study. *Journal of Research in Reading, 14*(1), 33–45.

Saracho, O.N., & Dayton, C.M. (1989). A factor analytic study of reading attitudes in young children. *Contemporary Educational Psychology, 14*, 12–21.

Saracho, O.N., & Spodek, B. (1998). A play foundation for family literacy. *International Journal of Educational Research, 29*, 41–50.

Sheldon, W.D.A., & Carrillo, L. (1952). Relation of parents, home, and certain developmental characteristics to children's reading ability. *The Elementary School Journal, 52*, 262–270.

Snow, C., & Tabors, P. (1996). Intergenerational transfer of literacy. In L.A. Benjamin & J. Lord (Eds.), *Family literacy: Directions in research and implications for practice* (pp. 73–80). Washington, DC: Office of Educational Research and Improvement, U.S. Department of Education.

Snow, C., & Tabors, P.O. (1993). Language skills that related to literacy development. In B. Spodek & O.N. Saracho (Eds.), *Language and literacy in early childhood education* (pp. 1–20). New York: Teachers College Press.

Stainthorp, R., & Hughes, D. (2000). Family literacy activities in the homes of successful readers. *Journal of Research in Reading, 23*(1), 41–54.

Talan, C. (2001). Family literacy: An investment in the future. *Managing Library Finances, 14*(1), 12–18.

Taylor, D., & Dorsey-Gaines, C. (1988). *Growing up literate: Learning from inner-city families.* Portsmouth, NH: Heinemann.

Teale, W.H., & Sulzby, E. (1986). Home background and young children's literacy development. In W.H. Teale & E. Sulzby (Eds.), *Emerging literacy: Writing and reading.* Norwood, NJ: Ablex.

Tett, L. (2000). Excluded voices: Class, culture, and family literacy in Scotland. *Journal of Adolescent and Adult Literacy, 44*(2), 122–128.

Tice, C.J. (2000). Enhancing family literacy through collaboration: Program considerations. *Journal of Adolescent and Adult Literacy, 44*(2), 138–145.

Tomasello, M., & Farrar, M.J. (1986). Joint attention and early language. *Child Development, 57,* 1454–1463.

Tolsoy, L. (1967). *Tolsoy on education* (L. Wiener, trans.). Chicago: University of Chicago Press.

U.S. Department of Education. (2000). Building literacy skills through early care and education. *Reading in the Early Years: Infancy through Kindergarten, 7*(2), 7–8.

U.S. Department of Education. (1993). *Goals 2000: Educate America.* Washington, DC: Author.

U.S. Department of Education and United States Department of Human Services. (1993). *Together we can* (pp. 1–4). Washington, DC: U.S. Department of Education and U.S. Department of Human Services.

Vacca, R.T., & Vacca, J.L. (2000). *Reading and learning to read.* New York: Longman.

Wan, G. (2000). Reading aloud to children: The past, the present and the future. *Reading Improvement, 37*(4), 148–160.

Wigfield, A., & Asher, S.R. (1984). Home, schools, and reading achievement: A social motivational analysis. In P. David Pearson et al. (Eds.), *Handbook of reading research* (pp. 423–452).

CHAPTER 8

CONTEMPORARY VIEWS OF RESEARCH AND PRACTICE IN EARLY CHILDHOOD LITERACY PROGRAMS

Olivia N. Saracho and Bernard Spodek

During most of the past 60 years, young children's literacy development has been considered a low priority in early childhood education. Over the last two decades researchers, theorists, and practitioners have reconstituted the field of literacy development in young children. Contemporary trends in reading instruction for young children vary dramatically from each other with each proponent affirming that their approach improves children's reading performance. Studies that are carefully conceived are cited to support or reject each trend. The reality is that children learn to read in spite of any approach. There is no one approach to reading instruction that is significantly better than all others. Many approaches to reading instruction were shown to be effective more than three decades ago (Stauffer, 1967). This holds true today as well.

LEARNING TO READ

Young children usually begin reading well before they are provided with formal reading instruction. Competent teachers note that today when children enroll in school, they may have a distinctive background, repertoire of information, and repertoire of skills (Vacca & Vacca, 2000). For example, young children may:

1. Have previously been in a group setting for three or four years or may be enrolling in school for the first time.
2. Have different ability levels (e.g., disabilities, exceptional abilities, independent readers, beginning readers, dominant language, literacy-related skills, and functioning).

Riley (1996) states that, "What this means is that some kindergartners may have the skills characteristic of the typical three-year-old, while others might be functioning at the level of the typical eight-year-old" (pp. 4–5). Consequently, teachers need to be flexible in providing young children with developmentally appropriate instruction in learning to read. Teachers can be guided by the International Reading Association (IRA) and the National Association of the Education of Young Children (NAEYC) (1998) position statement on literacy, which considers children's performance and presents a series of stages on children's literacy development. Vacca and Vacca (2000) summarize these stages:

1. *Awareness and Exploration Stage* (birth through the preschool years)—when young children (1) learn that print conveys meaning; (2) read environmental print (e.g., labels, signs, cereal boxes); (3) imitate reading; (4) explore writing (e.g., scribbling, writing expressions); (5) connect letters to their speech sound; and (6) inscribe letters or approximations of letters to depict the written language.
2. *Experimental Reading and Writing Stage* (kindergarten)—when young children experiment with oral and written language.
3. *Early Reading and Writing Stage* (first grade)—when children first encounter formal reading instruction.
4. *Transitional Reading and Writing Stage* (second grade)—when young children begin to become involve in complex literacy functions (e.g., word identification skills, sight word recognition, reading fluency, sustained silent reading, conventional spelling, proofreading).
5. *Independent and Productive Stage* (third grade)—when young children become independent and productive readers and writers.

Even before formal schooling, young children should be provided with rich literacy experiences where they can use their knowledge of language, literature, and the world to bring about countless operations in examining a text. They merge their reading experiences with their reading skills and knowledge with any text (National Reading Panel, 2000), which helps them to quickly acquire the prerequisite literacy skills needed to begin formal reading instruction (usually between the ages of five and seven). Young children begin their repertoire of reading knowledge and skills at an early age before they are confronted with the complex undertaking of decoding print. Some of these children memorize sight words. Most five-year-olds who are provided with rich literacy experiences usually learn their literacy skills all at once (Saracho, 2002).

Studies on the manner in which children develop an understanding of the features and shapes of written language extend to an evolving awareness of the children's beginning stages of literacy development. Young children discover the aspects and shapes of written language when they experiment with print as a cultural object (Ferreiro & Teberosky, 1983). The settings or circumstances where written language is used assists children in understanding print (Goodman, 1986; Harste, Woodward, & Burke, 1984). Gardner (1983) believes that "children acquire skills through observation and participation in the contexts in which these skills are customarily invoked. In contrast, in the standard classroom, teachers talk, often presenting material in abstract symbolic form and relying on inanimate media such as books and diagrams in order to convey information" (p. 357). Drawing on Gardner's (1983) concept of multiple intelligence, schools can adopt the kinds of experiences that encourage the children's emergent literacy in non-school settings.

Children's emergent literacy is developed as they are actively learning, solving problems, making meaning, and displaying their early literacy behaviors and knowledge (Saracho, 2002). Early childhood programs that use an emerging literacy approach present young children with a collection of print-related experiences early on (Watson, Layton, Pierce, & Abrams, 1994). Scribbling, printing, spelling, and copying are detectable features of emergent literacy. Children who scribble are striving to model adult writing. Scribbling and writing are precursors to reading. Pragmatic interactions with print and story-related activities are crucial in advancing the children's emergent writing and oral language skills (International Reading Association, 1986). Research suggests the importance of environmental influence on the children's literacy interactions, explorations, expressions, and behaviors (Saracho, 2002). Chambliss and McKillop (2000) believe that, "having a collection of well-chosen materials within a reading community can have an impact on children's engagement and achievement" (p. 104).

The National Research Council (1998) confirms from the literacy studies with preschoolers that (a) verbal interactions during adult-child shared book reading develops the children's vocabulary and conceptual knowledge concerning print and (b) learning to read is easier with activities that focus young children's concentration to the sound pattern within spoken words (e.g., rhyming, jokes, sound games). In addition, knowledge of word meanings, being aware that print communicates meaning, phonological awareness, and the relationship between letters and sounds contribute to successful reading (Saracho, 2002).

The play context can be used to teach young children to read, allowing them to learn in a natural context. When young children enroll in school, they possess a massive hearing and speaking vocabulary of meaningful words and phrases. They also command the fundamental grammar of their spoken language. Beginning reading strategies should embody those natural resources. Since many children learn to read without any apparent teaching from adults, research studies on the role of circumstantial reading instruction in the home has examined what actually happens. Young children see and hear family members (e.g., parents, siblings, grandparents) read and read to them and to other family members. They read print daily, reading advertising signs during their family travels or labels from food packages, toy boxes, and other household articles. They are able to read most of their children's books. Text in a story resembles their natural oral language and speaking patterns, which assist them in reading their books in a natural way. Such behavior denotes how teachers can read to children and assist them to read as literacy emerges.

INSTRUCTIONAL STRATEGIES

Researchers, theorists, and educators continue to assess the most dependable practices for initial reading instruction. As noted earlier, no one-best practice exists. A variety of reading strategies on emergent literacy can enrich teachers' repertoire of instructional strategies as they adopt those most favorably evaluated by scholars and researchers with divergent academic views. The practitioner's commitment is more crucial than either the specific materials or approaches used. A fusion of the best elements from several programs can be of most benefit when the fusion is based on an assessment of the students' individual needs.

Traditional teachers who teach reading based on the school's curriculum merely accept a convenient approach to teaching and learning. They detach themselves from "new" approaches and teach children to read as effortlessly as possible.

An emergent literacy approach is not an either/or condition. Teaching reading calls for a conscientious assessment and choice of reading materials and procedures. Many teachers base their reading instruction on phoneme-grapheme relationships. Limiting instruction to phonics alone usually forces children to read very slow, murmur, and babble without searching for meaning in the text. Reading instruction entails more than just the teaching of phonics.

An assortment of materials and methods can provide an efficient and effective approach to beginning reading instruction. The qualities that excel in each method and their ramifications need to be considered in making a conscientious selection. Results from research studies can provide information on (1) selecting material and methods, (2) the relationship between the reading process and acquisition patterns, (3) the effects of particular types of environmental incidents, (4) the students' role in constructing their own knowledge and skills in their environment, (5) a repository of knowledge obtained from the environment, (6) the interaction between student and environment such as those environmental qualities that interact with those the student's knowledge, (7) the systems that extend their cognitive competence, and (8) the new psychology of reading instruction concerning individual differences that describe and assess the instructional environmental impact on the students' learning and cognitive performance.

Emergent literacy needs to be supported by cognitive, learning, and developmental psychology. Current studies apply Vygostskian theory to language and literacy education, mainly with young children, and suggest a central transformation in young children's language and literacy development. Thomas Kuhn (1970) explains how, in science, distinct paradigms emerge as current theories are criticized and new theories are elaborated. Such paradigms establish how scientists perceive theories and launch contrasting research methods. The result of a recent paradigm shift in language and literacy education is *emergent literacy*, which replaces the previous paradigm of *reading readiness*.

The reading readiness paradigm meditates between two conflicting conceptions of human development and learning. One conception is grounded in Gesell's maturationist theory, suggesting that young children can only succeed in beginning reading when they reach a particular level of physical and intellectual maturity. This perspective suggests that readiness to learn to read is determined by the child's mental age. The other conflicting conception reflects the behaviorist developmental theory. This suggests that young children are only able to learn abstract functions if they have gained prerequisite knowledge and skills which are the basic elements of the reading process. These basic skills are integrated into the actual reading function.

Carroll (1970) operates within the reading readiness paradigm in determining an individual's requirements in becoming a good reader. He specifies knowledge of the language and the capacity to decode spoken words into their speech sounds, to identify and distinguish among letters, to match letters with sounds, to identify printed words, and to justify and conceptualize what is read. These requirements suggest that readiness for learning to read requires auditory and visual discrimination skills for letter-sound associations and knowledge of the essential language factors and capacity to understand text. Such a view of readiness conflicts with the emergent literacy position (Spodek & Saracho, 1993).

The reading readiness approach has controlled the views of kindergarten practitioners and countless early childhood educators interested for a considerable time. Numerous kindergarten reading and mathematics readiness programs are included in many early childhood curricula. These programs' dominant goal is learning academics (Karweit, 1993). Reading readiness programs match these interests. Numerous publishers of basal reading series prepare a variety of kindergarten materials to develop what have been identified as readiness skills and guide children into first grade reading instruction within the series. There is an element of legitimacy to these programs in that their tasks in the readiness programs coincide with those in the reading instructional programs. Children are taught these skills and workbooks or worksheets are used to provide skill practice before formal reading instruction. Many teachers believe that these materials prepare good readers (Spodek & Saracho, 1993).

The emergent literacy paradigm disputes this position on what should be a prelude to formal reading instruction. Emergent literacy proposes that young children participate in language experiences that prepare them to understand the reading process before they begin formal reading instruction. This paradigm closely parallels children's understanding of oral language and can be encouraged by a wide range of activities, some of which may not resemble reading at all. Advocates of the emergent literacy paradigm oppose the task analysis notion of preparation for reading instruction. They suggest that the reading process is a more complex intellectual operation. A knowledge of both the oral and written language and their relationship are essential in helping children in becoming effective readers and writers. Consequently, they prepare children for the intellectual undertaking of reading instead of involving them in mechanically undertaking "code-cracking." They also contend that the intellectual skills required emerge from a broad gamut of language and symbolic experiences, including rhetoric with others, play, and the arts (Spodek & Saracho, 1993).

The emergent literacy paradigm is consistent with the view that early childhood teachers should provide developmentally appropriate activities in their classrooms based on the notion that children learn from direct first-hand experience with the physical and social world. Children construct knowledge from their experiences (Spodek & Saracho, 1993).

The early childhood years are considered a period of rapid intellectual development. Children become both meaning makers and symbol makers at a very early age. They learn a broad vocabulary, the grammatical rules of their language, the uses of different and appropriate forms of language.

Their social experiences are critical to their cognitive and language growth and their social experience helps them understand symbols and employ symbols through play. Children's toys and art work are symbolic representations of objects from their world. However, the most crucial and abstract symbols are young children's words. They first utilize words audibly, they attempt to construct words and make an effort to create meaning out of the words they encounter in their world (Spodek & Saracho, 1993).

As young children attempt to bring meaning to their world, they become meaning and symbol makers. The meanings of symbols are gained from within the children's social environment, especially in their interactions with adults and other children. The context of composing and understanding symbols is where language and literacy learning occurs (Spodek & Saracho, 1993).

The chapters on literacy in this volume should contribute to a better understanding of the reading processes in early childhood education. They describe how educational environmental interventions interact with the cognitive processes that contribute to the children's reading competence. Both empirical and theoretical studies on emergent literacy are systematically and substantively reviewed, analyzed, and synthesized in these chapters which should appeal to a broad, multifaceted, interdisciplinary audience.

The volume adds to the body of knowledge on the effectiveness of various approaches to teaching children to read and indicate the extent to which effective approaches are applicable in classroom settings. The knowledge summarized and analyzed can expand the roles of the teachers in promoting literacy-related play and in recognizing contexts that stifle culturally and linguistically diverse learners. They present research regarding family literacy, allowing teachers to blend home and school literacy, understanding parental beliefs and practices, and be aware of literacy in settings beyond the classroom.

The material in this volume suggests, among others, the following educational implications:

1. *Meeting the Literacy Needs of Diverse Children in the Classroom.* Children in early childhood classrooms come from different communities and have divergent cultural and linguistic backgrounds. Some of these children are considered "at-risk" because they differ demographically, culturally or developmentally from the norm. These children have unique needs and need specific strategies to help them become competent and independent readers. Teachers need to be flexible in responding to them, based on an assessment of their strengths as well as their educational needs.

2. *Recognizing Changing Literacy Contexts and Learning Strategies.* Some learning contexts and strategies constrain substantive literacy learning, especially for culturally and linguistically unique children. Inappropriate literacy programs may offer reductive literacy practices, teaching skills in isolation of their contexts, and prohibit and limiting the use of the child's primary language in meaning making activities. In these programs second language learners and other working class children may be socialized to unproductive understandings and uses of literacy, because the literacy practices used fail to recognize differences and diversity as resources for learning. Such practices fail to recognize that language is the most powerful mediator in learning activity.

3. *Creating Literacy Opportunities for Children At-risk.* At-risk children need to be provided with appropriate literacy opportunities to apply their language and literacy skills in. Recent studies suggest strategies for at-risk children to develop their language, engage in book reading, conversations, and other educational literacy interventions to improve literacy skills through discourse.

4. *Using Developmentally Appropriate Literacy Strategies.* Prior to formal reading instruction, teachers need to choose developmentally appropriate literacy strategies and activities that include writing, story reading, creative dramatics, art, or any content area. In choosing the appropriate literacy strategies, teachers need to consider the importance of physical and social arrangements in the classroom.

5. *Modifying the Roles of the Classroom Teacher.* Teachers need to modify their instructional roles to cultivate literacy in a natural context such as during children's play. Studies suggest that teachers may assume the roles of discussion leader, storyteller, examiner, instructional guide, informer, learning center monitor, decision-maker, storyteller, guiding play, promoting literacy-related play, monitoring children's play, facilitating children's play, interacting in children's play, inquiring during children's play, initiating children's play, extending children's play, engaging children in discussion, and making decisions during play.

6. *Encouraging Storybook Reading for Social Practice.* Teachers need to be encouraged to use storybook reading as social practice to help children (1) recognize that important information can differ remarkably from one context to another, (2) understand that literacy practices differ across contexts, (3) understand that making universal assumptions about the importance of any particular literacy practice or event is unwise and can disadvantage them, (4) assume that literacy practices are socially constructed and particular literacy events or activities or practices are quite heterogeneous.

7. *Linking Home and School Literacy.* Teachers need to know how to cater to the needs of all students and acknowledge and build on the rich cultural diversity present within each early childhood setting. Family literacy initiatives can build effective relationships between home, school, and community. Aspects of home-based influences on children's literacy development such as parental beliefs about literacy and learning and the activities available at home to the children need to be considered. Literacy activities and interactions need to be considered to help children improve their reading, which may suggest that families need to learn the (1) importance of parent-child interactions in developing literacy, (2) language and literacy strategies and activities that can be used at home, and (3) value of extensive interventions in effective family literacy programs. Family members can reinforce the children's literacy learning when they are presented with literacy experiences in a myriad of settings and contexts.

8. *Promoting Reading in a Variety of Contexts.* Literacy can be developed in a variety of contexts within the community. Literacy experiences, instructional methods, and opportunities for students to practice their literacy skills within different contexts can be provided by the school and the family.

According to Spodek and Saracho (1993), the contemporary transformation of language and literacy programs will affect the roles of the teachers in literacy. Early childhood teachers will need to be active in providing literacy related activities for children rather than being passive and waiting for children to become "ready to read." Reading emerges as children, including two- and three-year-olds, develop oral language. Teachers should avoid using reading primers and workbooks with preschool children, instead providing them with emergent literacy experiences that are developmentally appropriate for their age, interest, culture, and language among other things.

Meanwhile primary teachers should come to understand that reading requires more than sounding out letters. Reading instruction can be integrated reading in all educational activities which should focus on writing, listening, and speaking. This can be done with thematic units and projects with instruction planned around a specific topic, and where all subject areas are applied in connection to the topic, and where language and literacy skills are presented.

The early childhood classroom should be a literacy-rich environment with teachers selecting materials that promote literacy. There should be books accessible to children in an appealing and equipped library area. These should be a dramatic play area to cultivate language and literacy learning, group discussions should be held where children develop expressive and receptive language skills, and an arts program that assists children to construct and symbolize meanings from their experiences.

Early childhood teachers must be sensitive to the impact their literacy program has on young children. Group time, discussions, book sharing, dramatic play, art, and music activities may all have different impacts on children. Teachers should be aware of what works for each individual child and build upon that knowledge.

Teachers should realize that they are not working alone in supporting literacy in their children. They should join parents in encouraging language and literacy learning. The family setting has a significant impact on young children's language and literacy development. In reality, the caliber of language and literacy experiences that young children get at home contributes significantly to their language and literacy proficiency. Support for the development of these proficiencies varies with each family.

ENCOURAGING INNOVATION

Adapting to these changes may be ambitious and challenging to both teachers and the schools' language and literacy programs. Schools as institutions resist any type of reform (Sarason, 1982). Teachers attempting to make modifications toward a more child-responsive education in their classrooms, even if they are not attempting to affect school policy, encounter opposition from both their teaching colleagues and administrators (Halliwell, 1992). Publishers of reading programs and test developers have a vested interest in conserving the language and literacy programs in the schools (Spodek & Saracho, 1993). All of these forces make it difficult for program innovation to take place.

Reform toward the emergent literacy paradigm requires that teachers use resources and materials that challenge formal reading readiness and publish beginning reading programs. Supportive classroom materials include Big Books, a range of children's books, and simple word processing programs for children (Spodek & Saracho, 1993).

Teachers also need to learn how to implement this innovative paradigm and have access to the appropriate materials. Teacher organizations, colleges, and universities need to offer both pre-service and in-service teachers workshops and courses in this new paradigm. Teacher organizations can make this information available to teachers through journal articles, separate publications, and conference program sessions. Teachers can create their own support systems, creating grassroots networks of teachers (Spodek & Saracho, 1993), such as emergent literacy or family literacy networks. Such networks allow teachers to generate and share skills in developing informal instructional techniques as well informal ways to assess children's language and literacy learning. Present language and literacy programs associated with standardized testing programs construct a damaging barrier to the implementation of optional educational programs. Frequently the school curriculum focuses on standardized tests (Shepard, 1999). Alternative methods of assessing children's language and literacy learning must be utilized and fully accepted (Spodek & Saracho, 1993).

SUMMARY

The contents of this volume on literacy has focused on the evolving body of knowledge relating to reading development and reading instruction in early childhood education. In carrying out its charge, the authors reviewed and critically analyzed studies. They address the evidence regarding this important aspect of education and, in doing this, knowledge about how those skills are best taught to beginning readers who vary in initial reading-related abilities. They also identify areas where significantly greater research effort is needed, and where the quality of the research efforts must improve in order to determine objectively the effectiveness of different types of reading instruction.

The area of language and literacy education is undergoing major changes today. Many of these changes suggest the importance of the early childhood years for children to become competent in language and successful readers. These changes provide a better understanding of bilingual as monolingual children as they develop competence in language and literacy.

These changes in views of language and literacy have significant implications for how children and teachers function in early childhood classes. Teachers need to reassess how they design their program and how they support children's learning. They also need to reassess how they evaluate language learning in young children.

The changes taking place can establish a new relationship between primary education and preprimary education. Developmentally appropriate programs can be created that are closely related at all levels, providing for a better vertical integration. Reading instruction will be reconceptualized. A broad range of educational experiences will be considered in preparing children in learning to read.

Programs can also have better horizontal integration. Integrated approaches to education and the use of units, projects or topics as the focus on instruction will help children understand the world and help them to become both meaning and symbol makers. All of this presents a challenge to early childhood educators at all levels, working with the broad range of children currently served in our many early childhood programs.

REFERENCES

Carroll, J.B. (1970). The nature of the reading process. In D.V. Gunderson (Ed.), *Language and reading*. Washington, DC: Center for Applied Linguistics.

Chambliss, M.J., & McKillop, A.M. (2000). Creating a print- and technology-rich classroom library to entice children to read. In L. Baker, M.J. Dreher, & J.T. Guthrie (Eds.), *Engaging young readers: Promoting achievement and motivation* (pp. 94–118). New York: Guildford Press.

Ferreiro, E., & Teberosky, A. (1983). *Literacy before schooling*. Portsmouth, NH: Heinemann.

Gardner, H. (1983). *Frames of mind: The theory of multiple intelligence*. New York: Basic Books.

Goodman, Y. (1986). Children coming to know literacy. In W. Teale & E. Sulzby (Eds.), *Emergent literacy* (pp. 1–14). Norwood, NJ: Ablex.

Halliwell, G.L. (1992). *Dilemmas and images: Gaining acceptance for child-responsive classroom practices*. Unpublished doctoral Dissertation, University of Queensland, Brisbane, Australia.

Harste, J., Woodward, V., & Burke, C. (1984). *Language stories & literacy lessons*. Portsmouth, NH: Heinemann.

International Reading Association [IRA] & National Association of the Education of Young Children [NAEYC]. (1998). Learning to read and write: Developmentally appropriate practices for young children. *The Reading Teacher, 52*, 193–216.

Karweit, N. (1993) Effective preschool and kindergarten programs for students at risk. In B. Spodek (Ed.), *Handbook of research on the education of young children* (pp. 385–411). New York: Macmillan.

Kuhn, T.S. (1970). *The structure of scientific revolutions*. Chicago: University of Chicago Press.

National Research Council. (1998). *Preventing reading difficulties in young children*. Washington, DC: National Academy of Sciences.

National Reading Panel. (2000). *Teaching children to read: An evidence-based assessment of the scientific research literature on reading and its implications for reading instructions*. Bethesda, MD: The National Reading Panel.

Riley, J.L. (1996). The ability to label the letters of the alphabet at school entry: A discussion on its value. *Journal of Research in Reading, 19*(2), 87–100.

Saracho, O.N. (2002). Young children's literacy development. In O. N. Saracho & B. Spodek (Eds.), *Contemporary perspectives in early childhood education* (Vol. 1, pp. ???). Greenwich, CT: Information Age.

Sarason, S.B. (1982), *The culture of the school and the problem of change*, Boston: Allyn and Bacon.

Shepard, L.A. (1999). The influence of standardized tests on the early childhood curriculum, teachers, and children. In B. Spodek & O.N. Saracho (Eds.), *Issues in early childhood curriculum* (pp. 166–189). Troy, NY: Educator's International Press, Inc.

Spodek, B., & Saracho, O.N. (1993). Language and literacy programs in early childhood education: A look to the future. In B. Spodek & O.N. Saracho (Eds.), *Yearbook of early childhood education: Early childhood language and literacy* (Vol. IV, pp. 196–200). New York: Teachers College Press.

Stauffer, R.G. (1967). *The first grade reading studies: Findings of individual studies.* Newark, DE: International Reading Association.

Vacca, R.T., & Vacca, J.L. (2000). *Reading and learning to read.* New York: Longman.

Watson, L.R., Layton, T.L., Pierce, P.L., & Abraham, L.M. (1994). Enhancing emerging literacy in a language preschool. *Language, speech and hearing services in schools, 25,* 136–145.

ABOUT THE AUTHORS

Ann Anderson is an associate professor in the Department of Curriculum Studies at the University of British Columbia. She teaches graduate and undergraduate courses in early mathematics learning, and mathematics education pre-K through grade 7. Prior to joining the department, she taught in the public education system. She is currently completing a research project with the co-authors in which they are examining how parents from different cultural groups mediate print literacy and mathematics with their three- and four-year-old children.

Jim Anderson is an associate professor in the Department of Language and Literacy Education at the University of British Columbia. Prior to joining the department, he worked for 15 years in the public education system as a classroom teacher, reading specialist, school principal, language arts consultant, and assistant superintendent of curriculum and instruction. He graduate and undergraduate courses in early literacy, family literacy, and reading-language arts. He is currently completing a research project with the co-authors in which they are examining how parents from different cultural groups mediate print literacy and mathematics with their three and four year old children.

Mary Alice Bond earned her master's degree in early childhood education from Towson University. She is a Senior Curriculum Specialist and Program Facilitator for the Early Learning Program at the Johns Hopkins University Center for Social Organization of Schools. She has been developing and training language and literacy pre-school programs for the last ten years.

Trevor Cairney is Chair of Education at the University of Western Sydney, Australia. His major research interests are in literacy education and the relationship between educational institutions and their communities. He has led 20 funded research projects in his 30 years as a teacher and educator and has written 7 books and over 150 papers in the field of education. These works include *Pathways to Literacy* (Cassell) and *Beyond Tokenism: Parents as partners in literacy* (Heinemann). He is a past President of the Australian Literacy Educators' Association, Director of the NSW Children's Literacy & ESL Research Network and a current director of the Australian Council for Educational Research. He has been conducting funded research concerned with the relationship between the literacy of home school and community for the past 10 years.

Kris D. Gutierrez is a Professor in the Graduate School of Education & Information Studies and director of the Center for the Study of Urban Literacies at the University of California, Los Angeles. Professor Gutierrez' research focuses on studying the literacy practices of urban schools. In particular, her research concerns itself with the social and cognitive consequences of literacy practices in formal and non-formal learning contexts. Across her work, she examines the relationship between literacy, culture, and human development. Professor Gutierrez' long-term ethnographic studies in Los Angeles area schools across various school districts have afforded her the opportunity to study the following: (1) the social and discursive practices of literacy instruction; (2) how effective literacy practices are constructed and sustained; (3) the policy issues and implications of urban schooling practices; and (4) the effects of Proposition 227 (ballot initiative to eliminate bilingual education) on the teaching and learning of literacy.

Annemarie Hindman is a Research Assistant with the Early Learning Program at the Center for Social Organization of Schools. Her past work includes experience with Head Start and other programs targeting disadvantaged young children, and she is currently working on a language and literacy training program for early childhood educators. She holds a bachelor's degree in history from Yale University.

Jon Shapiro is a professor of Language and Literacy Education and Associate Dean in the Faculty of Education at the University of British Columbia. His research interests are in the areas of emergent and early literacy, affective dimensions of literacy, and family literacy. He has published his research in journals in the United States, Canada, and Great Britain. He is currently completing two projects examining how parents from different cultural groups mediate print literacy and mathematics with their three and four year old children and the effects of a culturally sensitive family literacy program on parents and their children attending inner-city British Columbia schools.

Susan Sonnenschein is an associate professor in the Applied Developmental Psychology program at the University of Maryland, Baltimore County. She has a background in developmental psychology, educational psychology and school psychology. Her recent research interests have focused primarily on aspects of language and literacy and the socialization of children development in these areas. She, along with several colleagues, has recently completed a 5-year longitudinal study of literacy development in young children from different sociocultural groups. A large focus of that study was a consideration of parental beliefs and practices and their impact on children's literacy appropriation.

Lynda Stone is an assistant Professor of Child Development at California State University, Sacramento. Her current research interests focus on the role of language in literacy and cognitive development and the relationship between motivation and cultural practices.

Bernard Spodek is Professor Emeritus of Early Childhood Education at the University of Illinois. He received his doctorate from Teachers College, Columbia University. His research and scholarly interests are in the areas of curriculum, teaching, and teacher education in early childhood education. He has written and edited 31 books, 48 chapters in books, and 67 scholarly articles. Dr. Spodek's most recent books are *Multiple Perspectives on Play in Early Childhood Education,* with Olivia Saracho (SUNY Press), *Issues in Early Childhood Educational Research* (Teachers College Press), with Olivia Saracho and Anthony Pellegrini and the *Handbook of Research on the Education of Young Children* (Macmillan). Dr. Spodek has been president of the National Association for the Education of Young Children (1976–78) and is currently president of the Pacific Early Childhood Education Research Association.

Barbara A. Wasik is a Principal Research Scientist and the Director of the Early Learning Program at the Johns Hopkins University Center for Social Organization of Schools. Her area of research is emergent literacy and early intervention in beginning reading with a specific focus on disadvantaged children. She has extensive experience in program and curriculum development and was the original developer of the tutoring and early childhood program in Success for All, a school-wide restructuring program. Dr. Wasik has written extensively about tutoring as an early intervention strategy for children at risk of reading failure. Currently, she is developing a language and literacy training program for early childhood educators. Dr. Wasik has co-edited a book on *Early Prevention of School Failure* and is co-authoring a forthcoming book, *Kindergarten: Four-and Five-Year-Olds Go to School.* She received her Ph. D in developmental psychology.